SAINT MARY'S PRESS

ESSENTIAL
BIBLE
CONCORDANCE

NEW REVISED STANDARD VERSION: CATHOLIC EDITION

Saint Mary's Press™

Genuine recycled paper with 10% post-consumer waste.
Printed with soy-based ink. 5092400

The publishing team included Brian Singer-Towns, development editor; Paul Grass, FSC, copy
editor; James H. Gurley, production editor; Andy Palmer and Kimberly K. Sonnek, designers;
Alan S. Hanson, typesetter and prepress specialist; manufacturing coordinated by the production
services department of Saint Mary's Press.

This concordance was produced with the assistance of The Livingstone Corporation.

Printed in the United States of America

Printing: 9 8 7 6 5 4 3 2 1

Year: 2012 11 10 09 08 07 06 05 04

ISBN 0-88489-845-8

Library of Congress Cataloging-in-Publication Data

Saint Mary's Press essential Bible concordance : New Revised Standard Version / [edited by] Brian
Singer-Towns, Paul Grass.—Catholic ed.
     p. cm.
ISBN 0-88489-845-8 (pbk.)
     1. Bible—Concordances, English—New Revised Standard. 2. Bible. O.T. Apocrypha—
Concordances, English—New Revised Standard. I. Title: Essential Bible concordance. II. Singer-
Towns, Brian. III. Grass, Paul, FSC.
BS425.S25 2004
220.5'20433—dc22   2004010702

INTRODUCTION

A concordance serves as an index for finding specific verses in the Bible. The *Saint Mary's Press™ Essential Bible Concordance* lists key words in alphabetical order, followed by the Bible verses that contain the word. A complete concordance to the New Revised Standard Version: Catholic Edition would have over 300,000 entries covering 18,000 key words and would be fifty times the size of this present concordance! The SAINT MARY'S PRESS *Essential Bible Concordance,* selective and of a more manageable size, includes more than 675 key words that are most significant for personal Bible study.

Consider these suggestions for using the SAINT MARY'S PRESS *Essential Bible Concordance:*

- If you recall a key word from the Scripture passage or Bible story that you wish to locate, look up this key word in the concordance. If the concordance lists the word, you will see one or more verse references to help you locate the passage or the story.

- By looking up all the verse references for a particular key word, you can learn about the different ways the Bible uses the word and the various stories in which the word appears.

- You can use the concordance to find an appropriate Scripture reading for a prayer service. By looking up key words related to the theme of your prayer service, you can locate relevant verses and select the Scripture passages.

If you cannot find a particular key word, the one you are looking for might occur in a different translation of the Bible or might not be included in the SAINT MARY'S PRESS *Essential Bible Concordance.*

Understanding the Concordance Entries

The following example is a typical entry from the SAINT MARY'S PRESS *Essential Bible Concordance:*

ABOUND (ED) (ING)
Deut   28:11   LORD will make you **a** in
Rom   6:1   in order that grace may **a**?
1 Thess   3:12   increase and **a** in love for one

Each concordance entry lists the key word in boldface, followed by any alternative endings (in parentheses) that are also indexed. One or more context lines below the key word include the reference (book, chapter, and verse) and a short excerpt to indicate the context of the key word, which is represented by its initial letter in boldface. The abbreviations of the books of the Bible are listed on page 4.

ABBREVIATIONS

Abbreviation	Book
Acts	Acts
Am	Amos
Bar	Baruch
1 Chr	1 Chronicles
2 Chr	2 Chronicles
Col	Colossians
1 Cor	1 Corinthians
2 Cor	2 Corinthians
Dan	Daniel
Deut	Deuteronomy
Eccl	Ecclesiastes
Eph	Ephesians
Esth	Esther
Ex	Exodus
Ezek	Ezekiel
Ezra	Ezra
Gal	Galatians
Gen	Genesis
Hab	Habakkuk
Hag	Haggai
Heb	Hebrews
Hos	Hosea
Isa	Isaiah
Jas	James
Jdt	Judith
Jer	Jeremiah
Jn	John
1 Jn	1 John
2 Jn	2 John

Abbreviation	Book
3 Jn	3 John
Job	Job
Joel	Joel
Jon	Jonah
Josh	Joshua
Jude	Jude
Judg	Judges
1 Kings	1 Kings
2 Kings	2 Kings
Lam	Lamentations
Lev	Leviticus
Lk	Luke
1 Macc	1 Maccabees
2 Macc	2 Maccabees
Mal	Malachi
Mic	Micah
Mk	Mark
Mt	Matthew
Nah	Nahum
Neh	Nehemiah
Num	Numbers
Ob	Obadiah
1 Pet	1 Peter
2 Pet	2 Peter
Phil	Philippians
Philem	Philemon
Prov	Proverbs
Ps	Psalms
Rev	Revelation

Abbreviation	Book
Rom	Romans
Ruth	Ruth
1 Sam	1 Samuel
2 Sam	2 Samuel
Sir	Sirach
Song	Song of Solomon
1 Thess	1 Thessalonians
2 Thess	2 Thessalonians
1 Tim	1 Timothy
2 Tim	2 Timothy
Titus	Titus
Tob	Tobit
Wis	Wisdom of Solomon
Zech	Zechariah
Zeph	Zephaniah

ESSENTIAL CONCORDANCE

TO THE NRSV: CATHOLIC EDITION

A

ABANDON (ED)
Num	32:15	he will again **a** them
Deut	4:31	he will neither **a** you nor
Josh	10: 6	"Do not **a** your servants;
Judg	2:13	They **a** the LORD
1 Chr	28: 9	he will **a** you forever.
2 Chr	12: 5	You **a** me, so I have **a**
Tob	4: 3	your mother and do not **a** her
Ps	94:14	he will not **a** his heritage;
Sir	9:10	Do not **a** old friends,
Isa	54: 7	I **a** you, but with great
Mk	7: 8	You **a** the commandment
Acts	2:27	not **a** my soul to Hades,
Heb	10:35	therefore, **a** that confidence
Rev	2: 4	you have **a** the love you had at

ABBA
Mk	14:36	"**A**, Father, for you all things
Rom	8:15	When we cry, "**A**! Father!"
Gal	4: 6	our hearts, crying, "**A**! Father!"

ABIDE (S) (ABODE)
Gen	6: 3	shall not **a** in mortals forever,
Ex	15:17	your **a**, the sanctuary, O LORD,
Ps	26: 8	the place where your glory **a**.
	91: 1	Most High, who **a** in the
Prov	2:21	the upright will **a** in the land,
Wis	3:9	faithful will **a** with him in
Jer	31:23	bless you, O **a** of righteousness,
Hag	2: 5	My spirit **a** among you;
Jn	15: 4	**A** in me as I **a**
1 Cor	13:13	faith, hope, and love **a**, these
1 Jn	3:24	**a** in him, and he **a**
2 Jn	1: 9	not **a** in the teaching of Christ

ABILITY (ABLE)
Gen	15: 5	if you are **a** to count them."
Ex	18:25	Moses chose **a** men from all
Num	1: 3	Israel **a** to go to war. You
Josh	1: 5	shall be **a** to stand against you
1 Sam	7:33	"You are not **a** to go against
1 Kings	3: 9	your people, **a** to discern
1 Chr	29:14	we should be **a** to make this
2 Chr	25: 9	"The LORD is **a** to give you
Prov	27: 4	but who is **a** to stand before
Isa	36:14	he will not be **a** to deliver you.

Dan	2:26	you **a** to tell me the dream
Hos	5:13	he is not **a** to cure you or heal
Mt	9:28	I am **a** to do this?"
Mk	10:38	Are you **a** to drink the cup that
Lk	13:24	enter and will not be **a**.
Jn	9: 7	and came back **a** to see.
	18:28	defilement and to be **a** to eat
Acts	2: 4	as the Spirit gave them **a**.
Rom	4:21	convinced that God was **a** to do
2 Cor	1: 4	may be **a** to console those
	9: 8	And God is **a** to provide you
Eph	3:20	within us is **a** to accomplish
2 Tim	1:12	that he is **a** to guard until that
Heb	2:18	he is **a** to help those who are
	7:25	he is **a** for all time to save
Jas	3: 2	perfect, **a** to keep the whole
2 Pet	1:15	you may be **a** at any time to
Jude	1:24	to him who is **a** to keep you
Rev	6:17	and who is **a** to stand?"

ABOLISH (ED)
1 Macc	6:59	account of their laws that we **a**
2 Macc	2:22	laws that were about to be **a**,
Lam	2: 6	the LORD has **a** in Zion
Dan	11:31	They shall **a** the regular burnt
Hos	2:18	I will **a** the bow, the sword,
Mt	5:17	not to **a** but to fulfill.
Eph	2:15	He has **a** the law with its
2 Tim	1:10	who **a** death and brought life

ABOMINATION (S) (ABOMINABLE)
Gen	43:32	for that is an **a** to the Egyptians.
Lev	18:27	committed all of these **a**,
1 Kings	14:24	They committed all the **a** of
2 Chr	28: 3	according to the **a** practices of
Ezra	9: 1	their **a**, from the Canaanites
Ps	14: 1	they do **a** deeds; there is no
Prov	6:16	seven that are an **a** to him:
	26:25	there are seven **a** concealed
Sir	1:25	godliness is an **a** to a sinner
	13:20	poor are an **a** to the rich
Isa	6: 3	in their **a** they take delight;
Jer	4: 1	remove your **a** from my
Ezek	7:20	their **a** images, their detestable
	44: 7	my covenant with all your **a**.
Dan	9:27	shall be an **a** that desolates,
Lk	16:15	is an **a** in the sight of God
Rev	21:27	who practices **a** or falsehood,

ABOVE
Deut	4:39	LORD is God in heaven **a** and

Jdt	13:18	**a** all other women on earth;
Ps	8: 1	You have set your glory **a** the
	57: 5	O God, **a** the heavens.
Sir	32:13	But **a** all bless your Maker.
Isa	40:22	It is he who sits **a** the circle of
Ezek	1:26	seated **a** the likeness of a
	11:22	the God of Israel was **a** them.
Mt	10:24	"A disciple is not **a** the teacher,
Jn	3: 7	'You must be born from **a**.'
Eph	1:21	**a** every name that is named
Phil	2: 9	the name that is **a** every name,
Col	3: 2	things that are **a**, not on things
2 Thess	2: 4	exalts himself **a** every so-called
1 Tim	5: 7	they may be **a** reproach.
Heb	7:26	and exalted **a** the heavens.
Jas	1:17	every perfect gift, is from **a**,
1 Pet	4: 8	**A** all, maintain constant love

ABOUND (ED) (ING)
Ex	34: 6	and **a** in steadfast love and
Deut	28:11	LORD will make you **a** in
Neh	9:17	slow to anger and **a** in
Ps	103: 8	slow to anger and **a** in
Prov	8:24	were no springs **a** with water.
Joel	2:13	slow to anger, and **a** in
Rom	5:20	grace **a** all the more,
	6: 1	in order that grace may **a**?
2 Cor	3: 9	ministry of justification **a** in
Col	2: 7	were taught, **a** in thanksgiving.
1 Thess	3:12	increase and **a** in love for one

ABSTAIN
Acts	15:20	to **a** only from things polluted
Rom	14: 3	who **a**, and those who **a** must
1 Thess	5:22	**a** from every form of evil
1 Pet	2:11	exiles to **a** from the desires of

ABUNDANCE (ABUNDANTLY)
Deut	33:15	and the **a** of the everlasting
Job	36:31	peoples; he gives food in **a**.
Ps	36: 8	on the **a** of your house, and
Prov	11:14	but in an **a** of counselors there
Isa	33: 6	**a** of salvation, wisdom, and
Lam	3:32	according to the **a** of his
Mt	25:29	they will have an **a**;
Lk	6:45	out of the **a** of the heart
Jn	10:10	have life, and have it **a**.
2 Cor	9: 8	every blessing in **a**, so that by
Eph	3:20	to accomplish **a** far more than
1 Pet	1: 2	and peace be yours in **a**.
Jude	1: 2	and love be yours in **a**.

ABUSE (ABUSIVE)
Ex 22:22 not **a** any widow or orphan.
Prov 9: 7 corrects a scoffer wins **a**;
Sir 23:15 to using **a** language
Lk 6:28 pray for those who **a** you.
Col 3: 8 slander, and **a** language
2 Tim 3: 2 money, boasters, arrogant, **a**,
Heb 11:26 considered **a** suffered for the
1 Pet 3: 9 repay evil for evil or **a** for a;

ACCEPT (ED) (ACCEPTABLE)
Gen 4: 7 well, will you not be **a**?
Deut 16:19 you must not **a** bribes, for a
Job 42: 8 for I will **a** his prayer not to
Ps 19:14 meditation of my heart be **a** to
   119:108 **A** my offerings of praise, O
Prov 19:20 advice and **a** instruction,
   21: 3 justice is more **a** to the LORD
Isa 58: 5 a fast, a day **a** to the LORD?
Jer 6:20 Your burnt offerings are not **a**,
Ezek 43:27 and I will **a** you, says the Lord
Mal 1:10 and I will not **a** an offering
Mt 19:11 everyone can **a** this teaching,
Mk 4:20 hear the word and **a** it and
Lk 4:24 no prophet is **a** in the
Jn 1:11 his own people did not **a** him.
   5:43 you do not **a** me; if another
Acts 22:18 they will not **a** your testimony
Rom 12: 1 holy and **a** to God, which is
2 Cor 6: 2 "See, now is the **a** time;
Phil 4:18 a sacrifice **a** and pleasing to
Col 3:20 this is your **a** duty in the Lord.
1 Thess 2:13 you **a** it not as a human
1 Pet 2: 5 spiritual sacrifices **a** to God

ACCESS
Rom 5: 2 have obtained **a** to this grace
Eph 3:12 in whom we have **a** to God

ACCOMPLISH (ED)
Isa 55:11 shall **a** that which I purpose,
Ezek 17:24 LORD have spoken; I will **a** it.
Mt 5:18 the law until all is **a**.
Mk 13: 4 things are about to be **a**?"
Lk 18:31 by the prophets will be **a**.
Rom 15:18 what Christ has **a** through me
Eph 3:20 is able to **a** abundantly far

ACCOUNT (ABLE)
Mt 12:36 to give an **a** for every careless
Lk 1: 1 an orderly **a** of the events that
Rom 14:12 each of us will be **a** to God.
Col 3: 6 On **a** of these the wrath of
Heb 4:13 whom we must render an **a**.
1 Jn 2:12 sins are forgiven on **a** of his

ACKNOWLEDGE
Deut 4:35 you would **a** that the LORD is
Tob 12: 6 Do not be slow to **a** him.
Prov 3: 6 In all your ways **a** him, and he
Isa 26:13 but we **a** your name alone.
Jer 3:13 Only **a** your guilt, that you
Hos 5:15 until they **a** their guilt and
Mt 10:32 I also will **a** before my Father
Lk 12: 8 Son of Man also will **a** before
Rom 1:28 did not see fit to **a** God, God
3 Jn 1: 9 does not **a** our authority.

ACT (S) (ED)
Gen 19: 7 brothers, do not **a** so wickedly.

Ex 6: 6 with mighty **a** of judgment.
Josh 1: 8 be careful to **a** in accordance
Judg 19:23 do not **a** so wickedly.
2 Chr 6:37 we have **a** wickedly';
Neh 9:29 Yet they **a** presumptuously
Job 40:19 the great **a** of God— only its
Ps 31:23 repays the one who **a**
   71:15 your righteous **a**, of your
Prov 14:35 falls on one who **a** shamefully.
Eccl 7:16 and do not **a** too wise;
Sir 32:23 Guard yourself in every **a**,
Jer 9:24 the LORD; I **a** with steadfast
Ezek 20: 9 But I **a** for the sake of my
Dan 9:19 O Lord, listen and **a** and do
Mic 3: 4 because they have **a** wickedly.
Mt 7:24 words of mine and **a** on them
Jn 8: 4 very **a** of committing adultery.
Acts 3:17 you **a** in ignorance, as did also
Rom 1:27 shameless **a** with men and
Jas 1:25 doers who **a**—they will be

ADOPTION
Rom 9: 4 the **a**, the glory, the covenants,
Gal 4: 5 we might receive **a** as children.
Eph 1: 5 He destined us for **a** as his

ADORN (S) (ED) (MENT)
Ex 28: 2 the glorious **a** of your brother
2 Kings 9:30 and **a** her head, and looked
Ps 149: 4 he **a** the humble with victory.
Prov 3:22 your soul and **a** for your neck.
Isa 61:10 as a bride **a** herself with her
Ezek 16:11 I **a** you with ornaments: I put
Lk 21: 5 how it was **a** with beautiful
1 Pet 3: 4 let your **a** be the inner self
Rev 21: 2 prepared as a bride **a** for her

ADULTERY (ADULTRESS) (ADULTER-ER) (ADULTERERS)
Ex 20:14 You shall not commit **a**.
Lev 20:10 the **a** and the **a** shall be put to
Deut 5:18 Neither shall you commit **a**.
Prov 6:32 he who commits **a** has no
Sir 25: 2 an old fool who commits **a**.
Ezek 23:37 idols they have committed **a**;
Hos 3: 1 is an **a**, just as the LORD loves
Mal 3: 5 against the **a**, against those
Mt 5:27 'You shall not commit **a**.'
   15:19 murder, **a**, fornication,
Mk 10:11 commits **a** against her;
Lk 16:18 her husband commits **a**.
Jn 8: 3 caught in **a**; and making her
Rom 2:22 forbid **a**, do you commit **a**?
   7: 3 called an **a** if she lives with
1 Cor 6: 9 idolaters, **a**, male prostitutes,
Heb 13: 4 judge fornicators and **a**.
Jas 2:11 do not commit **a** but if you
2 Pet 2:14 They have eyes full of **a**,

ADVOCATE
Jn 14:16 another **A**, to be with you
   14:26 But the **A**, the Holy Spirit,
1 Jn 2: 1 we have an **a** with the Father,

AFFLICT (S) (ED) (ION) (IONS)
Gen 12:17 the LORD **a** Pharaoh and his
   16:11 has given heed to your **a**.
Deut 26: 7 saw our **a**, our toil, and our
2 Sam 7:10 evildoers shall **a** them no

Job 36:15 He delivers the **a** by their **a**,
Ps 25:16 for I am lonely and **a**.
   44:24 Why do you forget our **a** and
Isa 53: 7 he was **a**, yet he did not open
Lam 3:33 does not willingly **a** or grieve
Nah 1:12 have **a** you, I will **a** you no
2 Cor 1: 4 in all our **a**, so that we may be
   4:17 momentary **a** is preparing us
Col 1:24 lacking in Christ's **a** for the
2 Thess 1: 6 repay with **a** those who **a** you,
1 Tim 5:10 helped the **a**, and devoted
Rev 2: 9 your **a** and your poverty, even

AFRAID
Gen 3:10 I was **a**, because I was naked;
Ex 3: 6 for he was **a** to look at God.
   14:13 "Do not be **a**, stand firm, and
Deut 28:10 and they shall be **a** of you.
Josh 10:25 "Do not be **a** or dismayed;
Ruth 3:11 my daughter, do not be **a**, I
1 Sam 3:15 Samuel was **a** to tell the vision
1 Kings 19: 3 Then he was **a**; he got up and
1 Chr 13:12 David was **a** of God that day;
Ezra 4: 4 and made them **a** to build,
Ps 27: 1 of whom shall I be **a**?
   56: 3 when I am **a**, I put my trust in
Prov 3:24 you will not be **a**; when you
Isa 12: 2 and will not be **a**, for the LORD
   44: 8 Do not fear, or be **a**; have I not
Jer 1: 8 Do not be **a** of them, for I am
Ezek 34:28 no one shall make them **a**.
Mt 8:26 are you **a**, you of little faith?"
   14:27 is I; do not be **a**."
   28:10 "Do not be **a**; go and tell my
Lk 2:10 "Do not be **a**; for see—I am
   12:32 "Do not be **a**, little flock, for
Jn 14:27 do not let them be **a**.
Acts 27:24 'Do not be **a**, Paul; you must
Rom 13: 4 should be **a**, for the authority
Heb 13: 6 I will not be **a**. What can
2 Pet 2:10 they are not **a** to slander the

AGREE
Job 22:21 **A** with God, and be at
Mt 18:19 if two of you **a** on earth about
Mk 14:56 and their testimony did not **a**.
Rom 7:16 I do not want, I **a** that the law
2 Cor 13:11 **a** with one another, live in
1 Tim 6: 3 does not **a** with the sound
1 Jn 5: 8 and these three **a**.

ALIEN (S)
Gen 12:10 reside there as an **a**, for the
Ex 2:22 "I have been an **a** residing in a
   23: 9 **a**, for you were **a** in the land of
Lev 19:34 love the **a** as yourself, for you
Deut 24:17 not deprive a resident **a** or an
1 Macc 2: 7 the sanctuary given over to **a**?
Ps 144:11 the hand of **a**, whose mouths
Lam 5: 2 to strangers, our homes to **a**
Eph 2:19 strangers and **a**, but you are
1 Pet 2:11 Beloved, I urge you as **a** and

ALIVE
Gen 16:13 remained **a** after seeing him?"
Num 16:30 they go down **a** into Sheol;
Deut 5:26 as we have, and remained **a**?
2 Sam 12:18 "While the child was still **a**,
1 Kings 3:23 my son that is **a**, and your son
Ps 55:15 let them go down **a** to Sheol;

Prov	1:12	Sheol let us swallow them **a**
Zech	13: 8	one-third shall be left **a**.
Lk	15:24	mine was dead and is **a** again;
	24:23	who said that he was **a**.
Jn	4:51	him that his child was **a**.
Acts	1: 3	presented himself **a** to them
Rom	6:11	dead to sin and **a** to God in
	7: 9	I was once **a** apart from the
1 Cor	15:22	so all will be made **a** in Christ.
2 Cor	6: 9	and see—we are **a**; as punished,
Eph	2: 5	us **a** together with Christ—by
Col	2:13	God made you **a** together with
1 Thess	4:17	Then we who are **a**, who are
1 Pet	3:18	but made **a** in the spirit,
Rev	1:18	see, I am **a** forever and ever;

ALMIGHTY

Gen	17: 1	"I am God **A**; walk before me,
Ex	6: 3	Jacob as God **A**, but by my
Num	24: 4	sees the vision of the **A**, who
Ruth	1:20	for the **A** has dealt bitterly
Jdt	16:5	Lord **A** has foiled them by the
Job	6: 4	the arrows of the **A** are in me;
	21:15	What is the **A**, that we should
Ps	91: 1	in the shadow of the **A**,
Isa	13: 6	like destruction from the **A**!
Bar	3:1	O Lord **A**, God of Israel,
Joel	1:15	as destruction from the **A** it
Rev	4: 8	God the **A**, who was and is
	21:22	Lord God the **A** and the Lamb.

ALMS

Mt	6: 2	give **a**, do not sound a trumpet
Lk	12:33	your possessions, and give **a**.
Acts	3: 2	ask for **a** from those entering
Tob	4:16	Give all your surplus as **a**
	12: 8	better to give **a** than to
Sir	7:10	do not neglect to give **a**.

ALONE

Gen	2:18	the man should be **a**; I will
Ex	18:18	you cannot do it **a**.
Deut	8: 3	by bread **a**, but by every word
1 Kings	19:10	with the sword. I **a** am left,
Neh	9: 6	"You are the LORD, you **a**;
Ps	51: 4	you, you **a**, have I sinned, and
	148:13	for his name **a** is exalted;
Prov	16:33	decision is the LORD's **a**.
Eccl	4:11	how can one keep warm **a**?
Isa	2:11	and the LORD **a** will be exalted
Mt	4: 4	by bread **a**, but by every word
Mk	2: 7	can forgive sins but God **a**?"
	10:18	one is good but God **a**.
Jn	16:32	will leave me **a**. Yet I am not **a**
Rom	11: 3	your altars; I **a** am left,
Jas	2:24	works and not by faith **a**
Rev	15: 4	For you **a** are holy.

ALPHA

Rev	1: 8	"I am the **A** and the Omega,"
	21: 6	the **A** and the Omega, the
	22:13	I am the **A** and the Omega, the

ALTAR (S)

Gen	8:20	Noah built an **a** to the LORD,
	22: 9	laid him on the **a**, on top of
Ex	17:15	Moses built an **a** and called it,
	30: 1	You shall make an **a** on which
	37:25	the **a** of incense of acacia
Lev	8:11	anointed the **a** and all its

Deut	27: 5	build an **a** there to the LORD
Josh	8:30	built on Mount Ebal an **a** to
Judg	6:24	Gideon built an **a** there to the
1 Sam	14:35	Saul built an **a** to the LORD;
2 Sam	24:25	David built there an **a** to the
1 Kings	12:33	He went up to the **a** that he
	18:30	First he repaired the **a** of the
2 Kings	23:20	He slaughtered on the **a** all the
1 Chr	21:26	fire from heaven on the **a** of
2 Chr	32:12	one **a** you shall worship,
	33:16	restored the **a** of the LORD and
Ezra	3: 2	build the **a** of the God of
Neh	10:34	to burn on the **a** of the LORD
1 Macc	2:24	and killed him on the **a**.
2 Macc	1:32	light from the **a** shone back.
Ps	43: 4	go to the **a** of God, to God
	51:19	will be offered on your **a**.
Sir	35:8	of the righteous enriches the **a**,
Isa	6: 6	taken from the **a** with a pair of
	60: 7	shall be acceptable on my **a**,
Lam	2: 7	The Lord has scorned his **a**,
Ezek	6: 5	bones around your **a**.
Hos	8:11	became to him **a** for sinning.
Joel	1:13	ministers of the **a**. Come, pass
Am	9: 1	standing beside the **a**, and he
Mal	1: 7	polluted food on my **a**.
Mt	5:24	gift there before the **a** and go;
Lk	11:51	perished between the **a** and
Acts	17:23	an **a** with the inscription, 'To
1 Cor	10:18	the sacrifices partners in the **a**?
Heb	13:10	We have an **a** from which
Jas	2:21	his son Isaac on the **a**?
Rev	6: 9	under the **a** the souls of those
	11: 1	temple of God and the **a** and
	16: 7	the **a** respond, "Yes, O Lord

AMAZED (AMAZING)

Mt	8:27	were **a**, saying, "What sort of
	9:33	the crowds were **a** and said,
Mk	6: 6	And he was **a** at their unbelief.
	12:11	and it is **a** in our eyes'?"
Acts	2: 7	**A** and astonished, they asked,
Rev	15: 3	"Great and **a** are your deeds,
	17: 8	be **a** when they see the beast

AMBASSADORS

2 Cor	5:20	we are **a** for Christ, since God

AMEN

Deut	27:15	shall respond, saying, "**A**!"
1 Chr	16:36	Then all the people said "**A**!"
Tob	8: 8	they both said, "**A, A**."
Jdt	13:20	all the people said, "**A. A**."
Ps	89:52	be the LORD forever. **A** and **A**.
Rom	1:25	who is blessed forever! **A**.
Rom	11:36	him be the glory forever. **A**.
1 Cor	14:16	the "**A**" to your thanksgiving,
2 Cor	1:20	we say the "**A**," to the glory of
Rev	3:14	The words of the **A**, the
	5:14	living creatures said, "**A**!"
	22:20	coming soon." **A**. Come, Lord

ANCESTOR (S)

Gen	17: 4	be the **a** of a multitude of
Ex	3:13	'The God of your **a** has sent
Deut	1: 8	I swore to your **a**, to Abraham,
1 Kings	19: 4	am no better than my **a**."
Ps	22: 4	In you our **a** trusted; they
	106: 6	we and our **a** have sinned; we
Lam	5: 7	Our **a** sinned; they are no

Tob	8:5	are you, O God of our **a**,
Am	2: 4	lies after which their **a** walked.
Zech	1: 4	like your **a**, to whom the
Mt	3: 9	'We have Abraham as our **a**;
Lk	11:48	deeds of your **a**; for they killed
Jn	4:20	Our **a** worshiped on this
Acts	5:30	God of our **a** raised up Jesus,
Rom	4: 1	by Abraham, our **a** according
1 Cor	10: 1	our **a** were all under the cloud
Heb	11: 2	faith our **a** received approval.

ANGEL (S)

Gen	16: 7	The **a** of the LORD found her
	28:12	the **a** of God were ascending
Job	4:18	his **a** he charges with error;
Ps	91:11	command his **a** concerning
	148: 2	Praise him, all his **a**; praise
Mt	4: 6	command his **a** concerning
	18:10	their **a** continually see the face
Mk	8:38	his Father with the holy **a**."
	12:25	marriage, but are like **a** in
	13:27	the **a**, and gather his elect
Lk	2:15	When the **a** had left them and
	15:10	the presence of the **a** of God
Jn	20:12	she saw two **a** in white, sitting
Acts	7:53	law as ordained by **a**, and yet
Rom	8:38	nor life, nor **a**, nor rulers,
1 Cor	4: 9	world, to **a** and to mortals.
	6: 3	we are to judge **a**—to say
Gal	3:19	ordained through **a** by a
Col	2:18	worship of **a**, dwelling on
2 Thess	1: 7	from heaven with his mighty **a**
1 Tim	3:16	seen by **a**, proclaimed among
Heb	1: 4	become as much superior to **a**
	1:14	Are not all **a** spirits in the
	2: 9	was made lower than the **a**,
1 Pet	3:22	right hand of God, with **a**,
2 Pet	2: 4	God did not spare the **a** when
Jude	1: 6	And the **a** who did not keep
Rev	5:11	voice of many **a** surrounding
	7: 1	After this I saw four **a** standing
	8: 2	the seven **a** who stand before

ANGER (ANGRY)

Gen	18:30	the LORD be **a** if I speak.
	27:45	your brother's **a** against you
Ex	4:14	the **a** of the LORD was kindled
	34: 6	slow to **a**, and abounding in
Num	12: 9	the **a** of the LORD was kindled
	14:18	'The LORD is slow to **a**, and
Deut	6:15	The **a** of the LORD your God
	9:19	I was afraid that the **a** that the
Josh	7: 1	and the **a** of the LORD burned
Judg	2:12	they provoked the LORD to **a**.
1 Sam	20:30	Then Saul's **a** was kindled
2 Sam	12: 5	David's **a** was greatly kindled
1 Kings	11: 9	the LORD was **a** with Solomon,
Ps	30: 5	For his **a** is but for a moment
	37: 8	Refrain from **a**, and forsake
	90: 7	we are consumed by your **a**;
Prov	12:16	Fools show their **a** at once, but
	19:11	good sense are slow to **a**, and
Eccl	7: 9	not be quick to **a**, for **a** lodges
Sir	30:24	Jealousy and **a** shorten life.
Isa	5:25	the **a** of the LORD was kindled
Jer	3:12	I will not be **a** forever.
Lam	4:11	he poured out his hot **a**, and
Ezek	43: 8	have consumed them in my **a**.
Dan	9:16	let your **a** and wrath, we pray,
Hos	11: 9	will not execute my fierce **a**;

Jon 3: 9 may turn from his fierce **a**, so
Mic 7:18 does not retain his **a** forever,
Mt 5:22 if you are **a** with a brother or
Mk 3: 5 looked around at them with **a**;
Lk 15:28 Then he became **a** and refused
Jn 7:23 you **a** with me because I healed
2 Cor 12:20 quarreling, jealousy, **a**,
Gal 5:20 strife, jealousy, **a**, quarrels,
Eph 4:26 Be **a** but do not sin; do
6: 4 provoke your children to **a**,
Col 3: 8 such things—**a**, wrath, malice,
1 Tim 2: 8 holy hands without **a** or
Heb 3:11 As in my **a** I swore, 'They will
Jas 1:19 slow to speak, slow to **a**;
Rev 12:17 dragon was **a** with the woman,
14:10 into the cup of his **a**, and they

ANIMAL (S)

Gen 1:25 made the wild **a** of the earth
3:14 cursed are you among all **a**
Ex 20:15 has sexual relations with an **a**,
26:22 I will let loose wild **a** against
Deut 14: 4 These are the **a** you may eat:
2 Chr 25:18 but a wild **a** of Lebanon
Job 12: 7 "But ask the **a**, and they will
Ps 36: 6 you save humans and **a** alike,
50:10 For every wild **a** of the forest is
Eccl 3:19 humans and the fate of **a** is
Wis 11:15 serpents and worthless **a**,
Isa 43:20 The wild **a** will honor me,
Ezek 14:21 sword, famine, wild **a**, and
Dan 4:15 be with the **a** of the field
Joel 2:22 Do not fear, you **a** of the field,
Hab 2:17 destruction of the **a** will terrify
Mal 1: 8 you offer blind **a** in sacrifice, is
Lk 10:34 own **a**, brought him to an inn
Acts 11: 6 closely I saw four-footed **a**,
Heb 12:20 an **a** touches the mountain, it
Jude 1:10 like irrational **a**, they know by

ANNOUNCE (D) (S) (ANNOUNCING)

Deut 17: 9 shall **a** to you the decision
Isa 48: 5 I **a** them to you, so that
52: 7 messenger who **a** peace, who
Rom 1: 9 my spirit by **a** the gospel of his
Gal 4:13 that I first **a** the gospel to you;
1 Pet 1:25 good news that was **a** to you.
Rev 10: 7 fulfilled, as he **a** to his servants

ANOINT (ED) (ING)

Gen 31:13 God of Bethel, where you **a**
Ex 30:25 it shall be a holy **a** oil.
30:30 You shall **a** Aaron and his
Lev 4: 3 If it is the **a** priest who sins,
Deut 28:40 but you shall not **a** yourself
1 Sam 2:10 exalt the power of his **a**."
15: 1 LORD sent me to **a** you king
26: 9 against the LORD's **a**, and be
2 Sam 1:14 hand to destroy the LORD's **a**?"
19:21 he cursed the LORD's **a**?"
1 Kings 19:16 shall **a** Jehu son of Nimshi
19:16 and you shall **a** Elisha son of
2 Kings 9: 3 I **a** you king over Israel.'
1 Chr 16:22 "Do not touch my **a** ones;
2 Chr 6:42 do not reject your **a** one.
Ps 18:50 shows steadfast love to his **a**,
23: 5 my enemies; you **a** my head
105:15 "Do not touch my **a** ones; do
Isa 61: 1 because the LORD has **a** me;
Ezek 28:14 With an **a** cherub as guardian I

Dan 9:24 and to **a** a most holy place.
Hab 3:13 to save your **a**. You crushed
Zech 4:14 "These are the two **a** ones who
Mk 6:13 many demons, and **a** with oil
Lk 4:18 because he has **a** me to bring
7:46 You did not **a** my head with
Jn 12: 3 of pure nard, **a** Jesus' feet,
Acts 10:38 how God **a** Jesus of Nazareth
2 Cor 1:21 you in Christ and has **a** us,
Heb 1: 9 your God, has **a** you with the
1 Jn 2:20 have been **a** by the Holy One,
Rev 3:18 and salve to **a** your eyes so

ANSWER (ED)

1 Kings 18:26 "O Baal, **a** us!" But there was
18:37 **A** me, O LORD, **a** me
1 Chr 21:26 and he **a** him with fire from
Job 30:20 you and you do not **a** me;
Ps 20: 9 O LORD; **a** us when we call.
38:15 LORD my God, who will **a**.
118:21 thank you that you have **a** me
Prov 15: 1 A soft **a** turns away wrath,
18:13 If one gives **a** before hearing,
Isa 58: 9 call, and the LORD will **a**;
65:24 Before they call I will **a**, while
Hos 14: 8 It is I who **a** and look after
Mt 27:14 But he gave him no **a**, not
Lk 23: 9 but Jesus gave him no **a**.

ANTICHRIST

1 Jn 2:18 have heard that **a** is coming,
4: 3 is the spirit of the **a**, of which
2 Jn 1: 7 is the deceiver and the **a**!

APART

Ps 4: 3 the LORD has set **a** the faithful
Jn 15: 5 because **a** from me you can do
Rom 1: 1 an apostle, set **a** for the gospel
3:21 But now, **a** from law, the
Jas 2:20 faith **a** from works is barren?

APOSTLE (S)

Mt 10: 2 of the twelve **a**: first, Simon,
Mk 3:14 whom he also named **a**, to be
Lk 11:49 prophets and **a**, some of
Acts 2:43 were being done by the **a**.
4:33 With great power the **a** gave
8: 1 except the **a** were scattered
Rom 1: 1 called to be an **a**, set apart for
11:13 I am an **a** to the Gentiles,
1 Cor 9: 1 Am I not an **a**? Have I not seen
15: 9 be called an **a**, because I
2 Cor 11:13 For such boasters are false **a**,
Gal 2: 8 Peter making him an **a** to the
Eph 2:20 of the **a** and prophets,
4:11 some would be **a**, some
2 Tim 1:11 herald and an **a** and a teacher,
Heb 3: 1 Jesus, the **a** and high priest of
Jude 1:17 the predictions of the **a** of our
Rev 2: 2 claim to be **a** but are not,
21:14 of the twelve **a** of the Lamb.

APPEAR (ED) (ING) (S) (ANCE) (ANCES)

Gen 1: 9 and let the dry land **a**."
12: 7 Then the LORD **a** to Abram,
Ex 3: 2 the angel of the LORD **a** to him
16:10 the glory of the LORD **a** in the
Lev 16: 2 he will die; for I **a** in the cloud
Num 9:15 having the **a** of fire.
Num 16:19 the glory of the LORD **a** to the

Judg 6:12 The angel of the LORD **a** to
1 Sam 16: 7 "Do not look on his **a** or on
1 Kings 9: 2 the LORD **a** to Solomon a
2 Chr 1: 7 That night God **a** to Solomon,
Ps 21: 9 a fiery furnace when you **a**.
102:16 he will **a** in his glory.
Sir 35: 6 not **a** before the Lord empty-
Isa 53: 2 nothing in his **a** that we
Ezek 10:22 were the same faces whose **a**
Dan 5: 5 fingers of a human hand **a**
Hos 6: 3 his **a** is as sure as the
Joel 2: 4 They have the **a** of horses, and
Mt 1:20 an angel of the Lord **a** to him
Mk 12:40 the sake of **a** say long prayers.
13:22 false prophets will **a** and
Lk 1:11 Then there **a** to him an angel
19:11 kingdom of God was to **a**
Jn 7:24 Do not judge by **a**, but judge
21:14 the third time that Jesus **a** to
Acts 2: 3 tongues, as of fire, **a** among
12: 7 an angel of the Lord **a** and a
1 Cor 15: 5 and that he **a** to Cephas, then
2 Cor 5:10 must **a** before the judgment
Col 2:23 indeed an **a** of wisdom in
Titus 2:11 the grace of God has **a**,
Heb 9:24 to **a** in the presence of God
9:26 as it is, he has **a** once for all at
Rev 12: 1 A great portent **a** in heaven: a

APPOINT (ED)

Ex 18:25 all Israel and **a** them as heads
Lev 23: 2 These are the **a** festivals of the
1 Sam 8: 5 **a** for us, then, a king
1 Kings 1:35 for I have **a** him to be ruler
1 Chr 24: 3 according to the **a** duties in
Neh 5:14 I was **a** to be their governor in
10:33 the new moons, the festivals,
Esth 9:31 observed at their **a** seasons, as
Job 14: 5 you have **a** the bounds that
Ps 7: 6 you have **a** a judgment.
75: 2 the set time that I **a** I will
Eccl 3:17 for he has **a** a time for every
Isa 60:17 I will **a** Peace as your overseer
Jer 33:20 not come at their **a** time,
Dan 2:49 he **a** Shadrach, Meshach, and
8:19 for it refers to the **a** time of the
Hos 1:11 they shall **a** for themselves one
Hab 2: 3 still a vision for the **a** time;
Mk 3:16 So he **a** the twelve: Simon (to
Lk 10: 1 After this the Lord **a** seventy
Jn 15:16 I chose you. And I **a** you to go
Acts 3:20 send the Messiah **a** for you,
15: 2 others were **a** to go up to
1 Cor 6: 4 do you **a** as judges those who
12:28 God has **a** in the church first
1 Tim 1:12 and **a** me to his service,
Titus 1: 5 and should **a** elders in every
Heb 1: 2 whom he **a** heir of all things,
9:27 it is **a** for mortals to die once

APPROVAL (APPROVED)

Sir 32:10 **a** goes before one who is
Acts 8: 1 And Saul **a** of their killing
2 Cor 10:18 themselves that are **a**, but
Gal 1:10 seeking human **a**, or God's **a**?
1 Thess 2: 4 just as we have been **a** by God
2 Tim 2:15 as one **a** by him, a worker who
Heb 11: 2 faith our ancestors received **a**.
1 Pet 2:20 suffer for it, you have God's **a**.

ARGUE (ARGUMENT) (ARGUMENTS)

Job	13: 3	I desire to **a** my case with God.
Prov	25: 9	**A** your case with your
Isa	3:13	The LORD rises to **a** his case;
Mk	8:11	Pharisees came and began to **a**
Lk	9:46	An **a** arose among them as to
Acts	18: 4	Every sabbath he would **a** in
Rom	9:20	human being, to **a** with God?
2 Cor	10: 4	strongholds. We destroy **a**
Col	2: 4	deceive you with plausible **a**.
1 Tim	2: 8	hands without anger or **a**;

ARISE

Num	10:35	"**A**, O LORD, let your enemies
1 Kings	3:12	one like you shall **a** after you.
2 Kings	23:25	did any like him **a** after him.
1 Macc	14:41	trustworthy prophet should **a**,
Song	2:10	and says to me: "**A**, my love,
Isa	60: 1	**A**, shine; for your light has
Dan	7:17	four kings shall **a** out of the
Mic	4:13	**A** and thresh, O daughter Zion
Mt	24:11	false prophets will **a** and lead .

ARK

Gen	6:14	Make yourself an **a** of cypress
Ex	25:16	into the **a** the covenant that I
Num	3:31	to be the **a**, the table,
Deut	10: 5	put the tablets in the **a** that I
Josh	3: 3	you see the **a** of the covenant
Judg	20:27	for the **a** of the covenant of
1 Sam	4:11	The **a** of God was captured;
2 Sam	6:17	brought in the **a** of the LORD,
1 Kings	8: 9	nothing in the **a** except the
1 Chr	13: 9	to hold the **a**, for the oxen
2 Chr	35: 3	"Put the holy **a** in the house
Ps	132: 8	you and the **a** of your might.
Jer	3:16	say, "The **a** of the covenant
Lk	17:27	Noah entered the **a**, and the
Heb	9: 4	incense and the **a** of the
1 Pet	3:20	during the building of the **a**,
Rev	11:19	and the **a** of his covenant was

ASCEND (ED) (ING)

Gen	28:12	the angels of God were **a** and
Judg	13:20	the angel of the LORD **a** in the
2 Kings	2:11	and Elijah **a** in a whirlwind
Tob	12:20	I am **a** to him who sent me
Ps	24: 3	shall **a** the hill of the LORD
	139: 8	If I **a** to heaven, you are there
Isa	14:13	"I will **a** to heaven; I will raise
Ezek	11:23	glory of the LORD **a** from the
Jn	6:62	see the Son of Man **a** to where
	20:17	I have not yet **a** to the Father.
Acts	2:34	For David did not **a** into the
Rom	10: 6	'Who will **a** into heaven?'
Eph	4: 8	"When he **a** on high he made
Rev	7: 2	I saw another angel **a** from the
	17: 8	to **a** from the bottomless pit

ASK (ED)

Ex	3:13	they **a** me, 'What is his name?'
	12:26	And when your children **a**
Deut	32: 7	long past; **a** your father,
Judg	13:18	"Why do you **a** my name?
1 Kings	3:10	Solomon had **a** this.
1 Chr	4:10	And God granted what he **a**.
Ps	2: 8	**A** of me, and I will
	27: 4	One thing I **a** of the LORD, that
Prov	30: 7	Two things I **a** of you; do not
Isa	7:11	**A** a sign of the LORD

Jer	6:16	look, and **a** for the ancient
Mt	6: 8	you need before you **a** him.
	7: 7	**A**, and it will be given
Mk	6:23	"Whatever you **a** me, I will
	11:24	whatever you **a** for in prayer,
Lk	11:13	Holy Spirit to those who **a**
Jn	16:23	I tell you, if you **a** anything of
	16:24	you have not **a** for anything in
Rom	10:20	to those who did not **a** for me."
1 Cor	14:35	let them **a** their husbands at
Eph	3:20	all we can **a** or imagine,
Jas	1: 5	lacking in wisdom, **a** God,
	4: 3	You **a** and do not receive,
1 Jn	3:22	from him whatever we **a**,
	5:14	if we **a** anything according to

ASSEMBLY (ASSEMBLE)

Ex	12:16	you shall hold a solemn **a**,
Lev	4:21	the sin offering for the **a**.
Num	10: 3	congregation shall **a** before
Deut	23: 1	admitted to the **a** of the LORD.
1 Kings	18:19	Israel **a** for me at Mount
2 Chr	29:28	The whole **a** worshiped, the
Neh	8: 2	brought the law before the **a**,
Ps	149: 1	praise in the **a** of the faithful.
Isa	48:14	**A**, all of you, and hear
Joel	1:14	call a solemn **a**. Gather the
	2:15	a fast; call a solemn **a**;
Zeph	3: 8	nations, to **a** kingdoms,
Lk	23: 1	Then the **a** rose as a body and
Heb	12:23	the **a** of the firstborn who are
Jas	2: 2	into your **a**, and if a poor
Rev	16:14	world, to **a** them for battle

ASSURANCE

Deut	28:66	dread, with no **a** of your life.
Heb	10:22	a true heart in full **a** of faith,
	11: 1	Now faith is the **a** of things

ASSYRIA (ASSYRIANS)

Gen	10:11	into **A**, and built Nineveh,
2 Kings	15:19	King Pul of **A** came against the
	18:11	The king of **A** carried the
Tob	1:10	carried way captive to **A**
Isa	10: 5	Ah, **A**, the rod of my anger
	10:24	not be afraid of the **A** when
Jer	50:18	I punished the king of **A**.
Ezek	23: 5	lusted after her lovers the **A**,
Hos	14: 3	**A** shall not save us; we
Nah	3:18	O king of **A**; your nobles
Zech	10:10	gather them from **A**; I will

ASTRAY

Num	5:12	wife goes **a** and is unfaithful
Deut	30:17	but are led **a** to bow down to
Ps	14: 3	They have all gone **a**, they are
	119:176	I have gone **a** like a lost sheep;
Prov	10:17	who rejects a rebuke goes **a**
	20: 1	whoever is led **a** by it is not
Sir	31:5	pursues money will be led **a**
Isa	53: 6	we like sheep have gone **a**;
Jer	23:13	and led my people Israel **a**.
	50: 6	shepherds have led them **a**,
Ezek	14:11	Israel may no longer go **a**
Am	2: 4	they have been led **a** by the
Mt	18:12	one of them has gone **a**,
	24: 5	and they will lead many **a**.
Mk	13: 5	that no one leads you **a**.
1 Cor	12: 2	were enticed and led **a** to idols
2 Cor	11: 3	your thoughts will be led **a**

1 Pet	2:25	you were going **a** like sheep,
2 Pet	2:15	straight road and have gone **a**,

ATONE (D) (ATONING)

Prov	16: 6	iniquity is **a** for, and by the
Dan	4:27	**a** for your sins with
	9:24	and to **a** for iniquity,
1 Jn	2: 2	and he is the **a** sacrifice for our
	4:10	the **a** sacrifice for our sins.

ATONEMENT

Ex	29:36	as a sin offering for **a**.
	32:30	I can make **a** for your sin."
Lev	4:35	priest shall make **a** on your
Num	8:21	and Aaron made **a** for them to
	25:13	and made **a** for the Israelites.'
1 Chr	6:49	to make **a** for Israel, according
Neh	10:33	offerings to make **a** for Israel,
Rom	3:25	as a sacrifice of **a** by his blood,
Heb	2:17	sacrifice of **a** for the sins of the

AUTHORITY (AUTHORITIES)

Gen	41:45	Thus Joseph gained **a** over the
Prov	29: 2	When the righteous are in **a**,
Sir	20:8	pretends to **a** is hated.
Isa	9: 6	a son given to us; **a** rests upon
Mt	9: 6	the Son of Man has **a** on earth
	28:18	"All **a** in heaven and on earth
Mk	1:27	A new teaching—with **a**! He
	11:28	"By what **a** are you doing
Lk	5:24	the Son of Man has **a** on earth
	12:11	and the **a**, do not worry about
Jn	5:27	has given him **a** to execute
	12:42	many, even of the **a**, believed
Acts	1: 7	has set by his own **a**.
	5:29	God rather than any human **a**.
Rom	13: 1	be subject to the governing **a**;
	13: 2	whoever resists **a** resists what
1 Cor	7: 4	wife does not have **a** over her
	15:24	every ruler and every **a** and
2 Cor	10: 8	our **a**, which the Lord gave
Eph	1:21	far above all rule and **a** and
	3:10	rulers and the **a** in the heavenly
Col	2:10	head of every ruler and **a**.
	2:15	the rulers and **a** and made a
1 Tim	2:12	to teach or to have **a** over a
Titus	2:15	exhort and reprove with all **a**.
	3: 1	be subject to rulers and **a**, to
1 Pet	2:13	accept the **a** of every human
	3: 5	be the **a** of their husbands.
	5: 5	accept the **a** of the elders.
2 Pet	2:10	lust, and who despise **a**.
3 Jn	1: 9	does not acknowledge our **a**.
Jude	1: 8	defile the flesh, reject **a**, and
Rev	2:26	I will give **a** over the nations;
	13: 4	given his **a** to the beast,
	20: 4	on them were given **a** to judge.

AWAKE

Judg	5:12	**A**, **a**, Deborah!**a**, **a**, utter
Ps	44:23	O LORD? **A**, do not cast us off
	57: 8	**A**, my soul! **A**, O harp and
Prov	6:22	and when you **a**, they will talk
Song	5: 2	slept, but my heart was **a**.
Isa	51: 9	**A**, **a**, put on strength, O
	52: 1	**A**, **a**, put on your strength
Dan	12: 2	dust of the earth shall **a**,
Zech	13: 7	**A**, O sword, against my
Mt	24:42	Keep **a** therefore, for you do
	26:38	and stay **a** with me."

Mk 14:37 Could you not keep **a** one
Eph 5:14 "Sleeper, **a**! Rise from the
1 Thess 5: 6 but let us keep **a** and be sober;
5:10 whether we are **a** or asleep
Rev 16:15 who stays **a** and is clothed,

AWE (SOME)
Gen 28:17 "How **a** is this place! This is
Ex 15:11 in holiness, **a** in splendor,
34:10 for it is an **a** thing that I will
Deut 6:22 great and **a** signs and wonders
10:17 the great God, mighty and **a**, l
Josh 4:14 and they stood in **a** of him, as
2 Sam 7:23 doing great and **a** things for
1 Kings 3:28 they stood in **a** of the king,
Neh 1: 5 the great and **a** God who
9:32 mighty and **a** God, keeping
Job 37:22 around God is **a** majesty.
Ps 47: 2 the Most High, is **a**, a great
66: 3 Say to God, "How **a** are your
76: 7 But you indeed are **a**! Who
Sir 43:29 **A** is the Lord and very great,
Isa 29:23 and will stand in **a** of the God
64: 3 When you did **a** deeds that we
Ezek 1:18 Their rims were tall and **a**, for
Dan 9: 4 "Ah, LORD, great and **a** God,
Hos 3: 5 come in **a** to the LORD and to
Hab 3: 2 and I stand in **a**, O LORD, of
Mal 2: 5 and stood in **a** of my name.
Mt 9: 8 they were filled with **a**, and
Lk 5:26 God and were filled with **a**,
Acts 2:43 **A** came upon everyone,
Rom 11:20 become proud, but stand in **a**.
Heb 12:28 worship with reverence and **a**;

B

BAAL (S)
Num 25: 3 Israel yoked itself to the **B** of
Deut 4: 3 with regard to the **B** of Peor—
Judg 2:13 the LORD, and worshiped **B**
6:31 "Will you contend for **B**? Or
1 Sam 7: 4 So Israel put away the **B** and
1 Kings 16:32 altar for **B** in the house of **B**
18:25 said to the prophets of **B**,
2 Kings 3: 2 he removed the pillar of **B** that
10:28 Thus Jehu wiped out **B** from
2 Chr 17: 3 he did not seek the **B**,
23:17 killed Mattan, the priest of **B**,
Ps 106:28 themselves to the **B** of Peor,
Jer 2: 8 the prophets prophesied by **B**,
19: 5 the high places of **B** to burn
Hos 2:17 names of the **B** from her
13: 1 incurred guilt through **B** and
Rom 11: 4 not bowed the knee to **B**."

BABYLON
2 Kings 24:15 captivity from Jerusalem to **B**.
1 Chr 9: 1 into exile in **B** because of
2 Chr 36:18 all these he brought to **B**.
36:20 took into exile in **B** those who
Ps 137: 1 By the rivers of **B**—there we
137: 8 O daughter **B**, you devastator!
Isa 13: 1 concerning **B** that Isaiah son
21: 9 "Fallen, fallen is **B**; and all the
Jer 25:11 serve the king of **B** seventy

Jer 51:37 and **B** shall become a heap of
Bar 2:24 to serve the king of **B**;
Dan 2:48 whole province of **B** and chief
4:30 "Is this not magnificent **B**,
1 Pet 5:13 Your sister church in **B**, chosen
Rev 14: 8 "Fallen, fallen is **B** the great!
17: 5 "**B** the great, mother of whores
18: 2 "Fallen, fallen is **B** the great!

BAPTISM (S)
Mt 3: 7 Sadducees coming for **b**,
21:25 Did the **b** of John come from
Mk 1: 4 proclaiming a **b** of repentance
10:38 or be baptized with the **b** that
Lk 7:29 been baptized with John's **b**.
12:50 I have a **b** with which to be
Acts 13:24 proclaimed a **b** of repentance
18:25 knew only the **b** of John.
Rom 6: 4 with him by **b** into death,
1 Cor 15:29 receive **b** on behalf of the dead
Eph 4: 5 one Lord, one faith, one **b**,
Col 2:12 buried with him in **b**, you
Heb 6: 2 instruction about **b**, laying on
9:10 drink and various **b**, regulations
1 Pet 3:21 And **b**, which this prefigured,

BAPTIZE (D) (BAPTIZING)
Mt 3:11 "I **b** you with water for
3:16 And when Jesus had been **b**,
28:19 of all nations, **b** them in the
Mk 1: 8 **b** you with water; but he will **b**
1: 9 Galilee and was **b** by John in
16:16 one who believes and is **b** will
Lk 3: 7 that came out to be **b** by him,
3:16 He will **b** you with the Holy
Jn 3:23 kept coming and were being **b**
4: 2 but his disciples who **b**—
Acts 2:38 "Repent, and be **b** every one of
8:12 they were **b**, both men and
10:48 to be **b** in the name of Jesus
16:33 and his entire family were **b**
Rom 6: 3 **b** into Christ Jesus were **b**
1 Cor 1:13 were you **b** in the name of Paul
10: 2 and all were **b** into Moses in
12:13 we were all **b** into one body—
Gal 3:27 you as were **b** into Christ

BARREN (NESS)
Gen 11:30 Now Sarai was **b**; she had no
29:31 her womb; but Rachel was **b**.
Ex 23:26 miscarry or be **b** in your land;
Deut 7:14 neither sterility nor **b** among
Judg 13: 2 His wife was **b**, having borne
1 Sam 2: 5 The **b** has borne seven, but she
Ps 113: 9 He gives the **b** woman a home,
Prov 30:16 the **b** womb, the earth ever
Isa 49:21 I was bereaved and **b**, exiled
Lk 1: 7 because Elizabeth was **b**, and
23:29 'Blessed are the **b**, and the
Rom 4:19 considered the **b** of Sarah's
Heb 11:11 and Sarah herself was **b**—
Jas 2:20 faith apart from works is **b**?

BATTLE
Ex 13:18 land of Egypt prepared for **b**.
Josh 4:13 the plains of Jericho for **b**.
1 Sam 17:47 for the **b** is the LORD's
2 Sam 1:25 midst of the **b**! Jonathan lies
1 Kings 22:30 disguise myself and go into **b**,
2 Chr 20:15 the **b** is not yours but God's.

1 Macc 3:19 the army that victory in **b**
Ps 24: 8 mighty, the LORD, mighty in **b**
Eccl 9:11 swift, nor the **b** to the strong,
Ezek 13: 5 it might stand in **b** on the day
1 Cor 14: 8 who will get ready for **b**?
Rev 16:14 assemble them for **b** on the
20: 8 to gather them for **b**; they are

BEAR (S) (BORE)
Gen 4:13 is greater than I can **b**!
17:19 your wife Sarah shall **b** you a
Ex 19: 4 how I **b** you on eagles' wings
23: 2 when you **b** witness in a
Josh 3:17 the priests who **b** the ark of
Judg 13: 3 shall conceive and **b** a son.
1 Sam 17:36 has killed both lions and **b**
Job 9: 9 who made the **B** and Orion,
Ps 68:19 be the Lord, who daily **b**
Isa 7:14 and shall **b** a son, and shall
11: 7 The cow and the **b** shall graze,
Jer 30: 6 can a man **b** a child? Why
Ezek 3:14 spirit lifted me up and **b** me
14:10 they shall **b** their punishment
Dan 7: 5 that looked like a **b**.
Am 5:19 and was met by a **b**; or went
Mt 1:23 the virgin shall conceive and **b**
7:18 A good tree cannot **b** bad fruit,
8:17 "He took our infirmities and **b**
Lk 1:13 Elizabeth will **b** you a son,
11:46 with burdens hard to **b**,
Jn 15: 2 he prunes to make it **b** more
15: 8 that you **b** much fruit and
Acts 15:10 we have been able to **b**?
Rom 7: 4 that we may **b** fruit for God.
1 Cor 15:49 we will also **b** the image of the
Gal 6: 2 **B** one another's burdens,
Col 1:10 as you **b** fruit in every good
3:13 **B** with one another and, if
Heb 9:28 offered once to **b** the sins of
1 Pet 2:24 himself **b** our sins in his body
4:16 glorify God because you **b** this
Rev 12: 4 woman who was about to **b** a

BEAT (EN) (ING)
Ex 2:11 an Egyptian **b** a Hebrew, one
5:16 Look how your servants are **b**!
Deut 24:20 When you **b** your olive trees,
Neh 13:25 cursed them and **b** some of
Prov 23:35 they **b** me, but I did not
Song 5: 7 they **b** me, they wounded me,
Isa 2: 4 they shall **b** their swords into
Joel 3:10 **B** your plowshares into
Mic 4: 3 they shall **b** their swords into
Mt 7:25 winds blew and **b** on that
Mk 14:65 also took him over and **b** him.
Lk 10:30 who stripped him, **b** him, and
22:63 began to mock him and **b**
Acts 22:19 and **b** those who believed in
1 Cor 9:26 do I box as though **b** the air;
2 Cor 11:25 Three times I was **b** with rods.
1 Pet 2:20 endure when you are **b** for

BEAUTIFUL (BEAUTY)
Gen 12:11 a woman **b** in appearance;
Deut 21:11 among the captives a **b**
Josh 7:21 among the spoil a **b** mantle
1 Sam 16:12 he was ruddy, and had **b** eyes,
25: 3 The woman was clever and **b**,
2 Sam 11: 2 the woman was very **b**.
14:25 so much for his **b** as Absalom;

1 Kings	1: 3	they searched for a **b** girl
Jdt	10: 7	greatly astounded at her **b**
Esth	1:11	peoples and the officials her **b**;
	2: 7	the girl was fair and **b**, and
Job	42:15	no women so **b** as Job's
Ps	27: 4	to behold the **b** of the LORD,
	48: 2	**b** in elevation, is the joy
Prov	6:25	Do not desire her **b** in your
	31:30	Charm is deceitful, and **b** is
Song	1:15	Ah, you are **b**, my love; ah,
	4: 7	You are altogether **b**, my love;
Wis	13:3	If through delight in the **b** of
Isa	28: 1	fading flower of its glorious **b**,
	52: 7	How **b** upon the mountains
Jer	13:18	for your **b** crown has come
	13:20	was given you, your **b** flock?
Lam	2:15	was called the perfection of **b**,
Bar	5:1	the **b** of the glory from God.
Ezek	16:17	You also took your **b** jewels of
	28:12	of wisdom and perfect in **b**.
Dan	4:12	Its foliage was **b**, its fruit
	11:41	He shall come into the **b** land,
Hos	14: 6	his **b** shall be like the olive
Am	8:13	day the **b** young women
Zech	9:17	For what goodness and **b** are
Mt	23:27	on the outside look **b**, but
Lk	21: 5	it was adorned with **b** stones
Acts	3: 2	temple called the **B** Gate
	7:20	and he was **b** before God.
Rom	10:15	"How **b** are the feet of those
Heb	11:23	the child was **b**; and they were
Jas	1:11	flower falls, and its **b** perishes.
1 Pet	3: 4	with the lasting **b** of a gentle

BEFORE

Gen	18:22	remained standing **b** the
	45: 5	for God sent me **b** you to
Ex	20: 3	shall have no other gods **b** me.
	33: 2	I will send an angel **b** you,
Lev	10: 2	and they died **b** the LORD.
Num	17: 7	So Moses placed the staffs **b**
Deut	1:30	LORD your God, who goes **b**
	11:26	See, I am setting **b** you today a
1 Sam	4:7	like this has happened **b**.
Job	4:17	righteous **b** God? Can human
Ps	16: 8	I keep the LORD always **b** me;
	37: 7	Be still **b** the LORD, and wait
	139: 4	Even **b** a word is on my
Prov	16:18	Pride goes **b** destruction, and
	18:13	If one gives answer **b** hearing,
Isa	49: 1	The LORD called me **b** I was
	65:24	**B** they call I will answer
Jer	1: 5	**B** I formed you in the womb
Zeph	1: 7	Be silent **b** the Lord GOD!
Zech	2:13	Be silent, all people, **b** the
Mal	3: 1	to prepare the way **b** me,
Mt	6: 8	Father knows what you need **b**
	11:10	who will prepare your way **b**
Lk	12: 8	who acknowledges me **b**
	22:61	"**B** the cock crows today, you
Jn	8:58	**b** Abraham was, I am."
	13:19	I tell you this now, **b** it occurs,
Acts	2:25	'I saw the Lord always **b** me,
	8:32	and like a lamb silent **b** its
Rom	4:10	but **b** he was circumcised.
	14:10	all stand **b** the judgment seat
Gal	1:15	had set me apart **b** I was born
Col	1:17	He himself is **b** all things,
Titus	1: 2	who never lies, promised **b** the
Heb	12: 2	the joy that was set **b** him

1 Pet	1:20	destined **b** the foundation of
Rev	7: 9	standing **b** the throne and **b**

BEG (BEGGED) (BEGGAR)

Sir	40:28	do not lead the life of a **b**;
Lam	4: 4	the children **b** for food, but no
Mt	8:31	The demons **b** him, "If you
Mk	6:56	and **b** him that they might
	10:46	a blind **b**, was sitting by the
Lk	16: 3	and I am ashamed to **b**.
Jn	9: 8	who used to sit and **b**?"
	9: 8	before as a **b** began to ask,

BEGINNING

Gen	1: 1	In the **b** when God created the
Ps	111:10	of the LORD is the **b** of wisdom;
Prov	8:22	LORD created me at the **b** of
	9:10	fear of the LORD is the **b** of
Eccl	3:11	God has done from the **b** to
Wis	6:17	The **b** of wisdom is the most
Sir	1:14	the Lord is the **b** of wisdom;
Isa	46:10	declaring the end from the **b**
Mt	24: 8	is but the **b** of the birth pangs.
	24:21	been from the **b** of the world
Mk	1: 1	The **b** of the good news of
Lk	1: 2	from the **b** were eyewitnesses
Jn	1: 1	In the **b** was the Word, and
	15:27	been with me from the **b**.
Acts	1: 1	did and taught from the **b**
Col	1:18	he is the **b**, the firstborn from
Heb	7: 3	having neither **b** of days nor
1 Jn	1: 1	what was from the **b**, what we
2 Jn	1: 6	have heard it from the **b**—you
Rev	21: 6	Alpha and the Omega, the **b**

BEHIND

Ps	50:17	and you cast my words **b** you.
	139: 5	You hem me in, **b** and before,
Isa	38:17	cast all my sins **b** your back.
Ezek	3:12	I heard **b** me the sound of
Mt	16:23	"Get **b** me, Satan! You are a
Lk	2:43	the boy Jesus stayed **b** in
	8:44	She came up **b** him and
Phil	3:13	forgetting what lies **b** and
Heb	6: 1	leaving the basic teaching
Rev	1:10	and I heard **b** me a loud voice
	4: 6	of eyes in front and **b**:

BELIEVE (D) (S) (BELIEVING)

Gen	45:26	he could not **b** them.
Ex	4: 5	they may **b** that the LORD,
	14:31	people feared the LORD and **b**
Num	14:11	long will they refuse to **b** in
1 Kings	10: 7	but I did not **b** the reports
2 Kings	17:14	who did not **b** in the LORD
2 Chr	20:20	**B** in the LORD your God
Tob	2:14	But I did not **b** her
Job	9:16	I do not **b** that he would listen
Ps	78:32	they did not **b** in his wonders.
	106:12	Then they **b** his words; they
Prov	14:15	The simple **b** everything, but
Sir	19:15	do not **b** everything you hear
Isa	53: 1	Who has **b** what we have
Jer	12: 6	do not **b** them, though they
Jon	3: 5	And the people of Nineveh **b**
Hab	1: 5	that you would not **b** if you
Mt	9:28	"Do you **b** that I am able to
	21:32	and the prostitutes **b** him;
Mk	9:42	these little ones who **b** in me,
	11:24	in prayer, **b** that you have

Lk	1:45	And blessed is she who **b** that
	20: 5	'Why did you not **b** him?'
Jn	1: 7	so that all might **b** through
	11:40	if you **b**, you would see the
	20:31	through **b** you may have life
Acts	2:44	All who **b** were together and
	15:11	we **b** that we will be saved
	24:14	**b** everything laid down
Rom	4:11	who **b** without being
	10: 9	and **b** in your heart that God
1 Cor	13: 7	bears all things, **b** all things,
2 Cor	4:13	—we also **b**, and so we
Gal	3: 2	law or by **b** what you heard?
	3:22	be given to those who **b**.
Eph	1:19	his power for us who **b**,
Phil	1:29	not only of **b** in Christ,
1 Thess	4:14	For since we **b** that Jesus died
2 Thess	2:11	leading them to **b** what is
1 Tim	1:16	who would come to **b** in him
2 Tim	3:14	you have learned and firmly **b**,
Titus	3: 8	who have come to **b** in God
Heb	11: 6	must **b** that he exists and that
Jas	2:19	You **b** that God is one;
1 Pet	2: 7	who do not **b**, "The stone
1 Jn	4: 1	Beloved, do not **b** every spirit,
	5: 1	Everyone who **b** that Jesus is
Jude	1: 5	those who did not **b**.

BELIEVER (S)

Jn	7:39	about the Spirit, which **b** in
Acts	11:21	and a great number became **b**
	16:34	that he had become a **b** in
	18:27	through grace had become **b**
Rom	13:11	now than when we became **b**;
1 Cor	6: 6	but a **b** goes to court against a
2 Cor	6:15	a **b** share with an unbeliever?
Gal	2: 4	because of false **b** secretly
1 Thess	2:13	also at work in you **b**.
2 Thess	3: 6	away from **b** who are living in
1 Tim	4:12	but set the **b** an example in
Jas	1: 9	Let the **b** who is lowly boast in
1 Pet	2:17	Love the family of **b**.
1 Jn	2:11	whoever hates another **b** is

BELONG (S)

Gen	40: 8	"Do not interpretations **b** to
Deut	29:29	The secret things **b** to the
Ps	3: 8	Deliverance **b** to the LORD;
	89:18	For our shield **b** to the LORD,
Prov	16: 1	The plans of the mind **b** to
Dan	9: 9	To the Lord our God **b** mercy
Jon	2: 9	Deliverance **b** to the LORD!"
Mt	19:14	the kingdom of heaven **b**."
Jn	10:16	sheep that do **b** to this
	18:37	Everyone who **b** to the truth
Rom	8: 9	Spirit of Christ does not **b** to
1 Cor	1:12	"I **b** to Paul," or "I **b** to
2 Cor	10: 7	confident that you **b** to Christ,
Gal	3:29	And if you **b** to Christ, then
Col	2:17	but the substance **b** to Christ.
1 Thess	5: 8	But since we **b** to the day,
1 Jn	2:19	but they did not **b** to us; for if
Rev	7:10	"Salvation **b** to our God

BELOVED

Deut	33:12	The **b** of the LORD rests in
2 Sam	1:26	Jonathan; greatly **b** were you
Neh	13:26	and he was **b** by his God, and
Jdt	9:4	divided among your **b**
Ps	127: 2	he gives sleep to his **b**.

Song	2:16	My **b** is mine and I am
	7:11	Come, my **b**, let us go forth
Sir	20:13	The wise make themselves **b**
Isa	5: 1	My **b** had a vineyard on a
Jer	12: 7	I have given the **b** of my heart
Bar	4:16	led away the widow's **b** sons
Dan	9:23	for you are greatly **b**.
Mt	17: 5	"This is my Son, the **B**; with
Mk	9: 7	"This is my Son, the **B**; listen
Lk	20:13	I will send my **b** son;
Rom	12:19	**B**, never avenge yourselves,
1 Cor	15:58	Therefore, my **b**, be steadfast,
2 Cor	12:19	Everything we do, **b**, is for the
Eph	5: 1	be imitators of God, as **b**
Phil	4: 8	Finally, **b**, whatever is true,
Col	3:12	chosen ones, holy and **b**,
1 Thess	5:14	And we urge you, **b**, to
2 Thess	2:13	brothers and sisters **b** by the
1 Tim	6: 2	service are believers and **b**.
Philem	1:16	more than a slave, a **b**
Heb	6: 9	in this way, **b**, we are confident
Jas	5: 9	**B**, do not grumble against one
1 Pet	2:11	**B**, I urge you as aliens
2 Pet	3: 8	one fact, **b**, that with the Lord
1 Jn	4: 1	**B**, do not believe every spirit
3 Jn	1:11	**B**, do not imitate what is
Jude	1:20	But you, **b**, build yourselves
Rev	20: 9	of the saints and the **b** city.

BESIDES

Deut	32:39	there is no god **b** me.
1 Sam	2: 2	no one **b** you; there is no Rock
1 Chr	17:20	and there is no God **b** you,
Ps	18:31	who is a rock **b** our God?—
Isa	45:21	There is no other god **b** me, a

BETHLEHEM

Gen	35:19	way to Ephrath (that is, **B**),
Ruth	4:11	and bestow a name in **B**;
1 Sam	17:12	son of an Ephrathite of **B**
2 Sam	23:15	drink from the well of **B**
Mic	5: 2	But you, O **B** of Ephrathah,
Mt	2: 1	after Jesus was born in **B** of
Lk	2:15	"Let us go now to **B** and see
Jn	7:42	David and comes from **B**,

BETRAY (ED)

Mt	26:21	one of you will **b** me."
Mk	14:11	look for an opportunity to **b**
Lk	21:16	You will be **b** even by parents
Jn	13:11	he knew who was to **b** him;
1 Cor	11:23	the night when he was **b** took

BETTER

Num	11:18	Surely it was **b** for us in Egypt.'
Ruth	3:10	instance of your loyalty is **b**
1 Sam	15:22	Surely, to obey is **b** than
Tob	12:8	A little with righteousness is **b**
Ps	63: 3	your steadfast love is **b** than
Prov	16: 8	**B** is a little with righteousness
	16:19	It is **b** to be of a lowly
	19: 1	**B** the poor walking in integrity
	22: 1	favor is **b** than silver or gold.
Eccl	3:22	saw that there is nothing **b**
	5: 5	It is **b** that you should not vow
	7: 8	the patient in spirit are **b** than
Song	1: 2	For your love is **b** than wine,
Sir	23:27	is **b** than the fear of the Lord.
Jer	10: 8	given by idols is no **b** than
Dan	1:20	times **b** than all the magicians

Jon	4: 3	for it is **b** for me to die than
Mt	18: 6	it would be **b** for you if a great
Mk	14:21	It would have been **b** for that
Lk	10:42	Mary has chosen the **b** part,
Jn	11:50	it is **b** for you to have one
Rom	14: 5	judge one day to be **b** than
1 Cor	7: 9	For it is **b** to marry than to be
Phil	2: 3	regard others as **b** than
Heb	7:22	the guarantee of a **b** covenant.
	10:34	possessed something **b** and
1 Pet	3:17	For it is **b** to suffer for doing
2 Pet	2:21	would have been **b** for them

BEWARE

Job	36:21	**B**! Do not turn to iniquity
Eccl	12:12	beyond these, my child, **b**.
Jer	9: 4	**B** of your neighbors, and
Mt	7:15	**B** of false prophets, who come
Mk	13: 5	"**B** that no one leads you
Lk	20:46	**B** of the scribes, who like
Phil	3: 2	**B** of the dogs, **b** of
Rev	2:10	**B**, the devil is about to

BEYOND

Gen	31:52	I will not pass **b** this heap to
Num	22:18	I could not go **b** the command
Ps	147: 5	his understanding is **b**
Eccl	12:12	anything **b** these, my child,
Sir	3:23	meddle in matters that are **b**
	6:15	Faithful friends are **b** price
Isa	52:14	and his form **b** that of
Lam	5:22	and are angry with us **b**
1 Cor	10:13	not let you be tested **b** your
2 Cor	4:17	eternal weight of glory **b** all
2 Jn	1: 9	teaching of Christ, but goes **b**

BIND (S)

Deut	6: 8	**B** them as a sign on
Judg	15:10	"We have come up to **b**
Job	5:18	For he wounds, but he **b** up;
Ps	147: 3	and **b** up their wounds.
Prov	6:21	**B** them upon your heart
Isa	30:26	the LORD **b** up the injuries of
Ezek	34:16	I will **b** up the injured,
Mt	16:19	whatever you **b** on earth will
Col	3:14	love, which **b** everything

BIRTH

Deut	32:18	the God who gave you **b**.
Judg	13: 5	a nazirite to God from **b**.
Job	3: 1	cursed the day of his **b**.
Ps	22:10	I was cast from my **b**, and
Eccl	7: 1	death, than the day of **b**.
Isa	26:18	we writhed, but we gave **b**
Jer	2:27	a stone, 'You gave me **b**."
Mt	1:18	Now the **b** of Jesus the
Lk	1:14	many will rejoice at his **b**,
Jn	9: 1	saw a man blind from **b**.
Acts	3: 2	a man lame from **b** was being
1 Cor	1:26	not many were of noble **b**.
Eph	2:11	one time you Gentiles by **b**,
Jas	1:18	own purpose he gave us **b** by
1 Pet	1: 3	given us a new **b** into a living
Rev	12: 5	And she gave **b** to a son, a

BIRTHRIGHT

Gen	25:34	Thus Esau despised his **b**.
1 Chr	5: 2	yet the **b** belonged to Joseph.)
Heb	12:16	who sold his **b** for a single

BISHOP

1 Tim	3: 1	aspires to the office of **b**
	3: 2	Now a **b** must be above
Titus	1: 7	For a **b**, as God's steward,

BITTER (NESS)

Ex	12: 8	with unleavened bread and **b**
Num	5:18	shall have the water of **b** that
	5:24	shall enter her and cause **b**
Ruth	1:13	it has been far more **b** for me
Prov	14:10	The heart knows its own **b**,
	27: 7	a ravenous appetite even the **b**
Eccl	7:26	more **b** than death the woman
Isa	5:20	who put **b** for sweet and sweet
Zeph	1:14	day of the LORD is **b**,
Rom	3:14	are full of cursing and **b**."
Eph	4:31	Put away from you all **b** and
Heb	12:15	that no root of **b** springs up
Rev	10: 9	it will be **b** to your stomach,

BLAMELESS

Gen	6: 9	Noah was a righteous man, **b**
1 Sam	29: 9	know that you are as **b** in my
2 Sam	22:24	I was **b** before him, and I kept
Job	2: 3	a **b** and upright man who
	9:22	he destroys both the **b** and the
Ps	18:23	I was **b** before him, and I kept
	119: 1	those whose way is **b**,
Prov	11:20	but those of **b** ways are his
Wis	4: 9	and a **b** life is ripe old age.
	18:21	For a **b** man was quick to
Sir	11:10	you will not be held **b**.
Ezek	28:15	You were **b** in your ways from
Dan	6:22	because I was found **b** before
1 Cor	1: 8	so that you may be **b** on the
Eph	1: 4	to be holy and **b** before him
Phil	2:15	so that you may be **b** and
Col	1:22	to present you holy and **b** and
1 Thess	5:23	sound and **b** at the coming of
1 Tim	3:10	prove themselves **b**, let them
Titus	1: 6	someone who is **b**, married
Heb	7:26	such a high priest, holy, **b**,
Rev	14: 5	lie was found; they are **b**.

BLASPHEME (D) (S)

Lev	24:11	woman's son **b** the Name in a
	24:16	who **b** the name of the LORD
Ezek	20:27	In this again your ancestors **b**
Mt	26:65	said, "He has **b**! Why do we
Mk	3:29	whoever **b** against the Holy
Lk	12:10	whoever **b** against the Holy
Acts	26:11	tried to force them to **b**;
Rom	2:24	"The name of God is **b** among
1 Tim	6: 1	the teaching may not be **b**.
Jas	2: 7	they who **b** the excellent name
1 Pet	4: 4	of dissipation, and so they **b**.

BLASPHEMIES (BLASPHEMER)

Lev	24:16	congregation shall stone the **b**.
Neh	9:18	and had committed great **b**,
Mk	3:28	their sins and whatever **b** they
Lk	5:21	who is speaking **b**?
1 Tim	1:13	though I was formerly a **b**,
Rev	13: 6	mouth to utter **b** against God,

BLESS (ED)

Gen	1:22	God **b** them, saying, "Be
	22:17	I will indeed **b** you, and I will
Ex	20:11	the LORD **b** the sabbath day
	23:25	I will **b** your bread and your

Lev	9:22	the people and **b** them; and
Num	6:24	The Lord **b** you and keep you;
	22: 6	whomever you **b** is **b**, and
Deut	7:14	hall be the most **b** of peoples,
	28: 8	he will **b** you in the land that
Josh	8:33	should **b** the people of Israel.
Judg	13:24	boy grew, and the LORD **b** him.
Ruth	2: 4	They answered, "The LORD **b**
1 Sam	25:33	**B** be your good sense, and
2 Sam	7:29	you to **b** the house of your
1 Kings	1:48	on to pray thus, **B** be the
1 Chr	4:10	that you would **b** me and
2 Chr	31:10	for the Lord has **b** his people,
Neh	9: 5	**B** be your glorious name,
Tob	8:15	Let them **b** you forever
Job	42:12	The **b** the latter days of
Ps	89:52	**B** be the LORD forever. Amen
	104: 1	**B** the LORD, O my soul
Prov	22: 9	Those who are generous are **b**,
Sir	39:35	and **b** the name of the Lord.
Isa	30:18	**b** are all those who wait
Jer	31:23	"The LORD **b** you, O abode of
Ezek	37:26	and I will **b** them and
Dan	2:20	Daniel said: "**B** be the name of
Mt	5: 3	**B** are the poor in spirit
Mk	6:41	**b** and broke the loaves,
Lk	1:42	"**B** are you among women,
	6:28	**b** those who curse you, pray
Jn	20:29	**B** are those who have not
Acts	3:26	to you, to **b** you by turning
	20:35	'It is more **b** to give than to
Rom	4: 7	**B** are those whose iniquities
1 Cor	4:12	When reviled, we **b**; when
Gal	3: 8	"All the Gentiles shall be **b** in
Eph	1: 3	**B** be the God and Father
Titus	2:13	while we wait for the **b** hope
Heb	6:14	"I will surely **b** you and
	7: 7	that the inferior is **b** by the
Jas	1:12	**B** is anyone who endures
1 Pet	3:14	what is right, you are **b**.
Rev	22: 7	**B** is the one who keeps

BLESSING (S)

Gen	12: 2	that you will be a **b**.
Ex	32:29	have brought a **b** on
Lev	25:21	I will order my **b** for you in
Deut	11:26	setting before you today a **b**
	28: 2	all these **b** shall come upon
Josh	8:34	the words of the law, **b** and
2 Sam	7:29	with your **b** shall the house of
1 Chr	23:13	and pronounce **b** in his name
Neh	13: 2	turned the curse into a **b**.
Ps	24: 5	They will receive **b** from the
	144:15	the people to whom such **b**
Prov	10:22	The **b** of the LORD makes rich
Isa	44: 3	and my **b** on your offspring.
Ezek	34:26	they shall be showers of **b**.
Joel	2:14	and leave a **b** behind him, a
Zech	8:13	you shall be a **b**. Do not
Mal	2: 2	and I will curse your **b**;
	3:10	for you an overflowing **b**.
Mk	14:22	and after **b** it he broke it, gave
Lk	24:51	While he was **b** them, he
Rom	15:29	in the fullness of the **b** of
1 Cor	14:16	if you say a **b** with the spirit,
Gal	3:14	in Christ Jesus the **b** of
Eph	1: 3	with every spiritual **b** in the
Heb	12:17	he wanted to inherit the **b**, he
Jas	3:10	From the same mouth come **b**
1 Pet	3: 9	the contrary, repay with a **b**.

Rev	5:12	and honor and glory and **b**!"

BLIND (ED) (NESS)

Gen	19:11	And they struck with **b** the
Ex	4:11	mute or deaf, seeing or **b**?
Lev	19:14	block before the **b**;
Deut	27:18	be anyone who misleads a **b**
	28:28	you with madness, **b**, and
2 Sam	5: 8	attack the lame and the **b**,
2 Kings	6:18	this people, please, with **b**."
Tob	2:10	until I became completely **b**
Job	29:15	I was eyes to the **b**, and feet to
Ps	146: 8	opens the eyes of the **b**.
Isa	35: 5	Then the eyes of the **b** shall be
Zech	11:17	his right eye utterly **b**!
	12: 4	horse of the peoples with **b**.
Mal	1: 8	When you offer **b** animals in
Mt	11: 5	the **b** receive their sight, the
Mk	10:46	a **b** beggar, was sitting by the
Lk	6:39	"Can a **b** person guide a **b**
Jn	9:25	though I was **b**, now I see."
Rom	2:19	a guide to the **b**, a light to
2 Pet	1: 9	things is nearsighted and **b**,
1 Jn	2:11	darkness has brought on **b**.
Rev	3:17	are wretched, pitiable, poor, **b**,

BLOOD (SHED)

Gen	4:10	your brother's **b** is crying out
Ex	12:13	when I see the **b**, I will pass
Lev	17: 4	shall be held guilty of **b**;
Num	35:19	The avenger of **b** is the one
Deut	12:23	not eat the **b**; for the **b** is
1 Sam	14:32	troops ate them with the **b**.
1 Kings	21:19	will also lick up your **b**."
2 Kings	9:33	some of her **b** spattered on the
Ps	51:14	Deliver me from **b**, O God,
	72:14	precious is their **b** in his sight.
Prov	6:17	hands that shed innocent **b**,
Isa	5: 7	he expected justice, but saw **b**;
	34: 6	it is sated with **b**, it is gorged
Jer	48:10	keeps back the sword from **b**.
Ezek	33: 4	their **b** shall be upon their
Hos	4: 2	**b** follows **b**.
Joel	2:31	darkness, and the moon to **b**,
Hab	2: 8	because of human **b**, and
Zech	9:11	because of the **b** of my
Mt	27:24	innocent of this man's **b**."
Mk	14:24	"This is my **b** of the covenant,
Lk	22:20	the new covenant in my **b**.
Jn	1:13	who were born, not of **b** or of
Acts	18: 6	"Your **b** be on your own heads
Rom	3:25	of atonement by his **b**,
1 Cor	10:16	not a sharing in the **b** of
Eph	6:12	against enemies of **b** and flesh,
Col	1:20	making peace through the **b** of
Heb	9:22	without the shedding of **b**
	13:20	by the **b** of the eternal
1 Pet	1:19	but with the precious **b** of
1 Jn	5: 6	who came by water and **b**.
Rev	6:12	the full moon became like **b**,
	19:13	in a robe dipped in **b**,

BOAST (ING)

Ps	34: 2	My soul makes its **b** in the
Prov	27: 1	Do not **b** about tomorrow, for
Sir	25:6	and their **b** is the fear of the
Jer	9:24	but let those who **b b** in this,
Rom	11:18	do not **b** over the branches.
1 Cor	1:31	"Let the one who **b**, **b** in the

1 Cor	5: 6	Your **b** is not a good thing
2 Cor	11:30	If I must **b**, I will **b** of the
Gal	6:14	never **b** of anything except the
Eph	2: 9	so that no one may **b**.
Phil	2:16	that I can **b** on the day of
1 Thess	2:19	or crown of **b** before our Lord
Jas	1: 9	the believer who is lowly **b** in
	4:16	in your arrogance; all such **b** is

BOASTFUL

Ps	5: 5	The **b** will not stand before
Rom	1:30	haughty, **b**, inventors of evil,
1 Cor	13: 4	love is not envious or **b** or
Jas	3:14	do not be **b** and false to the

BODY (BODIES)

Num	14:29	your dead **b** shall fall in this
2 Sam	7:12	shall come forth from your **b**,
Ps	16: 9	my **b** also rests secure.
Prov	15:30	good news refreshes the **b**.
Isa	66:14	your **b** shall flourish like the
Ezek	1:23	had two wings covering its **b**.
Dan	3:27	any power over the **b** of those
Mic	6: 7	the fruit of my **b** for the sin of
Mt	6:22	is the lamp of the **b**. So, if
	27:52	and many **b** of the saints
Mk	14:22	said, "Take; this is my **b**."
Lk	12: 4	those who kill the **b**, and after
Jn	2:21	the temple of his **b**.
Rom	7:24	will rescue me from this **b** of
	12: 1	to present your **b** as a living
1 Cor	5: 3	For though absent in **b**, I am
	6:15	your **b** are members of Christ?
2 Cor	5: 8	rather be away from the **b** and
Gal	6:17	of Jesus branded on my **b**.
Eph	4: 4	There is one **b** and one Spirit,
Phil	3:21	transform the **b** of our
Col	2: 5	though I am absent in **b**, yet
1 Thess	4: 4	how to control your own **b** in
Heb	10: 5	but a **b** you have prepared
	10:22	and our **b** washed with pure
Jas	2:26	just as the **b** without the
1 Pet	2:24	bore our sins in his **b** on the
2 Pet	1:13	as I am in this **b**, to refresh
Jude	1: 9	disputed about the **b** of Moses,
Rev	11: 8	their dead **b** will lie in the

BOLD (NESS)

Deut	31: 6	Be strong and **b**; have no fear
Prov	21:29	The wicked put on a **b** face,
	28: 1	the righteous are as **b** as a
Acts	4:29	speak your word with all **b**,
2 Cor	10: 1	but **b** toward you when I am
Eph	3:12	have access to God in **b** and
Phil	1:14	speak the word with greater **b**
Philem	1: 8	though I am **b** enough in
Heb	4:16	the throne of grace with **b**,
1 Jn	4:17	we may have **b** on the day of

BONE (S)

Gen	2:23	"This at last is **b** of my **b** and
	50:25	you shall carry up my **b** from
Ex	12:46	not break any of its **b**.
Josh	24:32	The **b** of Joseph, which the
2 Kings	13:21	as the man touched the **b** of
Ps	22:14	and all my **b** are out of joint;
Prov	25:15	a soft tongue can break **b**.
Sir	28:17	of the tongue crushes the **b**.
Jer	20: 9	fire shut up in my **b**;

Ezek 37: 4 O dry **b**, hear the word of the
       37: 7 **b** came together, **b** to its **b**.
Mt 23:27 they are full of the **b** of the
Jn 19:36 "None of his **b** shall be

BOOK (S)

Ex 24: 7 Then he took the **b** of the
Deut 29:20 the curses written in this **b** will
Josh 1: 8 This **b** of the law shall not
2 Kings 22: 8 "I have found the **b** of the law
Neh 8: 8 So they read from the **b**, from
Ps 69:28 out of the **b** of the living;
Eccl 12:12 Of making many **b** there is no
Isa 34:16 Seek and read from the **b** of
Dan 7:10 sat in judgment, and the **b**
       12: 1 is found written in the **b**
Mk 12:26 you not read in the **b** of
Jn 20:30 are not written in this **b**.
       21:25 could not contain the **b** that
Phil 4: 3 names are in the **b** of life.
Heb 10: 7 (in the scroll of the **b** it is
Rev 3: 5 your name out of the **b** of life;
       20:12 before the throne, and **b** were

BORN

Gen 17:17 "Can a child be **b** to a man
Ex 1:22 "Every boy that is **b** to the
Job 14: 1 "A mortal, **b** of woman, few of
Prov 17:17 and kinsfolk are **b** to share
Eccl 3: 2 a time to be **b**, and a time to
Isa 9: 6 a child has been **b** for us, a
Jer 1: 5 before you were **b** I consecrated
Mt 1:16 Jesus was **b**, who is called the
Mk 14:21 one not to have been **b**."
Lk 2:11 to you is **b** this day in the city
Jn 3: 5 without being **b** of water
Rom 9:11 Even before they had been **b**
1 Cor 15: 8 as to one untimely **b**, he
Gal 4: 4 Son, **b** of a woman, **b** under
Phil 2: 7 being **b** in human likeness.
1 Pet 1:23 You have been **b** anew, not of
1 Jn 4: 7 who loves is **b** of God
Rev 12: 4 as soon as it was **b**.

BRANCH (ES)

Gen 40:10 the vine there were three **b**.
Num 13:23 cut down from there a **b** with
2 Sam 18: 9 mule went under the thick **b**
Sir 1:20 and her **b** are long life.
Isa 4: 2 On that day the **b** of the LORD
Jer 17: 6 I will cause a righteous **B** to
Ezek 17: 6 Its **b** turned toward him, its
Dan 11: 7 a **b** from her roots shall rise
Zech 6:12 name is **B**: for he shall **b** out
Mal 4: 1 leave them neither root nor **b**.
Jn 15: 2 He removes every **b** in me that
Rom 11:21 did not spare the natural **b**,

BREAD

Gen 3:19 you shall eat **b** until you
Ex 16: 4 "I am going to rain **b** from
Lev 7:13 cakes of leavened **b**.
Deut 8: 3 one does not live by **b** alone,
Judg 7:13 a cake of barley **b** tumbled
1 Sam 21: 4 "I have no ordinary **b** at hand,
1 Kings 17: 6 ravens brought him **b** and
2 Chr 4:19 the tables for the **b** of the
Neh 9:15 you gave them **b** from heaven,
Ps 78:25 Mortals ate of the **b** of angels;
Prov 9:17 and **b** eaten in secret is

Eccl 11: 1 Send out your **b** upon the
Wis 16:20 from heaven with **b** ready to
Sir 15:3 will feed him with the **b** of
Isa 55: 2 that which is not **b**, and your
Ezek 18: 7 gives his **b** to the hungry and
Am 8:11 not a famine of **b**, or a thirst
Ob 1: 7 those who ate your **b** have set
Mt 6:11 Give us this day our daily **b**.
Mk 14:20 who is dipping **b** into the
Lk 4: 4 'One does not live by **b** alone.'
Jn 6:35 "I am the **b** of life. Whoever
Acts 2:42 to the breaking of **b** and the
1 Cor 11:26 often as you eat this **b** and

BREAK (ING) (BROKEN)

Gen 17:14 he has **b** my covenant."
Ex 12:46 shall not **b** any of its bones.
Lev 26:44 utterly and **b** my covenant
Num 30: 2 he shall not **b** his word; he
Deut 7: 5 deal with them: **b** down their
       31:20 despising me and **b** my
Judg 2: 1 will never **b** my covenant with
Ezra 9:14 shall we **b** your
Neh 1: 3 the wall of Jerusalem is **b**
Ps 2: 9 You shall **b** them with a rod of
       51:17 a **b** spirit; a **b** and contrite
Prov 18:14 endure sickness; but a **b** spirit
       25:15 and a soft tongue can **b** bones.
Eccl 3: 3 a time to **b** down, and a time
Sir 10:19 Those who the **b**
Isa 42: 3 bruised reed he will not **b**,
Ezek 16:59 the oath, **b** the covenant;
       44: 7 You have **b** my covenant with
Mt 12:20 He will not **b** a bruised reed
       14:20 left over of the **b** pieces, twelve
Lk 5: 6 their nets were beginning to **b**.
       20:18 on that stone will be **b**
Jn 19:33 they did not **b** his legs.
Acts 2:42 to the **b** of bread and the
Rom 2:23 do you dishonor God by **b** the
1 Cor 10:16 The bread that we **b**, is it not a
Rev 5: 2 to open the scroll and **b** its

BREASTPLATE

1 Kings 22:34 the scale armor and the **b**;
Isa 59:17 put on righteousness like a **b**,
Eph 6:14 on the **b** of righteousness.
1 Thess 5: 8 and put on the **b** of faith and

BREATH

Gen 1:30 that has the **b** of life, I have
2 Sam 22:16 blast of the **b** of his nostrils.
Job 27: 3 as long as my **b** is in me
Ps 39:11 surely everyone is a mere **b**.
Eccl 12: 7 and the **b** returns to God who
Isa 40: 7 when the **b** of the LORD blows
Jer 10:14 and there is no **b** in them.
Lam 4:20 The LORD's anointed, the **b** of
Ezek 37: 9 "Prophesy to the **b**, prophesy,
Acts 17:25 to all mortals life and **b**
2 Thess 2: 8 Jesus will destroy with the **b** of
Rev 11:11 the **b** of life from God entered

BRIDE

Song 4: 8 me from Lebanon, my **b**;
Isa 62: 5 rejoices over the **b**,
Jer 2: 2 your love as a **b**, how you
Jn 3:29 He who has the **b** is the
Rev 21: 9 the **b**, the wife of the Lamb

BRIDEGROOM

Ex 4:25 "Truly you are a **b** of blood to
Ps 19: 5 comes out like a **b** from his
Jer 25:10 the voice of the **b** and the
Bar 2:23 the voice of the **b** and the
Mt 25: 1 and went to meet the **b**.
Mk 2:20 days will come when the **b** is
Jn 3:29 the **b**. The friend of the **b**
Rev 18:23 the voice of **b** and bride will

BRING (S) (ING)

Gen 6:19 you shall **b** two of every kind
Ex 36: 3 They still kept **b** him freewill
Lev 1: 2 When any of you **b** an offering
Num 14: 3 Why is the LORD **b** us into this
       20: 5 to **b** us to this wretched place
Deut 8: 7 your God is **b** you into a good
       24: 4 you shall not **b** guilt on the
1 Sam 2: 6 The LORD kills and **b** to life;
2 Sam 12:23 Can I **b** him back again?
1 Kings 21:21 I will **b** disaster on you;
Ps 25:17 and **b** me out of my distress
       34:21 Evil **b** death to the wicked,
Prov 18: 6 A fool's lips **b** strife, and a
       19: 4 Wealth **b** many friends, but
Eccl 12:14 For God will **b** every deed into
Isa 52: 7 announces peace, who **b** good
Jer 24: 6 I will **b** them back to this land
Dan 9:24 to **b** in everlasting
Mt 10:34 I have come to **b** peace to the
       12:35 The good person **b** good
Mk 15: 4 See how many charges they **b**
Lk 4:18 he has anointed me to **b** good
       11:26 goes and **b** seven other spirits
Jn 10:16 to this fold. I must **b** them
Rom 4:15 For the law **b** wrath; but where
       10:15 of those who **b** good news!"
1 Cor 8: 8 "Food will not **b** us close to
2 Cor 7:10 leads to salvation and **b** no
Titus 2:11 has appeared, **b** salvation to
Heb 1: 6 he **b** the firstborn into the
       2:10 in **b** many children to glory,
1 Pet 3:18 in order to **b** you to God.
2 Jn 1:10 and does not **b** this teaching;
Rev 21:24 kings of the earth will **b** their

BROKENHEARTED

Ps 34:18 LORD is near to the **b**, and
Isa 61: 1 to bind up the **b**, to proclaim

BROTHER (S)

Gen 4: 9 am I my **b** keeper?"
       27:29 Be lord over your **b**, and may
Deut 13: 6 even if it is your **b**, your
2 Sam 13:12 She answered him, "No, my **b**,
1 Macc 3:25 Judas and his **b** began to be
Ps 22:22 of your name to my **b** and
Song 8: 1 you were like a **b** to me, who
Wis 10:3 because in rage he killed his **b**.
Am 1:11 he pursued his **b** with the
Ob 1:10 violence done to your **b** Jacob,
Mal 1: 2 Is not Esau Jacob's **b**? says the
Mt 5:24 first be reconciled to your **b**
       12:49 are my mother and my **b**!
Mk 3:33 are my mother and my **b**?"
       3:35 will of God is my **b** and sister
Lk 22:32 back, strengthen your **b**."
Jn 7: 5 (For not even his **b** believed in
Rom 14:21 that makes your **b** or sister

1 Cor	5:11	bears the name of **b** or sister
2 Cor	11:26	from false **b** and sisters;
1 Tim	5: 1	father, to younger men as **b**,
Philem	1:16	than a slave, a beloved **b**—
Heb	2:11	ashamed to call them **b** and
Jas	2:15	If a **b** or sister is naked and
1 Jn	3:10	who do not love their **b** and
	3:17	and sees a **b** or sister in need

BUILD (S) (ER) (ERS) (BUILT)

Gen	8:20	Then Noah **b** an altar to the
	11: 4	"Come, let us **b** ourselves a
Ex	20:25	do not **b** it of hewn stones;
Deut	27: 5	And you shall **b** an altar there
Judg	6:24	Then Gideon **b** an altar there
1 Sam	7:17	and **b** there an altar to the
2 Sam	7: 5	Are you the one to **b** me a
1 Kings	6: 1	he began to **b** the house of the
Neh	7: 1	when the wall had been **b** and
Ps	118:22	The stone that the **b** rejected
	127: 1	Unless the LORD **b** the house,
Prov	24: 3	By wisdom a house is **b**,
Eccl	3: 3	and a time to **b** up;
Isa	5: 2	he **b** a watchtower in the
	62:10	**b** up, **b** up the highway
Jer	22:13	Woe to him who **b** his house
	31: 4	Again I will **b** you, and you
Dan	9:25	sixty-two weeks it shall be **b**
Mic	3:10	who **b** Zion with blood and
Zech	6:12	he shall **b** the temple of the
Mt	7:24	a wise man who **b** his house
	16:18	on this rock I will **b** my
Mk	12:10	The stone that the **b** rejected
	14:58	in three days I will **b** another,
Acts	20:32	message that is able to **b**
1 Cor	8: 1	puffs up, but love **b** up.
	14:17	the other person is not **b** up.
Eph	2:20	**b** upon the foundation of the
1 Thess	5:11	one another and **b** up each
Heb	3: 4	but the **b** of all things is God
Jude	1:20	But you, beloved, **b** yourselves
Rev	21:18	The wall is **b** of jasper, while

BUILDING

Josh	22:16	by **b** yourselves an altar today
1 Kings	6:12	this house that you are **b**,
Ezra	4: 1	exiles were **b** a temple to the
Neh	2:18	"Let us start **b**!" So they
Mic	7:11	A day for the **b** of your walls!
Lk	6:48	one is like a man **b** a house,
Rom	15: 2	good purpose of **b** up the
1 Cor	14:26	all things be done for **b** up.
2 Cor	10: 8	the Lord gave for **b** you up
Eph	4:12	for **b** up the body of Christ

BURDEN (S)

Gen	49:15	bowed his shoulder to the **b**,
Ex	18:22	and they will bear the **b** with
Num	11:11	you lay the **b** of all this people
Ps	55:22	Cast your **b** on the LORD,
Isa	10:27	On that day his **b** will be
Jer	23:33	"What is the **b** of the LORD?"
Mt	11:30	yoke is easy, and my **b** is
Lk	11:46	load people with **b** hard to
Acts	15:28	no further **b** than these
2 Cor	12:14	I will not be a **b**, because
2 Thess	3: 8	so that we might not **b** any of
Rev	2:24	lay on you any other **b**;

BURN (ED) (ING) (BURNT)

Gen	38:24	and let her be **b**."
Ex	3: 3	why the bush is not **b** up."
	32:10	my wrath may **b** hot against
Lev	6: 9	the altar shall be kept **b**.
	20:14	they shall be **b** to death,
Num	11: 3	the fire of the LORD **b** against
1 Sam	15:22	LORD as great delight in **b**
1 Kings	3: 4	offer a thousand **b** offerings
2 Kings	23:20	and **b** human bones on them.
2 Chr	36:19	They **b** the house of God,
Ezra	8:35	exiles, offered **b** offerings
Ps	89:46	long will your wrath **b** like
	140:10	Let **b** coals fall on them!
Prov	6:27	the bosom without **b** one's
Isa	1:11	had enough of **b** offerings of
Jer	6:20	Your **b** offerings are not
	36:29	You have dared to **b** this scroll,
Ezek	46:13	for a **b** offering to the LORD
Dan	7: 9	and its wheels were **b** fire.
Hos	6: 6	of God rather than **b** offerings.
Mal	4: 1	that comes shall **b** them up,
Mt	13:40	are collected and **b** up with
Mk	12:33	important than all whole **b**
Lk	3:17	he will **b** with unquenchable
	24:32	"Were not our hearts **b** within
Jn	15: 6	thrown into the fire, and **b**.
Acts	7:30	in the flame of a **b** bush.
Rom	12:20	you will heap **b** coals on their
1 Cor	3:15	If the work is **b** up, the builder
Heb	6: 8	its end is to be **b** over.
	10: 6	in **b** offerings and sin offerings
Rev	18: 8	she will be **b** with fire; for

C

CALL (ED) (ING)

Gen	3: 9	But the LORD God **c** to the
	22:11	the angel of the LORD **c** to him
Ex	3: 4	God **c** to him out of the
Deut	4:26	I **c** heaven and earth to witness
Ruth	1:20	"C me no longer Naomi, **c** me
1 Sam	3: 5	"I did not **c**; lie down again."
2 Sam	22: 4	I **c** upon the LORD, who is
1 Kings	18:24	Then you **c** on the name of
1 Chr	16: 8	**c** on his name, make known
2 Chr	7:14	if my people who are **c** by my
Ps	50:15	**C** on me in the day
	145:18	is near to all who **c** on him,
Prov	1:24	I have **c** and you refused,
	31:28	children rise up and **c** her
Sir	42:15	**c** to mind the works of the
Isa	43: 1	I have **c** you by name,
	55: 6	**c** upon him while he is
Jer	7:10	this house, which is **c** by my
	33: 3	**C** to me and I will
Lam	3:55	I **c** on your name, O LORD
Jon	1: 6	Get up, **c** on your god!
Zeph	3: 9	all of them may **c** on the name
Zech	13: 9	They will **c** on my name, and I
Mt	5: 9	they will be **c** children of God.
	27:47	"This man is **c** for Elijah."
Mk	10:18	"Why do you **c** me good?
	10:49	get up, he is **c** you."
Lk	6:46	"Why do you **c** me 'Lord,
	15:19	longer worthy to be **c** your
Jn	13:13	You **c** me Teacher and Lord—
Jn	15:15	I do not **c** you servants any
Acts	10:15	you must not **c** profane."
Rom	9:25	was not beloved I will **c**
	11:29	for the gifts and the **c** of God
1 Cor	1:26	Consider your own **c**, brothers
	7:24	condition you were **c**,
Gal	5:13	For you were **c** to freedom,
Eph	4: 1	worthy of the **c** to which you
Phil	3:14	the prize of the heavenly **c** of
Col	3:15	to which indeed you were **c** in
1 Thess	4: 7	For God did not **c** us to
2 Thess	2:14	For this purpose he **c** you
1 Tim	6:12	to which you were **c** and for
2 Tim	2:22	along with those who **c** on the
Heb	2:11	not ashamed to **c** them
Heb	9:15	those who are **c** may receive
Jas	2:23	and he was **c** the friend of
	5:14	They should **c** for the elders of
1 Pet	2: 9	him who **c** you out of
2 Pet	1:10	more eager to confirm your **c**
1 Jn	3: 1	that we should be **c** children
Rev	19:13	and his name is **c** The Word of

CAPTIVE (CAPTIVITY)

Gen	14:14	his nephew had been taken **c**,
Deut	28:41	for they shall go into **c**.
2 Kings	24:16	king of Babylon brought **c** to
2 Chr	6:38	in the land of their **c**, to which
Ezra	8:35	those who had come from **c**,
Neh	1: 2	those who had escaped the **c**,
Ps	106:46	by all who held them **c**.
Song	7: 5	a king is held **c** in the tresses.
Isa	52: 2	rise up, O **c** Jerusalem;
Jer	13:17	flock has been taken **c**.
Acts	20:22	And now, as a **c** to the Spirit,
Rom	7:23	making me **c** to the law of sin
2 Cor	10: 5	every thought **c** to obey Christ.
Eph	4: 8	he made captivity itself a **c**;
Col	2: 8	that no one takes you **c**
2 Tim	2:26	the devil, having been held **c**
Rev	13:10	taken captive, into **c** you go;

CARE (S) (FUL) (CARING)

Gen	39:22	committed to Joseph's **c** all
Ex	19:12	'Be **c** not to go up the
Deut	6:12	take **c** that you do not forget
	15: 9	Be **c** that you do not entertain
Josh	23:11	Be very **c**, therefore, to love the
2 Kings	21: 8	if only they will be **c** to do
Ps	8: 4	that you **c** for them?
	94:19	When the **c** of my heart are
Sir	38:27	and they are **c** to finish their
Jer	30:17	"It is Zion; no one **c** for her!"
Mt	13:22	hears the word, but the **c** of
	25:36	was sick and you took **c** of me,
Lk	10:34	to an inn, and took **c** of him.
1 Cor	12:25	have the same **c** for one
Eph	5:15	Be **c** then how you live, not
	5:29	he nourishes and tenderly **c**
1 Thess	2: 7	like a nurse tenderly **c** for her
1 Tim	3: 5	how can he take **c** of God's
Titus	3: 8	believe in God may be **c** to
Heb	2: 6	mortals, that you **c** for them?
Jas	1:27	**c** for orphans and widows in
1 Pet	1:10	to be yours made **c** search and
	5: 7	because he **c** for you.

CAST

Gen	21:10	"C out this slave woman with

Ex	32: 4	in a mold, and **c** an image of a
Lev	16: 8	and Aaron shall **c** lots on the
Josh	18: 6	and I will **c** lots for you here
1 Sam	14:42	"**C** the lot between me and
1 Kings	7:15	He **c** two pillars of bronze.
2 Kings	17:16	made for themselves **c** images
Neh	10:34	We have also **c** lots among the
Ps	42: 5	Why are you **c** down, O my
	55:22	**C** your burden on the LORD
Prov	16:33	The lot is **c** into the lap,
Isa	38:17	for you have **c** all my sins
Jer	7:15	And I will **c** you out of my
Joel	3: 3	and **c** lots for my people,
Ob	1:11	entered his gates and **c** lots
Jon	1: 7	So they **c** lots, and the lot fell
Hab	2:18	a **c** image, a teacher of lies
Mt	12:27	If I **c** out demons by Beelzebul,
Mk	3:23	"How can Satan **c** out Satan?
Jn	19:24	and for my clothing they **c**
Acts	1:26	And they **c** lots for them,
1 Pet	5: 7	**C** all your anxiety on him
Rev	4:10	they **c** their crowns before the

CELEBRATE

Ex	12:14	You shall **c** it as a festival to
Lev	23: 4	you shall **c** at the time
Num	29:12	You shall **c** a festival to the
Deut	26:11	shall **c** with all the bounty that
Neh	12:27	to Jerusalem to **c** the
Ps	145: 7	They shall **c** the fame of your
Ezek	45:21	you shall **c** the festival of the
Nah	1:15	**C** your festivals, O Judah,
Lk	15:24	And they began to **c**.
1 Cor	5: 8	Therefore, let us **c** the festival,
Rev	11:10	will gloat over them and **c** and

CHAINS (CHAINED)

Ex	28:14	and two **c** of pure gold, twisted
1 Kings	6:21	then he drew **c** of gold across,
Lam	3: 7	he has put heavy **c** on me;
Mk	5: 4	restrained with shackles and **c**,
Acts	12: 7	And the **c** fell off his wrists.
Eph	6:20	I am an ambassador in **c**.
Col	4:18	Remember my **c**. Grace be
2 Tim	2: 9	to the point of being **c** like a
Heb	11:36	and flogging, and even **c** and
2 Pet	2: 4	committed them to **c** of
Jude	1: 6	kept in eternal **c** in deepest

CHANGE (D) (CHANGERS)

Gen	31: 7	has cheated me and **c** my
Ex	32:14	the LORD **c** his mind about the
Num	23:19	that he should **c** his mind.
1 Sam	15:29	Israel will not recant or **c** his
Ps	110: 4	sworn and will not **c** his mind,
Jer	2:11	Has a nation **c** its gods, even
Dan	4:16	Let his mind be **c** from that of
Jon	3: 9	God may relent and **c** his
Mal	3: 6	I the LORD do not **c**;
Mt	18: 3	unless you **c** and become like
Mk	11:15	the tables of the money **c** and
Lk	9:29	the appearance of his face **c**
Jn	2:15	the coins of the money **c** and
1 Cor	15:51	but we will all be **c**,
Heb	1:12	like clothing they will be **c**.
Jas	1:17	variation or shadow due to **c**.

CHARGE

Gen	39: 4	and put him in **c** of all that he
Ex	23: 7	Keep far from a false **c**, and do

Num	4:16	Aaron the priest shall have **c**
Deut	23:19	You shall not **c** interest on
Job	34:13	Who gave him **c** over the earth
Ps	50:21	rebuke you, and lay the **c**
Mt	25:21	I will put you in **c** of many
Mk	15:26	The inscription of the **c**
Rom	8:33	Who will bring any **c** against
1 Cor	9:18	make the gospel free of **c**,
2 Cor	11: 7	news to you free of **c**?
Philem	1:18	anything, **c** that to my account.
1 Pet	5: 3	it over those in your **c**, but be

CHARIOT (S)

Gen	41:43	ride in the **c** of his second-in-
Ex	14:25	He clogged their **c** wheels so
Josh	11: 4	with very many horses and **c**.
Judg	4:15	Sisera got down from his **c**
2 Sam	8: 4	David hamstrung all the **c**
1 Kings	7:33	wheels were made like a **c**
2 Kings	2:11	a **c** of fire and horses of
1 Chr	28:18	plan for the golden **c** of the
2 Chr	1:14	Solomon gathered together **c**
Ps	104: 3	you make the clouds your **c**,
Song	6:12	fancy set me in a **c** beside my
Sir	48:9	in a **c** with horses of fire.
Isa	36: 9	you rely on Egypt for **c** and for
Joel	2: 5	As with the rumbling of **c**,
Nah	2: 3	The metal on the **c** flashes on
Hag	2:22	and overthrow the **c** and their
Zech	6: 2	The first **c** had red horses, the
Acts	8:28	seated in his **c**, he was reading
Rev	9: 9	like the noise of many **c** with

CHEERFUL

Prov	17:22	A **c** heart is a good medicine
Sir	13:26	The sign of a happy heart is a **c**
Zech	8:19	and gladness, and **c** festivals
2 Cor	9: 7	for God loves a **c** giver.
Jas	5:13	Are any **c**? They should sing

CHIEF PRIEST

2 Kings	25:18	the guard took the **c** Seraiah,
2 Chr	24:11	the officer of the **c** would
Ezra	7: 5	Eleazar, son of the **c** Aaron—
Jer	52:24	the guard took the **c** Seraiah,

CHILD (REN)

Gen	3:16	in pain you shall bring forth **c**,
Ex	2: 3	she put the **c** in it and
	12:26	And when your **c** ask you,
Deut	6: 7	Recite them to your **c** and talk
Josh	4: 6	When your **c** ask in time to
Judg	11:34	She was his only **c**; he had no
Ruth	4:16	Then Naomi took the **c** and
1 Sam	1:27	For this **c** I prayed; and the
2 Sam	12:16	pleaded with God for the **c**;
1 Kings	3: 7	I am only a little **c**; I do not
Ezra	10:44	sent them away with their **c**.
Neh	13:24	and half of their **c** spoke the
Job	3:16	not buried like a stillborn **c**,
Ps	34:11	Come, O **c**, listen to me; I will
Prov	1: 8	Hear, my **c**, your father's
Eccl	6: 3	a stillborn **c** is better off than
Isa	9: 6	For a **c** has been born for us
Jer	31:15	Rachel is weeping for her **c**;
Ezek	18:20	A **c** shall not suffer for the
Hos	11: 1	When Israel was a **c**, I loved
Joel	1: 3	Tell your **c** of it, and let your
Zech	12:10	one mourns for an only **c**,
Mal	4: 6	hearts of parents to their **c** and

Mt	2:11	they saw the **c** with Mary his
	5: 9	they will be called **c** of God.
Mk	10:15	kingdom of God as a little **c**
	13:12	and **c** will rise against parents
Lk	1:80	The **c** grew and became
	18:16	"Let the little **c** come to me,
Jn	1:12	power to become **c** of God,
Acts	2:39	is for you, for your **c**, and
Rom	8:14	the Spirit of God are **c** of God.
1 Cor	13:11	I was a **c**, I spoke like a **c**
Gal	4: 7	but a **c**, and if a **c** then
Eph	5: 8	you are light. Live as **c** of
Phil	2:15	blameless and innocent, **c** of
Col	3:21	do not provoke your **c**,
1 Tim	3:12	and let them manage their **c**
Titus	1: 6	once, whose **c** are believers,
Heb	12:6	and chastises every **c** whom he
1 Pet	1:14	Like obedient **c**, do not be
1 Jn	3: 8	commits sin is a **c** of the devil;
3 Jn	1: 4	to hear that my **c** are walking
Rev	12: 4	that he might devour her **c** as

CHOOSE (S) (CHOSE) (CHOSEN)

Gen	13:11	So Lot **c** for himself all the
	18:19	for I have **c** him, that he may
Num	17: 5	of the man whom I **c** shall
Deut	7: 6	your God has **c** you out of all
	30:19	blessings and curses. **C** life so
Josh	24:15	**c** this day whom you will
	24:22	you have **c** the LORD, to serve
Judg	10:14	the gods whom you have **c**;
1 Sam	17:40	and **c** five smooth stones from
Neh	1: 9	I have **c** to establish my name.'
Ps	65: 4	those whom you **c** and bring
	119:30	I have **c** the way of faithfulness;
Prov	3:31	and do not **c** any of their ways;
Isa	7:15	to refuse the evil and **c** the
	42: 1	whom I uphold, my **c**, in
Ezek	20: 5	On the day when I **c** Israel, I
Zech	3: 2	The LORD who has **c** Jerusalem
Mt	11:27	anyone to whom the Son **c** to
	22:14	are called, but few are **c**."
Mk	13:20	of the elect, whom he **c**, he
Lk	6:13	he called his disciples and **c**
	10:22	to whom the Son **c** to reveal
Jn	3: 8	The wind blows where it **c**,
	15:16	You did not **c** me but I chose
Acts	9:15	an instrument whom I have **c**
Rom	9:18	has mercy on whomever he **c**,
	11: 5	time there is a remnant, **c** by
1 Cor	1:27	But God **c** what is foolish in
	12:11	just as the Spirit **c**.
Eph	1: 4	just as he **c** us in Christ
Col	3:12	As God's **c** ones, holy and
1 Thess	1: 4	by God, that he has **c** you
2 Thess	2:13	because God **c** you as the first
Jas	2: 5	Has not God **c** the poor in the
1 Pet	2: 9	But you are a **c** race, a royal
Rev	17:14	with him are called and **c** and

CHRIST ('S)

Mk	1: 1	the good news of Jesus **C**, the
Jn	4:25	is coming" (who is called **C**).
Acts	3: 6	in the name of Jesus **C** of
Rom	5: 8	while we still were sinners **C**
	8:35	separate us from the love of **C**?
1 Cor	1:23	we proclaim **C** crucified, a
	9:21	God's law but am under **C**
	15:14	and if **C** has not been raised,
2 Cor	5:14	For the love of **C** urges us on,

16

2 Cor 10: 1 and gentleness of **C**—
Gal 3:28 all of you are one in **C** Jesus.
Eph 4:15 who is the head, into **C**,
5:23 wife just as **C** is the head of
Phil 1:21 living is **C** and dying is gain.
2: 5 in you that was in **C** Jesus,
Col 1:27 which is **C** in you, the hope of
3:15 let the peace of **C** rule in your
1 Thess 4:16 and the dead in **C** will rise
2 Thess 2: 1 coming of our Lord Jesus **C**
1 Tim 2: 5 God and humankind, **C**, Jesus,
2 Tim 1: 9 was given to us in **C** Jesus
Titus 2:13 great God and Savior, Jesus **C**.
Philem 1:20 Refresh my heart in **C**.
Heb 5: 5 So also **C** did not glorify
13: 8 Jesus **C** is the same yesterday
1 Pet 3:18 For **C** also suffered for sins
4:13 you are sharing **C** sufferings,
1 Jn 2:22 denies that Jesus is the **C**?
5: 6 by water and blood, Jesus **C**,
2 Jn 1: 7 do not confess that Jesus has **C**
Jude 1: 4 only Master and Lord, Jesus **C**.
Rev 20: 4 and reigned with **C** a

CHRISTIAN (S)

Acts 11:26 disciples were first called "**C**."
26:28 me to become a **C**?"
1 Pet 4:16 of you suffers as a **C**, do not

CHURCH (ES)

Mt 16:18 rock I will build my **c**, and the
Acts 5:11 great fear seized the whole **c**
16: 5 So the **c** were strengthened in
Rom 16: 5 Greet also the **c** in their house.
1 Cor 11:18 you come together as a **c**,
14:34 should be silent in the **c**.
2 Cor 11: 8 I robbed other **c** by accepting
Gal 1:13 violently persecuting the **c** of
Eph 5:23 is the head of the **c**, the body
Phil 3: 6 a persecutor of the **c**; as to
Col 1:18 head of the body, the **c**; he is
1 Thess 2:14 imitators of the **c** of God in
2 Thess 1: 4 boast of you among the **c** of
1 Tim 3:15 the **c** of the living God,
Jas 5:14 for the elders of the **c** and have
3 Jn 1: 9 written something to the **c**;
Rev 1: 4 John to the seven **c** that are in
22:16 with this testimony for the **c**.

CIRCUMCISE (D)

Gen 17:11 You shall **c** the flesh
Deut 10:16 **C**, then, the foreskin of
Josh 5: 2 flint knives and **c** the Israelites
Jdt 14:10 he was **c**, and joined the house
Lk 1:59 eighth day they came to **c** the
Acts 21:21 not to **c** their children or
Rom 3:30 justify the **c** on the ground of
Col 3:11 and Jew, **c** and uncircumcised,

CIRCUMCISION

Ex 4:26 "A bridegroom of blood by **c**."
Acts 7: 8 covenant of **c**. And so
Rom 2:25 **C** indeed is of value if
1 Cor 7:19 **C** is nothing
Col 2:11 of the flesh in the **c** of Christ;

CLAY

Job 10: 9 you fashioned me like **c**; and
Wis 15: 7 same **c** both the vessels that
Sir 33:13 Like **c** in the hand of the

Isa 45: 9 Does the **c** say to the one who
Jer 18: 4 **c** was spoiled in the potter's
Rom 9:21 potter no right over the **c**,
2 Tim 2:20 but also of wood and **c**,

CLEAN (CLEANSED) (CLEANSING)

Gen 7: 2 seven pairs of all **c** animals,
Lev 20:25 the unclean bird and the **c**;
Job 15:14 mortals, that they can be **c**?
Ps 51: 7 shall be **c**; wash me, and I
Prov 20: 9 "I have made my heart **c**;
Jer 4:14 wash your heart of **c**
Mk 1:40 you can make me **c**."
Jn 13:10 is entirely **c**. And you are **c**,
Rom 14:20 of God. Everything is indeed **c**,
Heb 10: 2 worshipers, **c** once for all,

CLOTHE (S) (CLOTHED) (CLOTHING)

Gen 37:29 the pit, he tore his **c**.
Lev 8: 7 **c** him with the robe,
1 Kings 21:27 he tore his **c** and put sackcloth
Neh 9:21 their **c** did not wear out and
Ps 22:18 and for my **c** they cast lots.
Prov 6:27 without burning one's **c**?
Jer 52:33 put aside his prison **c**, and
Mk 15:24 and divided his **c** among
Acts 10:30 suddenly a man in dazzling **c**
1 Tim 2: 9 and decently in suitable **c**,
Jas 2: 2 in fine **c** comes into your
Rev 3: 4 who have not soiled their **c**;

CLOUD (S)

Ex 13:21 them in a pillar of **c** by day,
1 Kings 18:45 black with **c** and wind; there
Job 38:37 the wisdom to number the **c**?
Ps 57:10 faithfulness extends to the **c**.
Prov 25:14 Like **c** and wind without rain
Joel 2: 2 a day of **c** and thick darkness!
Mt 24:30 of Man coming on the **c** of
1 Thess 4:17 up in the **c** together with them
Jude 1:12 waterless **c** carried along
Rev 1: 7 He is coming with the **c**;

COIN (S)

Mt 17:27 you will find a **c**; take that
Lk 15: 8 woman having ten silver **c**,
Jn 2:15 poured out the **c** of the money

COME (S) (COMING)

Ex 19:11 the LORD will **c** down upon
Deut 28:45 All these curses shall **c** upon
2 Sam 7:12 who shall **c** forth from your
Ps 96:13 for he is **c**, for he is **c** to
Prov 24:34 poverty will **c** upon you
Isa 1:18 **C** now, let us argue it
Jer 51:45 **C** out of her, my people
Hos 3: 5 they shall **c** in awe to the LORD
Mic 6: 6 what shall I **c** before the LORD,
Zech 10: 4 them shall **c** the cornerstone,
Lk 7:20 When the men had **c** to him,
Jn 6:37 and anyone who **c** to me I will
Acts 1:11 will **c** in the same way as
Gal 4: 4 the fullness of time had **c**,
Heb 12:22 you have **c** to Mount Zion
2 Pet 3: 9 but all to **c** to repentance.
Rev 4: 1 like a trumpet, said, "**C** up

COMFORT

Gen 37:35 daughters sought to **c** him;
1 Chr 7:22 his brothers came to **c** him.

Job 2:11 to go and console and **c** him.
Ps 71:21 and **c** me once again.
Eccl 4: 1 with no one to **c** them!
Jer 31:13 I will **c** them, and give
Lam 1: 9 with none to **c** her.
Acts 9:31 in the **c** of the Holy Spirit,
Col 4:11 they have been a **c** to me.
2 Thess 2:16 gave us eternal **c** and good ,

COMMAND (ED)

Gen 2:16 God **c** the man, "You may
Deut 12:32 everything that I **c** you;
Josh 1: 9 I hereby **c** you: Be strong
Ps 33: 9 he **c**, and it stood firm.
Eccl 8: 2 king's **c** because of your sacred
Isa 13: 3 have **c** my consecrated ones,
Dan 3:28 the king's **c** and yielded up
Mt 4: 3 these stones to become
1 Cor 7:25 I have no **c** of the Lord, but I
1 Tim 6:17 are rich, **c** them not to be

COMMANDMENT (S)

Ex 34:28 of the covenant, the ten **c**.
Josh 22: 5 to keep his **c**, and to hold
1 Sam 12:14 rebel against the **c** of the LORD,
Tob 3: 4 and disobeyed your **c**.
Ps 119:98 Your **c** makes me wiser than my
Prov 2: 1 and treasure up my **c** within
Sir 15:15 choose, you can keep the **c**,
Jn 13:34 I give you a new **c**,
Gal 5:14 single **c**, "You shall love your
Heb 7:18 an earlier **c** because it was
2 Jn 1: 6 his **c**; this is the **c** just as
Rev 14:12 those who keep the **c** of God

COMMIT (S)

Ex 20:14 You shall not **c** adultery.
Lev 18:29 whoever **c** any of these
2 Kings 17:21 and made them **c** great sin.
Ps 22: 8 **C** your cause to the LORD
Prov 6:32 he who **c** adultery has no
Mt 5:27 'You shall not **c** adultery.'
1 Cor 6:18 Every sin that a person **c** is
Rev 2:22 and those who **c** adultery with

COMMON

Lev 10:10 between the holy and the **c**,
2 Chr 9:27 as **c** in Jerusalem as stone,
Prov 22: 2 the poor have this in **c**:
Ezek 22:26 between the holy and the **c**,
Acts 2:44 and had all things in **c**;
1 Cor 12: 7 of the Spirit for the **c** good.

COMPASSION

Deut 13: 8 Show them no pity or **c**
Judg 21:15 The people had **c** on Benjamin
1 Sam 23:21 the LORD for showing me **c**!
Tob 8:17 you had **c** on two only
1 Macc 3:44 pray and ask for mercy and **c**.
2 Macc 7:6 he will have **c** on his
Ps 77: 9 in anger shut up his **c**?"
Wis 10:5 him strong in the face of his **c**
Sir 18:14 **c** on those who accept his
Isa 49:13 and will have **c** on his
Jer 21: 7 or spare them, or have **c**.
Mic 7:19 He will again have **c** upon us;
Mk 6:34 and he had **c** for them,
Rom 9:15 I will have **c** on whom I have **c**
Col 3:12 clothe yourselves with **c**,

CONCEIT (ED)
Job 37:24 are wise in their own **c**."
Phil 2: 3 from selfish ambition or **c**,
2 Tim 3: 4 swollen with **c**, lovers of

CONDEMN (ATION) (ED)
Job 9:20 my own mouth would **c** me;
Ps 94:21 and **c** the innocent to death.
Prov 19:29 **C** is ready for scoffers,
Jn 8:11 "Neither do I **c** you. Go your
Acts 26:10 they were being **c** to death.
Rom 2:27 but keep the law will **c** you
1 Cor 11:34 will not be for your **c**.
1 Jn 3:20 whenever our hearts **c** us;
Jude 1: 9 dare to bring a **c** of slander

CONDUCT
Tob 4:14 yourself in all your **c**.
Ps 112: 5 who **c** their affairs with justice.
Prov 21: 8 but the **c** of the pure is right
Eccl 8:14 to the **c** of the wicked, and
Sir 11:26 according to their **c**.
Rom 13: 3 not a terror to good **c**,
1 Pet 3: 1 a word by their wives' **c**,

CONFESS (ES)
Lev 5: 5 you shall **c** the sin that you
1 Kings 8:33 **c** your name, pray and plead
Ps 38:18 I **c** my iniquity; I am sorry
Jn 12:42 they did not **c** it, for fear
Rom 10: 9 you **c** with your lips that Jesus
Phil 2:11 every tongue should **c** that
Jas 5:16 **c** your sins to one another
1 Jn 4:15 in those who **c** that Jesus
Rev 3: 5 I will **c** your name before my

CONFIDENCE (CONFIDENT)
Judg 9:26 of Shechem put **c** in him.
2 Kings 18:19 you base this **c** of yours?
Job 4: 6 fear of God your **c**, and the
Sir 5:5 not be so **c** of forgiveness
27:16 betrays secrets destroys **c**,
Ps 118: 8 than to put **c** in mortals.
Prov 11:13 trustworthy in spirit keeps a **c**.
Mic 7: 5 have no **c** in a loved one;
2 Cor 3: 4 the **c** that we have through
Eph 3:12 in boldness and **c** through
Heb 3: 6 hold firm the **c** and the pride
1 Jn 2:28 we may have **c** and not be

CONQUER (ED)
Jn 16:33 I have **c** the world!"
Heb 11:33 through faith **c** kingdoms,
1 Jn 2:13 because you have **c** the evil
Rev 12:11 they have **c** him by the

CONSCIENCE
1 Sam 25:31 or pangs of **c**, for having shed
Wis 17:11 distressed by **c**, it has always
Acts 24:16 have a clear **c** toward God
Rom 2:15 to which their own **c** also
1 Cor 10:28 and for the sake of **c**—
1 Tim 3: 9 the faith with a clear **c**.
Heb 10:22 clean from an evil **c** and our
1 Pet 3:16 Keep your **c** clear,

CONSECRATE (D)
Ex 13: 2 **C** to me all the firstborn
Lev 8:15 Thus he **c** it, to make
1 Kings 9: 3 I have **c** this house that you

Neh 3: 1 Sheep Gate. They **c** it and set
Jer 1: 5 you were born I **c** you; I

CONSIDER (ED)
Ex 33:13 **C** too that this nation is
Deut 32: 7 **c** the years long past; ask
1 Sam 12:24 for **c** what great things he has
Ps 13: 3 **C** and answer me, O LORD
Prov 6: 6 **c** its ways, and be wise
Eccl 7:13 **C** the work of God;
Dan 11:36 and **c** himself greater than
Lk 12:27 **C** the lilies, how they grow
Rom 6:11 must **c** yourselves dead to sin
Heb 10:24 let us **c** how to provoke
1 Pet 4:16 do not **c** it a disgrace,

CONSUME (D) (CONSUMING)
Lev 9:24 and **c** the burnt offering and
2 Chr 7: 1 and **c** the burnt offering
Ps 69: 9 house that has **c** me; the
Lam 4:11 that **c** its foundations.
Rom 1:27 were **c** with passion for one
Rev 20: 9 down from heaven and **c**

CONTEMPT
Gen 16: 4 looked with **c** on her mistress.
1 Sam 2:17 offerings of the LORD with **c**.
1 Macc 1:39 reproach, her honor into **c**.
Ps 107:40 he pours **c** on princes
Dan 12: 2 shame and everlasting **c**.
Mk 9:12 and be treated with **c**?
1 Cor 11:22 you show **c** for the church
Heb 6: 6 are holding him up to **c**.

CONTRITE
Ps 51:17 a broken and **c** heart,
Isa 57:15 those who are **c** and humble

CONVINCE (D) (CONVINCING)
Lk 16:31 will they be **c** even if someone
Acts 18: 4 try to **c** Jews and Greeks.
Rom 14: 5 fully **c** in their own minds.
Phil 1:25 I am **c** of this, I know that

CORNERSTONE
Job 38: 6 or who laid its **c**
Isa 28:16 a precious **c**, a sure foundation:
Mt 21:42 has become the **c**;
Eph 2:20 Christ Jesus himself as the **c**.

CORRUPT (ION)
Gen 6:11 Now the earth was **c**
Ps 14: 1 They are **c**, they
Dan 6: 4 and no negligence or **c** could
Acts 2:40 from this **c** generation."
Eph 4:22 your old self, **c** and deluded

COUNSEL (OR) (ORS)
2 Sam 15:34 will defeat for me the **c**
Job 38: 2 darkens **c** by words without
Ps 33:11 The **c** of the LORD stands
Prov 15:22 Without **c**, plans go wrong,
Sir 37:7 All **c** praise the **c** they
Isa 11: 2 the spirit of **c** and might,
Rom 11:34 Or who has been his **c**?"
Rev 3:18 Therefore I **c** you to buy

COURAGE
Josh 2:11 and there was no **c** left in any
2 Sam 7:27 servant has found **c** to pray

2 Chr 15: 7 take **c**! Do not let your hands
Ezra 7:28 I took **c**, for the hand of the
Tob 5:10 young man said, "Take **c**;
Ps 107:26 **c** melted away in their
Hag 2: 4 take **c**, O Zerubbabel,
Jn 16:33 But take **c**; I have conquered
Acts 23:11 "Keep up your **c**! For just as

COVENANT (S)
Gen 6:18 establish my **c** with you;
Deut 4:13 He declared to you his **c**,
Josh 3: 6 up the ark of the **c**,
1 Sam 20:16 Jonathan made a **c** with
Ezra 10: 3 let us make a **c** with our
Job 31: 1 "I have made a **c** with my eyes;
Ps 78:37 were not true to his **c**.
Jer 11: 2 Hear the words of this **c**,
Mal 2: 4 that my **c** with Levi may hold,
Mt 26:28 is my blood of the **c**,
Acts 7: 8 him the **c** of circumcision.
1 Cor 11:25 cup is the new **c** in my blood.
Heb 7:22 the guarantee of a better **c**.
Rev 11:19 ark of his **c** was seen

COVET
Ex 20:17 not **c** your neighbor's house;
Prov 21:26 the wicked **c**, but the righteous
Rom 13: 9 You shall not **c**";
Jas 4: 2 And you **c** something and

CREATE (D)
Gen 1: 1 when God **c** the heavens and
Jdt 13:18 who **c** the heavens and the
Ps 148: 5 commanded and they were **c**.
Prov 8:22 The LORD **c** me at the
Wis 2:23 for God **c** us for incorruption
Sir 33:10 humankind was **c** out of the
Jer 31:22 For the LORD has **c** a new
Mk 13:19 creation that God **c** until now,
Eph 4:24 **c** according to the likeness
Heb 12:27 **c** things—so that what cannot
Rev 10: 6 who **c** heaven and what is in

CREATION
Gen 2: 3 that he had done in **c**.
Tob 8:5 and the whole **c** bless you
Jdt 9:12 King of all your **c**.
Sir 16:17 for what am I in a boundless **c**?
Mk 10: 6 from the beginning of **c**,
Rom 1:20 Ever since the **c** of the world
2 Cor 5:17 there is a new **c**: everything
2 Pet 3: 4 from the beginning of **c**!"

CREATOR
2 Macc 13:14 the decision to the **C** of
Eccl 12: 1 Remember your **c** in the days
Sir 24:8 my **C** chose the place for my
Isa 40:28 everlasting God, the **C** of the
Col 3:10 to the image of its **c**.

CREATURE (S)
Gen 2:19 the man called every living **c**,
Rom 1:25 the **c** rather than the Creator,
Jas 1:18 of first fruits of his **c**.
Rev 5:13 I heard every **c** in heaven

CROOKED
Deut 32: 5 a perverse and **c** generation.
Ps 125: 5 turn aside to their own **c** ways
Prov 17:20 The **c** of mind do not prosper

Eccl	7:13	straight what he has made **c**?
Lam	3: 9	he has made my paths **c**.
Acts	13:10	will you not stop making **c**
Phil	2:15	of a **c** and perverse generation,

CRY (CRIED)

Ex	2:23	slavery their **c** for help
Josh	24: 7	When they **c** out to the LORD,
1 Macc	4:10	Let us **c** to Heaven.
Ps	130: 1	Out of the depths I **c** to you,
Prov	21:13	you will **c** out and not be
Jer	14:12	I do not hear their **c**,
Hos	7:14	They do not **c** to me
Mk	15:37	Then Jesus gave a loud **c**
Rom	8:15	When we **c**, "Abba! Father!"
1 Thess	4:16	with a **c** of command,

CROSS

Num	32: 5	do not make us **c** the Jordan."
Mt	10:38	does not take up the **c**
Lk	14:27	not carry the **c** and follow me
Gal	6:14	boast of anything except the **c**
Heb	12: 2	endured the **c**, disregarding its
1 Pet	2:24	on the **c**, so that, free from sins

CROWN (ED)

Lev	8: 9	holy **c**, as the LORD
Job	31:36	it on me like a **c**;
Ps	8: 5	and **c** them with glory and
Prov	14:18	clever are **c** with knowledge.
Song	3:11	**c** with which his mother **c** him
Mt	27:29	twisting some thorns into a **c**,
1 Thess	2:19	hope or joy or **c** of boasting
Jas	1:12	receive the **c** of life that
Rev	12: 1	on her head a **c** of twelve stars.

CRUCIFY (CRUCIFIED)

Lk	24: 7	and be **c**, and on the third day
Acts	2:36	this Jesus whom you **c**."
Rom	6: 6	old self was **c** with him so
Gal	5:24	Christ Jesus have **c** the flesh
Rev	11: 8	where also their Lord was **c**.

CRUSH (ED)

Num	24:17	it shall **c** the borderlands of
Job	6: 9	would please God to **c** me,
Ps	89:23	I will **c** his foes before him
Isa	53: 5	transgressions, **c** for our
Mt	21:44	and it will **c** anyone on whom
Rom	16:20	will shortly **c** Satan under your
2 Cor	4: 8	but not **c**; perplexed,

CRY (ING) (CRIED)

Ex	2:23	the slavery their **c** for help
Judg	10:14	Go and **c** to the gods whom
1 Kings	18:27	"**C** aloud! Surely he is a
Ps	130: 1	Out of the depths I **c** to you,
Prov	21:13	your ear to the **c** of the poor,
Lam	2:18	**C** aloud to the Lord!
Mk	15:37	Jesus gave a loud **c** and
Rom	8:15	When we **c**, "Abba! Father!"
1 Thess	4:16	Lord himself, with a **c** of
Jas	5: 4	**c** out, and the cries of

CUP

Gen	40:11	**c** was in my hand;
2 Sam	12: 3	and drink from his **c**, and
Ps	23: 5	my head with oil; my **c**
Prov	23:31	sparkles in the **c** and goes
Jer	25:15	my hand this **c** of the wine

Lam	4:21	you also the **c** shall pass;
Ezek	23:31	I will give her **c** into your
Mk	14:36	remove this **c** from me; yet,
1 Cor	11:27	drinks the **c** of the Lord
Rev	16:19	the wine-**c** of the fury of his

CURE (D)

2 Kings	5: 3	He would **c** him of his
Tob	12:3	to you safely, he **c** my wife,
Hos	5:13	he is not able to **c** you
Mt	8: 7	him, "I will come and **c** him."
Acts	28: 9	also came and were **c**.

CURSE

Num	22: 6	**c** this people for me,
Josh	24: 9	Balaam son of Beor to **c** you,
2 Sam	16: 9	"Why should this dead dog **c**
Job	2: 9	integrity? **C** God, and die."
Ps	109:28	Let them **c**, but you will bless.
Prov	30:11	those who **c** their fathers
Jer	23:10	because of the **c** the land
Mt	26:74	Then he began to **c**, and
Gal	3:10	the law are under a **c**;
Jas	3: 9	and with it we **c** those who

D

DANCE (S)

Judg	21:21	Shiloh come out to **d** in the **d**,
Ps	150: 4	him with tambourine and **d**;
Jer	31: 4	in the **d** of the merrymakers.
Mt	11:17	and you did not **d**; we wailed,

DARK (NESS)

Gen	1: 2	a formless void and **d** covered
Ex	10:21	there may be **d** over the land
Josh	24: 7	**d** between you and the
Tob	5:10	but I lie in **d** like the dead
Job	12:22	out of **d**, and brings deep **d**
Ps	139:12	even the **d** is not **d** to you;
Prov	4:19	the wicked is like deep **d**;
Eccl	2:13	excels folly as light excels **d**.
Isa	5:20	who put **d** for light
Joel	2:31	sun shall be turned to **d**,
Jn	1: 5	The light shines in the **d**,
Acts	2:20	to **d** and the moon to blood
Rom	2:19	to those who are in **d**,
Eph	5: 8	For once you were **d**, but now
Heb	12:18	a blazing fire, and **d**, and
1 Jn	1: 5	in him there is no **d** at all.
Rev	16:10	kingdom was plunged into **d**;

DAUGHTER

Ex	2: 5	The **d** of Pharaoh came
Judg	11:34	and there was his **d** coming
Ruth	2: 2	said to her, "Go, my **d**."
2 Sam	6:16	the city of David, Michal **d** of
Jdt	10:12	replied, "I am a **d** of the
Esth	2: 7	adopted her as his own **d**.
Ps	9:14	in the gates of **d** Zion,
Isa	62:11	Say to **d** Zion, "See, your
Zech	9: 9	Rejoice greatly, O **d** Zion!
Mk	7:29	—the demon has left your **d**."
Heb	11:24	be called a son of Pharaoh's **d**,

DAY (S)

Ex	34:28	the LORD forty **d** and forty

Num	14:34	forty **d**, for every day a year
Judg	17: 6	In those **d** there was no
1 Kings	19: 8	food forty **d** and forty nights
Ps	21: 4	length of **d** forever and ever.
Prov	31:12	all the **d** of her life.
Eccl	12: 1	before the **d** of trouble come,
Dan	12:12	three hundred thirty-five **d**.
Lk	4: 2	where for forty **d** he was
Acts	2:17	'In the last **d** it will be,
2 Tim	3: 1	that in the last **d** distressing
2 Pet	3: 3	that in the last **d** scoffers will
Rev	12: 6	thousand two hundred sixty **d**.
Tob	12:18	Bless him each and every **d**;
Sir	5:8	you on the **d** of calamity

DEAD

Ex	12:30	a house without someone **d**.
Ruth	4: 5	the widow of the **d** man,
Ps	115:17	The **d** do not praise the LORD
Eccl	9: 4	dog is better than a **d** lion.
Isa	26:19	give birth to those long **d**.
Jn	20: 9	he must rise from the **d**.
Eph	5:14	Rise from the **d**, and Christ
2 Tim	4: 1	judge the living and the **d**,
Jas	2:26	body without the spirit is **d**,
Rev	14:13	Blessed are the **d** who from

DECEIT

Deut	32: 4	A faithful God, without **d**,
Job	27: 4	my tongue will not utter **d**.
Ps	101: 7	No one who practices **d** shall
Dan	8:25	he shall make **d** prosper under
Mk	7:22	wickedness, **d**, licentiousness,
Rom	1:29	Full of envy, murder, strife, **d**,
1 Pet	2:22	no **d** was found in his mouth

DECEIVE (S)

Josh	9:22	"Why did you **d** us, saying,
Job	13: 9	you **d** him, as one person **d**
Jer	37: 9	Do not **d** yourselves,
Zech	13: 4	hairy mantle in order to **d**,
1 Cor	3:18	Do not **d** yourselves.
Col	2: 4	so that no one may **d** you
1 Jn	3: 7	let no one **d** you. Everyone
Rev	20: 8	and will come out to **d** the

DECLARE

Deut	5: 5	you to **d** to you the words of
1 Chr	16:24	**D** his glory among the nations
Job	38:18	**D**, if you know all this
Ps	50: 6	heavens **d** his righteousness,
Sir	16:25	and **d** knowledge accurately
Isa	66:19	and they shall **d** my glory
Jn	16:14	what is mine and **d** it to you.
Col	4: 3	may **d** the mystery of Christ,
1 Jn	1: 3	we **d** to you what we have

DEDICATED

Num	18: 6	as a gift, **d** to the LORD,
1 Kings	7:51	that his father David had **d**,
Lk	21: 5	stones and gifts **d** to God,

DEED (S)

Deut	3:24	earth can perform **d** and
Ezra	9:13	for our evil **d** and for
Ps	66: 3	"How awesome are your **d**!
Eccl	1:14	I saw all the **d** that
Sir	16:12	a person according to one's **d**.
Isa	63: 7	recount the gracious **d** of the
Hos	5: 4	Their **d** do not permit them

Mt	13:58	he did not do many **d** of
Lk	10:13	For if the **d** of power
Acts	26:20	turn to God and do **d**
Rom	8:13	you put to death the **d** of the
Col	1:21	hostile in mind, doing evil **d**,
Titus	2:14	who are zealous for good **d**.
1 Pet	2:12	see your honorable **d**
Rev	18: 6	repay her double for her **d**;

DELIGHT

Gen	3: 6	that it was a **d** to the eyes,
1 Sam	15:22	Has the LORD as great **d** in
Job	27:10	Will they take **d** in the
Ps	147:10	His **d** is not in the strength
Prov	2:14	in doing evil and **d** in the
Sir	1:27	fidelity and humility are his **d**.
Isa	1:11	I do not **d** in the blood of
Jer	9:24	for in these things I **d**,
Ezek	24:16	from you the **d** of your eyes;
Mk	12:37	was listening to him with **d**.

DELIVER

Ex	3: 8	to **d** them from the Egyptians,
Deut	32:39	no one can **d** from my hand.
Ps	109:21	steadfast love is good, **d** me.
Eccl	8: 8	nor does wickedness **d** those
Isa	50: 2	have I no power to **d**?
Dan	3:17	is able to **d** us from the
Mt	27:43	let God **d** him now,

DELIVERANCE

Ex	14:13	and see the **d** that the LORD
Ps	53: 6	O that **d** for Israel would
	72: 4	give **d** to the needy,
Jon	2: 9	**D** belongs to the LORD!"

DEMON (S)

Deut	32:17	They sacrificed to **d**, not God,
Ps	106:37	and their daughters to the **d**;
Mt	7:22	and cast out **d** in your name,
Mk	16:17	name they will cast out **d**;
Lk	4:33	the spirit of an unclean **d**,
Jn	10:21	has a **d**. Can a **d** open
1 Cor	10:20	sacrifice to **d** and not to God.
Jas	2:19	Even the **d** believe—and
Rev	18: 2	become a dwelling place of **d**,

DENY (DENIES)

Lev	16:29	you shall **d** yourselves, and
Num	29: 7	and **d** yourselves; you shall do
Sir	14:4	What he **d** himself he collects
Mt	16:24	let them **d** themselves and
Lk	12: 9	but whoever **d** me before
Acts	4:16	we cannot **d** it.
2 Tim	2:13	for he cannot **d** himself.
2 Pet	2: 1	They will even **d** the Master
Jude	1: 4	licentiousness and **d** our only

DESCENDANTS

Gen	9: 9	with you and your **d** after you,
Ex	28:43	for him and for his **d** after
2 Sam	22:51	to David and his **d** forever.
Ps	112: 2	Their **d** will be mighty in the
Isa	44: 3	pour my spirit upon your **d**,
Lk	1:55	Abraham and to his **d**
Rom	9: 7	children are his true **d**;
Gal	3: 7	believe are the **d** of Abraham.

DESCENDED

Ex	19:18	the LORD had **d** upon it in fire;
Lk	3:22	Holy Spirit **d** upon him in
Rom	1: 3	who was **d** from David
Heb	7:14	our Lord was **d** from Judah,

DESIRE (D) (S)

Gen	3:16	**d** shall be for your husband
Deut	5:21	Neither shall you **d** your
2 Sam	19:38	and all that you **d** of me I will
Job	13: 3	and I **d** to argue my case with
Ps	73:25	nothing on earth that I **d**
Prov	3:15	nothing you **d** can compare
Eccl	12: 5	drags itself along and **d** fails;
Isa	53: 2	appearance that we should **d**
Hos	6: 6	For I **d** steadfast love and not
Mal	2:15	what does the one God **d**?
Mt	9:13	I **d** mercy, not sacrifice.
Rom	10: 1	my heart's **d** and prayer to
2 Cor	8:10	even to **d** to do something—
Heb	11:16	they **d** a better country, that is
Jas	1:14	tempted by one's own **d**,
1 Jn	2:16	the **d** of the flesh, the **d**

DESPISE (D)

Num	14:11	long will this people **d** me?
Job	5:17	do not **d** the discipline
Ps	102:17	and will not **d** their prayer.
Prov	1: 7	fools **d** wisdom and
Mt	6:24	devoted to the one and **d** the
Rom	2: 4	Or do you **d** the riches of his
2 Pet	2:10	who **d** authority.

DESTROY (ED) (ING) (S)

Gen	6:13	I am going to **d** them along
Deut	6:15	you and he would **d** you from
1 Sam	15: 9	would not utterly **d** them;
Esth	3: 6	Haman plotted to **d** all the
1 Macc	3:8	he **d** the ungodly out of the
Ps	145:20	all the wicked he will **d**.
Isa	11: 9	They will not hurt or **d** on all
Jer	1:10	to **d** and to overthrow,
Lk	4:34	Have you come to **d** us?
Jn	10:10	to steal and kill and **d**.
1 Cor	3:17	anyone **d** God's temple,
Jas	4:12	able to save and to **d**.
Rev	11:18	for **d** those who **d** the earth."

DESTRUCTION

Josh	6:17	devoted to the LORD for **d**.
Ps	107:20	and delivered them from **d**.
Prov	16:18	Pride goes before **d**, and a
Sir	36:11	harm your people meet **d**.
Isa	14:23	it with the broom of **d**,
Hos	13:14	O Sheol, where is your **d**?
Hab	2:17	the **d** of the animals will
Mt	7:13	is easy that leads to **d**,
1 Cor	5: 5	to Satan for the **d** of the flesh,
1 Thess	5: 3	then sudden **d** will come
2 Pet	2: 1	bringing swift **d** on themselves.
Rev	17:11	and it goes to **d**.

DEVIL

Mt	4:11	Then the **d** left him,
Lk	8:12	then the **d** comes and takes
Jn	13: 2	The **d** had already put it into
Acts	13:10	"You son of the **d**, you enemy
Eph	6:11	against the wiles of the **d**.
1 Tim	3: 7	and the snare of the **d**.
Jas	4: 7	Resist the **d**, and he

1 Pet	5: 8	adversary the **d** prowls
1 Jn	3:10	children of the **d** are revealed
Rev	20: 2	who is the **D** and Satan,

DIE (D) (DEAD)

Gen	2:17	eat of it you shall **d**."
Ex	14:11	away to **d** in the wilderness?
Num	23:10	**d** the death of the upright
Tob	3:6	For it is better for me to **d**
Job	14:14	If mortals **d**, will they live
Ps	118:17	I shall not **d**, but I shall live,
Prov	5:23	They **d** for lack of discipline,
Eccl	3: 2	and a time to **d**; a time to
Sir	40:28	it is better to **d** than to beg.
Isa	66:24	look at the **d** bodies of the
Ezek	3:18	"You shall surely **d**," and you
Jon	4: 8	and asked that he might **d**.
Jn	6:50	eat of it and not **d**.
Rom	5: 7	rarely will anyone **d** for a
1 Cor	15:22	for as all **d** in Adam,
Heb	9:27	appointed for mortals to **d**
Rev	14:13	from now on **d** in the Lord.

DISCIPLE (S)

Isa	8:16	seal the teaching among my **d**.
Mt	26:56	Then all the **d** deserted him
Mk	3: 7	Jesus departed with his **d** to
Lk	6:13	he called his **d** and chose
Jn	2:11	and his **d** believed
Acts	14:20	But when the **d** surrounded

DISCIPLINE

Deut	4:36	you hear his voice to **d** you.
1 Kings	12:11	will **d** you with scorpions.'
Job	5:17	despise the **d** of the Almighty,
Ps	6: 1	or **d** me in your wrath.
Prov	3:11	do not despise the LORD's **d**
Sir	6:18	from your youth choose **d**.
Jer	31:18	I took the **d**; I was like a calf
Eph	6: 4	in the **d** and instruction
Heb	12:11	**d** always seems painful rather
1 Pet	5: 8	**D** yourselves, keep alert.

DISEASE (S)

Ex	15:26	any of the **d** that I brought
Deut	28:60	you all the **d** of Egypt,
2 Chr	16:12	and his **d** became severe;
Ps	103: 3	who heals all your **d**,
Isa	53: 4	carried our **d**;
Mt	10: 1	and to cure every **d** and every
Mk	1:34	who were sick with various **d**,
Lk	6:18	to be healed of their **d**;
Acts	28: 9	**d** also came and were cured

DISHONEST

Ex	18:21	trustworthy, and hate **d** gain;
Sir	5:8	Do not depend on **d** wealth.
Ezek	22:27	destroying lives to get **d** gain.
Mic	6:11	and a bag of **d** weights?
Lk	16:10	little is **d** also in much.

DISOBEY (DISOBEDIENT)

Lev	26:27	despite this, you **d** me, and
Esth	3: 3	"Why do you **d** the king's
Rom	11:31	have now been **d** in order
Eph	5: 6	comes on those who are **d**.
1 Tim	1: 9	but for the lawless and **d**,
Titus	3: 3	were once foolish, **d**,
Heb	3:18	not to those who were **d**?

DISTRESS (ED)

Deut	4:30	In your **d**, when all these
Judg	2:15	and they were in great **d**.
2 Sam	22: 7	In my **d** I called upon the
Ps	119:50	is my comfort in my **d**,
Prov	1:27	when **d** and anguish come
Sir	2:11	and saves in time of **d**.
Isa	37: 3	day is a day of **d**, of rebuke,
Jon	2: 2	the LORD out of my **d**, and he
Lk	21:23	For there will be great **d** on
Rom	8:35	hardship, or **d**, or persecution,
Jas	1:27	and widows in their **d**,
2 Pet	2: 7	a righteous man greatly **d** by

DISTRIBUTED

Josh	13:32	Moses **d** in the plains of Moab
Ps	112: 9	They have **d** freely, they have
Acts	4:35	and it was **d** to each as any

DIVORCE

Deut	22:19	permitted to **d** her as long
Sir	7:26	Do not **d** her;
Isa	50: 1	your mother's bill of **d**
Mt	5:31	give her a certificate of **d**.'
Mk	10: 4	of dismissal and to **d**
1 Cor	7:13	she should not **d** him.

DOCTRINE

Eph	4:14	about by every wind of **d**,
2 Tim	4: 3	not put up with sound **d**,
Titus	2:10	to the **d** of God our Savior.

DOMINION

Gen	1:26	them have **d** over the fish of
Job	25: 2	**D** and fear are with God
Ps	22:28	For **d** belongs to the LORD,
Sir	17:4	gave them **d** over beasts and
Dan	7:14	His **d** is an everlasting **d**
Rom	5:17	exercise **d** in life
Eph	1:21	authority and power and **d**,
Rev	1: 6	glory and **d** forever and ever.

DREAM (S) (ER)

Gen	40: 5	each his own **d**, and each **d**
Judg	7:13	man telling a **d** to his
1 Kings	3: 5	Solomon in a **d** by night;
Jer	23:27	forget my name by their **d**
Dan	7: 1	Then he wrote down the **d**:
Mt	2:13	appeared to Joseph in a **d** and
Acts	2:17	and your old men shall **d d**.

DRINK (DRANK)

Gen	19:33	their father **d** wine that night;
Ex	32:20	and made the Israelites **d** it.
Num	4: 7	flagons for the **d** offering;
Judg	7: 5	those who kneel down to **d**,
2 Sam	23:15	would give me water to **d**
Tob	4:15	Do not **d** wine to excess
Jdt	12:17	"Have a **d** and be merry
Ps	50:13	or **d** the blood of goats?
Prov	5:15	**D** water from your own cistern
Eccl	9: 7	and **d** your wine with a merry
Sir	15:3	him the water of wisdom to **d**
Jer	35: 2	then offer them wine to **d**.
Dan	1:12	to eat and water to **d**.
Hab	2:15	make your neighbors **d**,
Mt	27:34	they offered him wine to **d**,
Lk	22:18	I will not **d** of the fruit
Jn	7:38	one who believes in me **d**.
Rom	14:17	food and **d** but righteousness

1 Cor	12:13	all made to **d** of one Spirit.
1 Tim	5:23	No longer **d** only water,
Rev	16: 6	have given them blood to **d**.

DRUNK

Gen	9:21	of the wine and became **d**,
Ruth	3: 7	When Boaz had eaten and **d**,
1 Sam	25:36	him, for he was very **d**;
1 Kings	16: 9	drinking himself **d** in the
Song	5: 1	drink, and be **d** with love.
Sir	31:28	Wine **d** at the proper time
Isa	29: 9	Be **d**, but not from wine;
Jn	2:10	guests have become **d**.
1 Cor	11:21	and another becomes **d**.
1 Thess	5: 7	and those who are **d** get **d** at
Rev	18: 3	the nations have **d** of the wine

DUST

Gen	13:16	count the **d** of the earth,
Num	23:10	Who can count the **d** of Jacob,
1 Sam	2: 8	up the poor from the **d**;
Ps	90: 3	You turn us back to **d**,
Eccl	3:20	from the **d**, and all turn to **d**
Sir	17:32	all human beings are **d** and
Isa	65:25	serpent—its food shall be **d**!
Mic	7:17	they shall lick **d** like a snake,
Mt	10:14	shake off the **d** from your
Acts	18: 6	he shook the **d** from his
Rev	18:19	And they threw **d** on their

DWELL (ING) (S)

Ex	25: 8	so that I may **d** among them.
1 Kings	6:13	I will **d** among the children
1 Macc	1:38	she became a **d** of strangers;
Ps	23: 6	and I shall **d** in the house
Isa	57:15	I **d** in the high and holy
Joel	3:17	the LORD your God, **d** in Zion,
Zech	2:11	and I will **d** in your midst.
Acts	7:48	not **d** in houses made with
2 Cor	12: 9	power of Christ may **d**
Col	3:16	word of Christ **d** in you richly;
Rev	21: 3	He will **d** with them;

E

EAGLE

Deut	14:12	you shall not eat: the **e**,
Prov	30:19	the way of an **e** in the sky,
Ezek	17: 3	A great **e**, with great wings
Rev	12:14	two wings of the great **e**,

EAR (S)

Ex	21: 6	shall pierce his **e** with an awl;
2 Kings	19:16	Incline your **e**, O LORD, and
Neh	1:11	let your **e** be attentive
Ps	116: 2	he inclined his **e** to me,
Prov	25:12	wise rebuke to a listening **e**.
Eccl	1: 8	or the **e** filled with hearing.
Wis	15:15	nor **e** with which to hear
Bar	3:9	give **e**, and learn wisdom
Dan	9:18	Incline your **e**, O my God, and
Lk	22:51	touched his **e** and healed him.
1 Cor	2: 9	nor **e** heard, nor the human
Rev	13: 9	Let anyone who has an **e**

EARTH

Gen	1: 1	created the heavens and the **e**,
Deut	5: 8	in the water under the **e**.
Josh	3:13	the LORD of all the **e**,
1 Kings	8:27	God indeed dwell on the **e**?
1 Chr	16:23	to the Lord, all the **e**.
Job	26: 7	and hangs the **e** upon nothing.
Ps	97: 1	Let the **e** rejoice;
Isa	37:16	all the kingdoms of the **e**;
Jer	33:25	ordinances of heaven and **e**,
Dan	12: 2	in the dust of the **e** shall
Joel	2:30	the heavens and on the **e**,
Am	9: 5	he who touches the **e** and it
Hab	2:20	the **e** keep silence before him!
Hag	2:21	shake the heavens and the **e**,
Mt	5:18	until heaven and **e** pass away,
Lk	5:24	authority on **e** to forgive sins"
Jn	12:32	am lifted up from the **e**,
Acts	7:49	and the **e** is my footstool.
1 Cor	15:47	first man was from the **e**,
Eph	3:15	family in heaven and on **e**
Heb	12:26	time his voice shook the **e**;
2 Pet	3:13	new heavens and a new **e**,
Rev	20:11	the **e** and the heaven fled

EAT (ER) (ING)

Gen	2:16	"You may freely **e** of every tree
Ex	32: 6	people sat down to **e** and
Lev	11: 4	you shall not **e** the following:
Num	11:13	and say, 'Give us meat to **e**!'
Deut	14: 4	are the animals you may **e**:
Judg	14:14	the **e** came something to **e**.
2 Sam	9: 7	yourself shall **e** at my table
2 Kings	9:10	The dogs shall **e** Jezebel
Tob	1:11	from **e** the food of the
1 Macc	1:62	not to **e** unclean food.
Ps	22:26	The poor shall **e** and be
Eccl	5:18	it is fitting to **e** and drink
Isa	65:25	lion shall **e** straw like the ox;
Jer	19: 9	and all shall **e** the flesh of
Ezek	3: 1	O mortal, **e** what is offered
Hag	1: 6	you **e**, but you never
Mt	15: 2	their hands before they **e**."
Lk	10: 8	**e** what is set before you
Acts	10:13	"Get up, Peter; kill and **e**."
Rom	14:20	others fall by what you **e**;
1 Cor	10:31	whether you **e** or drink,
2 Thess	3:10	to work should not **e**.
Rev	10: 9	"Take it, and **e**; it will be

EGYPT

Gen	12:10	So Abram went down to **E**
Ex	32: 1	out of the land of **E**,
Num	24: 8	who brings him out of **E**,
Deut	16:12	you were a slave in **E**,
Josh	15:47	villages; to the Wadi of **E**,
1 Kings	14:25	King Shishak of **E** came up
2 Chr	36: 3	Then the king of **E** deposed
Neh	9:18	brought you up out of **E**,
Ps	78:51	struck all the firstborn in **E**,
Isa	19: 1	An oracle concerning **E**.
Jer	46: 2	of Pharaoh Neco, king of **E**,
Ezek	29: 2	against Pharaoh king of **E**,
Hos	11: 1	and out of **E** I called my son.
Mt	2:15	"Out of **E** I have called my son
Heb	11:27	By faith he left **E**, unafraid
Rev	11: 8	called Sodom and **E**, where

ELDER (S)

Gen	25:23	the **e** shall serve the younger."

Ex	24: 1	and seventy of the **e** of Israel,
Deut	25: 7	shall go up to the **e** at the gate
Josh	24: 1	and summoned the **e**, the
Judg	2: 7	the **e** who outlived Joshua,
Ruth	4: 2	took ten men of the **e** of the
Ps	105:22	and to teach his **e** wisdom.
Isa	3:14	with the **e** and princes of his
Mt	15: 2	break the tradition of the **e**?
Mk	7: 3	the tradition of the **e**;
Acts	21:18	and all the **e** were present.
1 Tim	5:17	Let the **e** who rule well be
Titus	1: 5	appoint **e** in every town,
1 Pet	5: 5	accept the authority of the **e**.
Rev	19: 4	twenty-four **e** and the four

ELECT
Wis	4:15	grace and mercy are with his **e**.
Sir	46:1	a great savior of God's **e**.
Mt	24:31	gather his **e** from the four
Mk	13:22	lead astray, if possible, the **e**.
Rom	11: 7	The **e** obtained it, but the rest
2 Tim	2:10	for the sake of the **e**,
2 Jn	1:13	The children of your **e** sister

EMPEROR
Mk	12:17	"Give to the **e** the things that
Jn	19:12	are no friend of the **e**.
Acts	25:11	them. I appeal to the **e**."
1 Pet	2:17	Fear God. Honor the **e**.

ENCOURAGE (MENT)
Deut	1:38	shall enter there; **e** him,
2 Sam	11:25	and overthrow it.' And **e** him."
1 Macc	12:9	we have as **e** the holy books
Acts	4:36	(which means "son of **e**").
Rom	15: 4	steadfastness and by the **e** of
1 Cor	14: 3	upbuilding and **e** and
Philem	1: 7	much joy and **e** from your

ENDURE (D) (S)
Gen	8:22	As long as the earth **e**,
Job	20:21	their prosperity will not **e**.
Ps	72:17	May his name **e** forever,
Jer	10:10	cannot **e** his indignation.
Lam	5:19	throne to all generations.
Joel	2:11	terrible indeed—who can **e** it?
Lk	17:25	first he must **e** much suffering
Jn	6:27	food that **e** for eternal life,
Rom	9:22	has **e** with much patience the
1 Cor	10:13	you may be able to **e** it.
2 Cor	9: 9	his righteousness **e** forever."
2 Tim	2:10	I **e** everything for the sake of
Heb	12: 7	**E** trials for the sake of
1 Pet	2:19	you **e** pain while suffering

ENEMY (ENEMIES)
Ex	1:10	join our **e** and fight against us
Deut	6:19	thrusting out all your **e** from
Josh	21:44	had given all their **e** into
Judg	2:14	power of their **e** all around,
2 Sam	7: 1	from all his **e** around him,
Jdt	8:35	to take vengeance on our **e**."
Esth	9: 5	all their **e** with the sword,
1 Macc	4:36	said, "See, our **e** are crushed;
Ps	74:10	Is the **e** to revile your name
Prov	16: 7	even their **e** to be at peace
Sir	6:9	friends who change into **e**.
Isa	59:18	requital to his **e**;
Dan	4:19	interpretation for your **e**!
Mt	5:44	Love your **e** and pray for those

Acts	2:35	make your **e** your footstool."
Rom	12:20	"if your **e** are hungry, feed
1 Cor	15:25	put all his **e** under his feet.
Heb	10:13	"until his **e** would be made a
Jas	4: 4	becomes an **e** of God.

ENTER
Ex	40:35	not able to **e** the tent of
Num	20:24	For he shall not **e** the land
Ps	118:19	that I may **e** through them
Isa	26: 2	keeps faith may **e** in.
Joel	3: 2	and I will **e** into judgment
Mt	5:20	you will never **e** the kingdom
Mk	10:15	a little child will never **e** it."
Jn	3: 5	no one can **e** the kingdom of
Acts	14:22	that we must **e** the kingdom of
Heb	4:11	every effort to **e** that rest,
Rev	21:27	But nothing unclean will **e** it,

ENVY
Prov	24: 1	Do not **e** the wicked, nor
Eccl	4: 4	one person's **e** of another.
Wis	2:24	through the devil's **e** death
Sir	9:11	Do not **e** the success of
Mk	7:22	deceit, licentiousness, **e**,
Rom	1:29	Full of **e**, murder, strife, deceit,
Phil	1:15	proclaim Christ from **e** and
Titus	3: 3	our days in malice and **e**,
Jas	3:16	there is **e** and selfish
1 Pet	2: 1	and all guile, insincerity, **e**,

ESCAPE
Gen	7: 7	the ark to **e** the waters
1 Sam	23:28	was called the Rock of **E**.
Job	11:20	all way of **e** will be lost
Ps	89:48	can **e** the power of Sheol?
Prov	12:13	but the righteous **e** from
Jer	11:11	upon them that they cannot **e**;
Joel	2:32	there shall be those who **e**,
Mt	23:33	How can you **e** being
Rom	2: 3	you will **e** the judgment of
2 Tim	2:26	and that they may **e** from the
Heb	12:25	not **e** when they refused
2 Pet	1: 4	may **e** from the corruption

ETERNAL (ETERNITY)
Gen	49:26	blessings of the **e** mountains,
Eccl	12: 5	go to their **e** home,
Jer	20:11	Their **e** dishonor will never
Hab	3: 6	The **e** mountains were
Mt	25:41	depart from me into the **e** fire
Mk	3:29	but is guilty of an **e** sin"—
Jn	3:16	not perish but may have **e** life.
Acts	13:46	unworthy of **e** life,
Rom	2: 7	he will give **e** life;
2 Cor	5: 1	**e** in the heavens.
Eph	3:11	accordance with the **e** purpose
2 Thess	2:16	gave us **e** comfort and good
1 Tim	6:16	honor and **e** dominion.
Titus	3: 7	according to the hope of **e** life.
Heb	13:20	the blood of the **e** covenant,
1 Pet	5:10	called you to his **e** glory in
1 Jn	3:15	murderers do not have **e** life
Jude	1:21	that leads to **e** life.
Rev	14: 6	with an **e** gospel to proclaim

EVERLASTING
Gen	9:16	remember the **e** covenant
2 Sam	23: 5	with me an **e** covenant,
1 Chr	16:17	to Israel as an **e** covenant,

Ps	119:142	righteousness is an **e**
Isa	24: 5	broken the **e** covenant.
Ezek	37:26	shall be an **e** covenant with
Dan	12: 2	some to **e** life,

EVERYTHING
Gen	6:17	**e** that is on the earth
Deut	29: 9	you may succeed in **e** that
Ps	150: 6	Let **e** that breathes praise the
Eccl	3:11	made **e** suitable for its time;
Sir	15:18	mighty in power and sees **e**;
	19:15	so do not believe **e** you hear
Mt	28:20	teaching them to obey **e**
Lk	1: 3	after investigating **e** carefully
Jn	14:26	will teach you **e**, and remind
Rom	14:20	**E** is indeed clean, but it
1 Cor	10:31	do **e** for the glory of God
Gal	6:15	but a new creation is **e**!
1 Thess	5:21	but test **e**; hold fast
1 Tim	4: 4	For **e** created by God is good
2 Pet	1: 3	power has given us **e** needed

EVIL
Gen	44: 4	'Why have you returned **e** for
Num	32:13	had done **e** in the sight of
Deut	28:20	account of the **e** of your deeds,
Judg	4: 1	what was **e** in the sight of
1 Sam	19: 9	Then an **e** spirit from the LORD
1 Kings	11: 6	Solomon did what was **e**
Job	2: 3	turns away from **e**. He
Ps	141: 4	turn my heart to any **e**,
Prov	3: 7	and turn away from **e**.
Eccl	12:14	whether good or **e**.
Isa	13:11	punish the world for its **e**,
Jer	18:10	if it does **e** in my sight,
Am	5:14	Seek good and not **e**,
Mic	3: 2	love the **e**, who tear
Mt	12:35	the **e** person brings **e** things
Lk	11:13	If you then, who are **e**, know
Jn	3:20	For all who do **e** hate the light
Rom	16:19	and guileless in what is **e**.
1 Cor	14:20	be infants in **e**, but in thinking
Eph	6:12	spiritual forces of **e** in
1 Thess	5:22	abstain from every form of **e**.
1 Tim	6:10	root of all kinds of **e**,
Heb	5:14	distinguish good from **e**.
Jas	4:16	all such boasting is **e**.
1 Pet	3:10	their tongues from **e** and their
1 Jn	2:13	you have conquered the **e** one.
2 Jn	1:11	participate in the **e** deeds of

EVILDOER (S)
2 Sam	7:10	and **e** shall afflict them no
Job	34:22	where **e** may hide themselves.
Ps	34:16	of the Lord is against **e**,
Prov	24:19	Do not fret because of **e**.
Jer	23:14	strengthen the hands of **e**,
Mt	7:23	go away from me, you **e**.'
1 Pet	2:12	though they malign you as **e**,

EXALT (ED)
Ex	15: 2	and I will **e** him.
Josh	3: 7	I will begin to **e** you in the
1 Sam	2:10	and **e** the power of his anointed
1 Chr	25: 5	the promise of God to **e** him;
Ps	66: 7	rebellious not **e** themselves.
Isa	25: 1	I will **e** you, I will praise your
Dan	11:36	He shall **e** himself and
Lk	14:11	humble themselves will be **e**."

Jas 4:10 the Lord, and he will **e** you.

EXIST (S) (ED)

Ps 119:89 The Lord **e** forever;
Rom 4:17 the things that do not **e**.
1 Cor 8: 6 for whom we **e**, and one Lord,
Heb 2:10 through whom all things **e**,
Rev 4:11 will they **e** and were created."

EYE (S)

Gen 3: 7 Then the **e** of both were
Num 33:55 as barbs in your **e** and thorns
Deut 11:12 The **e** of the Lord your God
Josh 23:13 and thorns in your **e**, until you
Judg 16:28 the Philistines for my two **e**."
1 Kings 10: 7 I came and my own **e** had
2 Chr 16: 9 For the **e** of the Lord range
Tob 6:9 and the **e** will be healed."
Job 36: 7 He does not withdraw his **e**
Ps 119:37 Turn my **e** from looking at
Prov 15: 3 The **e** of the Lord are in
Sir 23:4 do not give me haughty **e**.
Isa 42: 7 to open the **e** that are blind,
Jer 24: 6 set my **e** upon them for good,
Ezek 24:16 you the delight of your **e**;
Dan 10: 6 his **e** like flaming torches,
Zech 4:10 "These seven are the **e** of the
Mt 9:30 And their **e** were opened.
Jn 9:10 "Then how were your **e**
Acts 28:27 might not look with their **e**,
Rom 11:10 let their **e** be darkened
Eph 1:18 with the **e** of your heart
1 Jn 2:16 the desire of the **e**, the pride in
Rev 7:17 away every tear from their **e**."

F

FACE

Gen 32:20 I shall see his **f**; perhaps he
Num 14:14 are seen **f** to **f**, and your cloud
Deut 5: 4 you **f** to **f** at the mountain
2 Kings 14: 8 look one another in the **f**."
Esth 7: 8 they covered Haman's **f**.
Ps 27: 8 my heart says, "seek his **f**!"
Song 2:14 and your **f** is lovely.
Isa 8:17 who is hiding his **f** from the
Jer 32: 4 speak with him **f** to **f** and see
Ezek 39:29 never again hide my **f** from
Dan 10: 6 his **f** like lightning,
Hos 5:15 their guilt and seek my **f**.
Mt 17: 2 before them, and his **f** shone
Lk 9:29 appearance of his **f** changed,
Jn 19: 3 and striking him on the **f**.
Acts 6:15 that his **f** was like the **f** of
1 Cor 13:12 we will see **f** to **f**. Now I know
2 Cor 10: 1 who am humble when **f** to **f**
3 Jn 1:14 talk together **f** to **f**. Peace to
Rev 22: 4 see his **f**, and his name will be
Jdt 10:23 at the beauty of her **f**.
Sir 13:26 happy heart is a cheerful **f**,

FAIL

Num 15:22 unintentionally **f** to observe
Josh 1: 5 I will not **f** you
1 Chr 28:20 He will not **f** you or forsake
Tob 14:4 none of all their words will **f**.
Isa 58:11 whose waters never **f**.

Zeph 3: 5 each dawn without **f**;
Lk 22:32 your own faith may not **f**;
2 Cor 13: 5 unless, indeed, you **f**

FAITH

Num 5: 6 breaking **f** with the Lord,
Deut 32:51 you broke **f** with me
Josh 2:12 a sign of good **f**
22:20 break **f** in the matter
Judg 9:15 in good **f** you are anointing
Ezra 10: 2 We have broken **f**
1 Macc 10:27 Now continue still to keep **f**
Job 39:12 Do you have **f** in it
Ps 78:22 they had no **f** in God,
116:10 I kept my **f**,
Sir 27:17 your friend and keep **f** with
Isa 7: 9 stand firm in **f**,
Hab 2: 4 the righteous live by their **f**.
Mt 6:30 you of little **f**?
21:21 if you have **f**
Mk 2: 5 When Jesus saw their **f**,
11:22 Have **f** in God.
Lk 5:20 When he saw their **f**,
18:42 your **f** has saved you.
Acts 3:16 by **f** in his name,
14: 9 seeing that he had **f**
24:24 concerning **f** in Christ Jesus.
Rom 1: 5 **f** among all the Gentiles
16:26 the obedience of **f**—
1 Cor 2: 5 your **f** might rest not on
16:13 stand firm in your **f**,
2 Cor 1:24 lord it over your **f**;
13: 5 you are living in the **f**.
Gal 1:23 the **f** he once tried to destroy
6:10 those of the family of **f**.
Eph 1:15 I have heard of your **f**
6:16 the shield of **f**,
Phil 1:25 progress and joy in **f**,
3: 9 from God based on **f**.
Col 1: 4 your **f** in Christ Jesus
1:23 steadfast in the **f**,
1 Thess 1: 3 your work of **f**
3:10 whatever is lacking in your **f**.
2 Thess 1: 3 your **f** is growing abundantly,
1:11 good resolve and work of **f**,
1 Tim 1: 2 my loyal child in the **f**:
3: 9 to the mystery of the **f**
6:12 the good fight of the **f**;
2 Tim 1: 5 your sincere **f**, a **f** that lived
3:15 through **f** in Christ Jesus.
Titus 1: 1 for the sake of the **f**
1:13 may become sound in the **f**,
Philem 1: 5 your **f** toward the Lord Jesus.
Heb 4: 2 united by **f**
11: 1 **f** is the assurance of things
11:13 these died in **f**
12: 2 pioneer and perfecter of our **f**,
Jas 1: 3 **f** produces endurance;
2:26 **f** without works is also dead
1 Pet 1: 5 the power of God through **f**
5: 9 steadfast in your **f**,
2 Pet 1: 1 a **f** as precious as ours
1 Jn 5: 4 conquers the world, our **f**.
Jude 1: 3 contend for the **f**
Rev 2:13 you did not deny your **f**

FAITHFUL (NESS)

Deut 7: 9 the **f** God who maintains
Judg 5:15 and Issachar **f** to Barak;
1 Sam 2: 9 guard the feet of his **f** ones,

1 Sam 20:14 show me the **f** love
2 Sam 2: 6 steadfast love and **f**
2 Chr 6:41 your **f** rejoice in your
31:20 **f** before the Lord his God
Neh 7: 2 he was a **f** man
Ps 4: 3 Lord has set apart the **f**
16:10 let your **f** one see the Pit.
116:15 the death of his **f** ones.
Prov 2: 8 the way of his **f** ones.
28:20 The **f** will abound with
Wis 3:9 the **f** will abide with him in
Sir 6:15 **f** friends are beyond price;
Isa 1:21 How the **f** city has become a
25: 1 formed of old, **f** and sure.
Jer 31: 3 I have continued my **f** to you.
Dan 6: 4 because he was **f**,
Hos 2:20 my wife in **f**;
Mic 7: 2 The **f** have disappeared from
Zech 8: 3 Jerusalem shall be called the **f**
Mt 24:45 "Who then is the **f** and wise
Lk 12:42 Who then is the **f** and prudent
16:11 you have not been **f**
Acts 11:23 to remain **f** to the Lord
1 Cor 1: 9 God is **f**;
2 Cor 1:18 As surely as God is **f**,
Eph 1: 1 **f** in Christ Jesus:
6:21 a dear brother and a **f** minister
Col 1: 2 **f** brothers and sisters in Christ
4: 7 a **f** minister, and a fellow
1 Thess 5:24 one who calls you is **f**,
1 Tim 1:12 because he judged me **f**
2 Tim 2: 2 many witnesses entrust to **f**
Heb 2:17 a merciful and **f** high priest
11:11 he considered him **f**
1 Pet 4:19 entrust themselves to a **f**
1 Jn 1: 9 he who is **f** and just will
Rev 1: 5 Jesus Christ, the **f** witness,
2:13 of Antipas my witness, my **f**
17:14 are called and chosen and **f**."

FALL (S) (EN)

Gen 2:21 caused a deep sleep to **f**
Ex 5: 3 our God, or he will **f** upon us
Lev 19:10 gather the **f** grapes of your
Num 11: 9 the manna would **f** with it.
1 Sam 3:19 of his words **f** to the ground.
1 Chr 10: 8 found Saul and his sons **f** on
Ps 5:10 let them **f** by their own
91: 7 A thousand may **f** at your side,
Prov 16:18 a haughty spirit before a **f**.
Eccl 4:10 for if they **f**, one will lift up
Sir 28:23 who forsake the Lord will **f**
Isa 40:30 and the young will **f**
Jer 6:15 shall **f** among those who **f**;
Dan 11:35 some of the wise shall **f**,
Hos 10: 8 to the hills, **f** on us.
Mt 7:25 but it did not **f**, because it had
Mk 4:17 immediately they **f** away.
Lk 10:18 I watched Satan **f** from heaven
Acts 5:15 Peter's shadow might **f** on
Rom 3:23 all have sinned and **f** short of
11:11 they stumbled so as to **f**?
1 Cor 8:13 cause one of them to **f**.
1 Tim 6: 9 who want to be rich **f** into
Heb 10:31 a fearful thing to the **f**
1 Pet 2: 8 a rock that makes them **f**.
Rev 6:16 **f** on us and hide us

FAMILY (FAMILIES)

Gen 8:19 out of the ark by **f**.

Ex	1:21	feared God, he gave them **f**.
Ps	107:41	and makes their **f** like flocks.
Am	3: 2	known of all the **f** of the earth;
Titus	1:11	they are upsetting whole **f**

FAMINE

Gen	12:10	Now there was a **f** in the land.
	43: 1	Now the **f** was severe in the
Ruth	1: 1	there was a **f** in the land,
1 Kings	8:37	If there is **f** in the land,
2 Kings	4:38	to Gilgal, there was a **f** in the
Job	5:20	In **f** he will redeem you from
Ps	37:19	in the days of **f** they have
Jer	14:15	Sword and **f** shall not come
Am	8:11	when I will send a **f** on the
Acts	11:28	there would be a severe **f**
Rom	8:35	distress, or persecution, or **f**,
Rev	18: 8	pestilence and mourning and **f**

FAST (ED)

Deut	10:20	you shall hold **f**, and by his
Josh	22: 5	his commandments, and to
		hold **f** to him, and to serve
2 Kings	18: 6	For he held **f** to the LORD; he
1 Chr	10:12	the oak in Jabesh, and **f** seven
2 Chr	20: 3	and proclaimed a **f** throughout
Ezra	8:21	Then I proclaimed a **f** there, at
Esth	4:16	in Susa, and hold a **f** on my
Ps	17: 5	My steps have held **f** to your
Prov	4: 4	me, "Let your heart hold **f** my
Sir	49:4	Job who held **f** to all the ways
Isa	56: 4	that please me and hold **f** my
Mt	6:16	"And whenever you **f**, do not
Lk	18:12	I **f** twice a week; I give
Rom	12: 9	hate what is evil, hold **f** to
Col	2:19	and not holding **f** to the head,
1 Thess	5:21	but test everything; hold **f** to
1 Tim	3: 9	they must hold **f** to the
Heb	4:14	of God, let us hold **f** to our
Rev	14:12	hold **f** to the faith of Jesus

FATHER

Gen	2:24	Therefore a man leaves his **f**
	26:24	am the God of your **f**
Ex	20:12	Honor your **f** and your
	21:17	Whoever curses **f** or mother
Deut	5:16	Honor your **f** and your
Judg	17:10	and be to me a **f** and a priest,
1 Kings	2:12	on the throne of his **f** David;
1 Chr	17:13	I will be a **f** to him, and he
Job	38:28	"Has the rain a **f**, or who has
Ps	27:10	If my **f** and mother forsake
	109:14	May the iniquity of his **f** be
Prov	3:12	one he loves, as a **f** the son in
	20:20	If you curse **f** or mother, your
Wis	2:16	and boasts that God is his **f**.
Sir	3:3	who honor their **f** atone for
Isa	8: 4	knows how to call "My **f**" or
	9: 6	Everlasting **F**, Prince of Peace.
Jer	2:27	"You are my **f**," and to a stone,
Ezek	16: 3	your **f** was an Amorite, and
Mic	7: 6	for the son treats the **f** with
Mal	1: 6	A son honors his **f**, and
Mt	5:16	and give glory to your **F** in
	11:27	over to me by my **F**; and no
	23: 9	And call no one your **f** on
Lk	6:36	Be merciful, just as your **F** is
	11: 2	you pray, say: **F**, hallowed be
	18:20	Honor your **f** and mother.' "
Jn	3:35	The **F** loves the Son and has

Jn	6:46	that anyone has seen the **F**
	14: 9	can you say, 'Show us the **F**?
Rom	4:16	Abraham (for he is the **f** of all
2 Cor	6:18	and I will be your **f**, and you
Eph	6: 2	"Honor your **f** and mother"—
1 Thess	2:11	like a **f** with his children,
1 Tim	5: 1	to him as to a **f**, to younger
Heb	1: 5	again, "I will be his **F**, and he
Jas	1:17	**F** of lights, with whom there
1 Jn	1: 3	our fellowship is with the **F**
Rev	3: 5	before my **F** and before his

FAVOR

Gen	6: 8	But Noah found **f** in the sight
Ex	33:12	and you have also found **f** in
Lev	26: 9	I will look with **f** upon you
Judg	6:17	"If now I have found **f** with
2 Chr	33:12	in distress he entreated the **f** of
1 Macc	4:10	to see whether he will **f** us
Ps	5:12	you cover them with **f** as with
Prov	3:34	to the humble he shows **f**.
	13:15	Good sense wins **f**, but the
Sir	32:14	to seek him will find **f**.
Isa	49: 8	LORD: In a time of **f** I have
Zech	11: 7	two staffs; one I named **F**, the
Lk	1:30	Mary, for you have found **f**
Acts	7:10	and enabled him to win **f** and

FEAR (S)

Gen	9: 2	The **f** and dread of you shall
Ex	9:30	that you do not yet **f** the LORD
Deut	2:25	to put the dread and **f** of you
	10:12	Only to **f** the LORD your God,
Josh	2:24	of the land melt in **f**
1 Sam	12:14	If you will **f** the LORD and
2 Chr	19: 7	Now, let the **f** of the LORD be
Job	1: 9	"Does Job **f** God for nothing?
Ps	2:11	Serve the LORD with **f**, with
	46: 2	Therefore we will not **f**,
	147:11	those who **f** him, in those who
Prov	1: 7	The **f** of the LORD is the
	10:27	The **f** of the LORD prolongs life
Eccl	8:12	be well with those who **f** God,
Sir	7:29	With all your soul **f** the Lord,
Isa	8:12	and do not **f** what it **f**,
	51: 7	do not **f** the reproach of
Jer	5:22	Do you not **f** me? says the
Mk	5:36	"Do not **f**, only believe."
Lk	12: 5	you whom to **f**: **f** him
Jn	7:13	for **f** of the Jews.
Rom	8:15	slavery to fall back into **f**,
2 Cor	5:11	knowing the **f** of the Lord,
Phil	2:12	with **f** and trembling;
Heb	2:15	slavery by the **f** of death.
1 Pet	1:17	live in reverent **f** during the
1 Jn	4:18	There is no **f** in love,
Rev	2:10	Do not **f** what you are about

FEET

Ex	3: 5	the sandals from your **f**,
	24:10	Under his **f** there was
Ruth	3: 8	lying at his **f**, was a woman!
1 Sam	2: 9	guard the **f** of his faithful
Ps	8: 6	put all things under their **f**,
	40: 2	and set my **f** upon a rock,
Prov	1:16	for their **f** run to evil,
Isa	6: 2	with two they covered their **f**,
Dan	2:33	its **f** partly of iron and partly
Nah	1: 3	are the dust of his **f**.
Zech	14: 4	his **f** shall stand on the Mount

Mt	10:14	the dust from your **f**
Lk	1:79	to guide our **f** into the way of
	8:35	sitting at the **f** of Jesus,
Acts	5: 2	and laid it at the apostles' **f**.
Rom	3:15	Their **f** are swift to shed blood
1 Cor	12:21	the head to the **f**,
Eph	1:22	put all things under his **f**
Heb	1:13	a footstool for your **f**"?
Rev	1:15	his **f** were like burnished

FIELD (S)

Gen	4: 8	us go out to the **f**.
	23:17	So the **f** of Ephron
Lev	19: 9	the very edges of your **f**,
Ruth	2: 3	came and gleaned in the **f**
Ps	50:11	all that moves in the **f**
Prov	24:30	I passed by the **f** of one
Isa	1: 8	a shelter in a cucumber **f**,
	40: 6	like the flower of the **f**.
Mt	6:28	Consider the lilies of the **f**,
	13:38	the **f** is the world,
2 Cor	10:13	but will keep within the **f**

FIGHT

Ex	14:14	The LORD will **f** for you,
Deut	1:30	is the one who will **f** for you,
Judg	1: 1	to **f** against them?
Neh	4:20	Our God will **f** for us."
1 Macc	2:40	and refuse to **f** with the
Sir	4:28	**F** to the death for truth, and
Jer	21: 5	I myself will **f** against you
1 Tim	1:18	you may **f** the good **f**,

FILL (ED)

Gen	1:28	**f** the earth and subdue it
Ps	72:19	may his glory **f** the whole
Jer	23:24	Do I not **f** heaven and earth?
Ezek	10: 2	**f** your hands with burning
Hag	2: 7	and I will **f** this house with
Jn	6:26	you ate your **f** of the loaves.
Rom	15:13	May the God of hope **f** you
Eph	4:10	so that he might **f** all things.)

FIND

Gen	18:26	If I **f** at Sodom fifty righteous
Num	32:23	be sure your sin will **f** you out.
Job	37:23	The Almighty—we cannot **f**
Ps	61: 4	**f** refuge under the shelter of
	132: 5	until I **f** a place for the LORD
Prov	2: 5	**f** the knowledge of God.
	8:17	who seek me diligently **f** me.
Eccl	12:10	sought to **f** pleasing words,
Jer	6:16	and **f** rest for your souls.
Mt	7: 7	search, and you will **f**;
Lk	23: 4	I **f** no basis for an accusation
Eph	5:10	Try to **f** out what is pleasing to

FIRE

Gen	15:17	a smoking **f** pot and a flaming
Ex	3: 2	a flame of **f** out of a bush; he
	40:38	and **f** was in the cloud by
Lev	9:24	**F** came out from the LORD
Num	16:35	And **f** came out from the LORD
Deut	4:24	your God is a devouring **f**,
Judg	6:21	and **f** sprang up from the rock
1 Kings	18:38	Then the **f** of the LORD fell
2 Kings	1:10	let **f** come down from heaven
	6:17	horses and chariots of **f**
2 Chr	7: 1	**f** came down from heaven
Ps	11: 6	he will rain coals of **f**

Sir	7:17	of the ungodly is **f**
Isa	5:24	the tongue of **f** devours the
Jer	23:29	Is not my word like **f**,
Dan	3:25	in the middle of the **f**,
Zech	3: 2	a brand plucked from the **f**?"
Mt	3:11	with the Holy Spirit and **f**.
	18: 8	be thrown into the eternal **f**.
Mk	9:43	to hell, to the unquenchable **f**.
Lk	3:16	with the Holy Spirit and **f**.
Heb	10:27	judgment, and a fury of **f**
Jas	3: 6	And the tongue is a **f**.
Jude	1:23	snatching them out of the **f**;
Rev	1:14	were like a flame of **f**,
	20:14	thrown into the lake of **f**.

FIRST

Gen	1: 5	and there was morning, the **f**
	13: 4	made an altar at the **f**;
Ex	12: 2	the **f** month of the year
	34:19	All that **f** opens the womb is
Prov	3: 9	with the **f** fruits of all your
Sir	11:7	examine **f**, and then criticize.
Isa	41: 4	I, the LORD, am **f**,
Dan	7: 4	The **f** was like a lion
Mt	5:24	**f** be reconciled to your brother
	19:30	many who are **f** will be last,
Mk	9:11	that Elijah must come **f**?"
	13:10	good news must **f** be
Jn	2:11	Jesus did this, the **f** of his
Rom	1:16	to the Jew **f** and also to the
1 Cor	15:45	The **f** man, Adam, became a
Eph	1:12	we, who were the **f** to set our
Heb	3:14	we hold our **f** confidence
	10: 9	He abolishes the **f**
1 Jn	4:19	We love because he **f** loved us.
Rev	1:17	I am the **f** and the last,
	20: 5	This is the **f** resurrection.

FIRSTBORN

Gen	27:19	I am Esau your **f**.
Ex	4:22	Israel is my **f** son.
	34:20	All the **f** of your sons you shall
Josh	6:26	At the cost of his **f**
1 Kings	16:34	the cost of Abiram his **f**,
Ps	78:51	He struck all the **f** in Egypt,
Ezek	20:26	their offering up all their **f**,
Zech	12:10	as one weeps over a **f**.
Lk	2: 7	she gave birth to her **f** son
Col	1:15	the **f** of all creation;
Heb	1: 6	when he brings the **f** into the

FISH

Gen	1:26	dominion over the **f** of the
Ex	7:18	The **f** in the river shall die
Num	11: 5	We remember the **f** we used to
Tob	8:3	odor of the **f** so repelled the
Jon	1:17	a large **f** to swallow up Jonah;
Mt	7:10	for a **f**, will give a snake?
Lk	5: 6	so many **f** that their nets
Jn	6: 9	five barley loaves and two **f**.

FLESH

Gen	2:23	my bones and **f** of my **f**;
	17:13	in your **f** an everlasting
1 Sam	17:44	your **f** to the birds of the
2 Chr	32: 8	an arm of **f**; but with us
Ps	50:13	Do I eat the **f** of bulls,
Mal	2:15	Both **f** and spirit are his.
Mt	16:17	For **f** and blood has not
	26:41	willing, but the **f** is weak."

Lk	24:39	a ghost does not have **f** and
Jn	1:14	And the Word became **f**
Acts	2:17	my Spirit upon all **f**,
Rom	7: 5	we were living in the **f**,
	8:13	you live according to the **f**,
1 Cor	6:16	The two shall be one **f**.
	15:39	but there is one **f** for human
2 Cor	12: 7	was given me in the **f**,
Gal	3: 3	you now ending with the **f**?
Eph	2: 3	in the passions of our **f**,
	6:12	enemies of blood and **f**,
1 Pet	1:24	All **f** is like grass
1 Jn	2:16	the desire of the **f**,
Jude	1: 8	dreamers also defile the **f**,
Rev	19:18	to eat the **f** of kings, the **f** of

FLOCK

Gen	4: 4	of the firstlings of his **f**,
Ex	2:17	defense and watered their **f**.
Ps	77:20	led your people like a **f**
	80: 1	who lead Joseph like a **f**!
Song	4: 1	Your hair is like a **f** of goats,
Isa	40:11	He will feed his **f** like a
Jer	10:21	and all their **f** is scattered.
Zech	11: 7	the shepherd of the **f**
Mal	1:14	has a male in the **f**
Lk	2: 8	watch over their **f** by night.
Acts	20:28	over all the **f**,
1 Pet	5: 2	to tend the **f** of God

FLOOD

Gen	9:15	a **f** to destroy all flesh.
Ps	29:10	LORD sits enthroned over the **f**;
Sir	40:10	on their account the **f** came
Mt	24:38	in those days before the **f**
2 Pet	2: 5	when he brought a **f** on a

FOLLOW

Ex	16: 4	they will **f** my instruction
Judg	2:17	they did not **f** their example.
1 Kings	11:10	he should not **f** other gods;
1 Macc	1:44	to **f** customs strange to the
Prov	20: 7	happy are the children who **f**
Sir	18:30	self-control. Do not **f** your
Mt	4:19	"**F** me, and I will make
Lk	9:23	their cross daily and **f** me.
Jn	10: 4	and the sheep **f** him because
	21:19	this he said to him, "**F** me."
1 Tim	5:15	already turned away to **f** Satan.
2 Pet	2: 2	many will **f** their licentious

FOOD

Gen	1:30	given every green plant for **f**.
Gen	9: 3	shall be **f** for you;
Num	21: 5	For there is no **f** and no water,
Ps	42: 3	My tears have been my **f** day
	104:27	to give them their **f** in due
Prov	12: 9	be self-important and lack **f**.
	23: 3	for they are deceptive **f**.
Mt	3: 4	and his **f** was locusts and wild
Jn	4:32	I have **f** to eat that you do
	6:27	the **f** that endures for eternal
1 Cor	3: 2	you with milk, not solid **f**,
	8: 1	Now concerning **f** sacrificed to
2 Cor	11:27	often without **f**, cold and
Heb	5:14	But solid **f** is for the mature,

FOOL

Ps	49:10	**f** and dolt perish together
Prov	10:18	whoever utters slander is a **f**.

Prov	20: 3	but every **f** is quick to quarrel.
Hos	9: 7	The prophet is a **f**,
Mt	5:22	You **f**, you will be liable to
2 Cor	11:21	I am speaking as a **f**

FOREVER

Gen	3:22	eat, and live **f**"—
Ex	3:15	This is my name **f**,
2 Sam	7:13	the throne of his kingdom **f**.
1 Kings	2:33	the head of his descendants **f**;
	9: 3	and put my name there **f**;
1 Chr	16:15	Remember his covenant **f**,
2 Chr	5:13	steadfast love endures **f**,
	33: 7	I will put my name **f**;
Tob	3:11	Blessed is your name **f**!
Ps	9: 7	But the LORD sits enthroned **f**,
	44: 8	give thanks to your name **f**.
	77: 8	Has his steadfast love ceased **f**?
	111: 3	righteousness endures **f**.
Prov	10:25	righteous are established **f**.
Eccl	3:14	whatever God does endures **f**;
Wis	5:15	But the righteous live **f**,
Sir	51:12	for his mercy endures **f**;
Isa	26: 4	Trust in the LORD **f**,
	51: 8	but my deliverance will be **f**,
Jer	3: 5	will he be angry **f**,
Bar	3: 3	For you are enthroned **f**,
Ezek	27:36	and shall be no more **f**.
Dan	2:44	and it shall stand **f**;
Jn	6:51	of this bread will live **f**;
Rom	9: 5	over all, God blessed **f**.
Heb	5: 6	You are a priest **f**,
	7:24	because he continues **f**.
1 Pet	1:25	word of the Lord endures **f**.
1 Jn	2:17	the will of God live **f**.
Rev	1:18	I am alive **f** and ever;
	22: 5	and they will reign **f** and ever.

FORGIVE

Gen	18:24	not **f** it for the fifty righteous
	50:17	I beg you, **f** the crime of your
Ex	10:17	Do **f** my sin just this once
Num	14:19	**F** the iniquity of this people
	30:12	and the LORD will **f** her.
1 Sam	25:28	Please **f** the trespass of your
1 Kings	8:30	heed and **f**.
	8:50	and **f** your people who have
2 Chr	6:21	hear and **f**.
	6:27	**f** the sin of your servants
Ps	25:18	and **f** all my sins.
Jer	18:23	Do not **f** their iniquity,
	33: 8	and I will **f** all the guilt
Hos	1: 6	the house of Israel or **f** them.
Mt	6:12	And **f** us our debts,
	18:35	if you do not **f** your brother
Mk	2: 7	Who can **f** sins but God
	11:25	**f**, if you have anything against
Lk	5:21	Who can **f** sins but God
	23:34	Father, **f** them; for they do not
2 Cor	2: 7	you should **f** and console him,
	12:13	**F** me this wrong!
Col	3:13	**f** each other; just as the

FORGIVENESS

Ps	130: 4	But there is **f** with you,
Dan	9: 9	our God belong mercy and **f**,
Mt	26:28	for many for the **f** of sins.
Mk	1: 4	repentance for the **f** of sins.
Lk	1:77	by the **f** of their sins.
Acts	5:31	repentance to Israel and **f** of

Col 1:14 redemption, the **f** of sins.
Heb 9:22 there is no **f** of sins.

FORNICATION

Mk 7:21 **f**, theft, murder,
1 Cor 6:13 body is meant not for **f**
Col 3: 5 whatever in you is earthly: **f**,
Rev 14: 8 of the wrath of her **f**.

FORSAKE (N)

Deut 31: 6 will not fail you or **f** you."
Josh 1: 5 will not fail you or **f** you.
1 Chr 28: 9 but if you **f** him, he will
Jdt 9:11 protector of the **f**,
Ps 27:10 If my father and mother **f** me,
Prov 4: 6 Do not **f** her, and she will
Sir 17:25 to the Lord and **f** your sins;
Isa 1:28 and those who **f** the LORD
shall be consumed
Heb 13: 5 will never leave you or **f** you."

FORTY

Gen 7: 4 earth for **f** days and **f** nights;
Ex 16:35 The Israelites ate manna **f**
Deut 25: 3 **F** lashes may be given
1 Sam 4:18 He had judged Israel **f** years.
Neh 9:21 **F** years you sustained them in
Jon 3: 4 **F** days more, and Nineveh
Mt 4: 2 He fasted **f** days and **f** nights,

FOUNDATION

1 Kings 6:37 In the fourth year the **f** of the
Ezra 3: 6 But the **f** of the temple of the
Ps 97: 2 and justice are the **f**
Isa 28:16 am laying in Zion a **f** stone,
Lk 14:29 when he has laid a **f**
1 Cor 3:10 master builder I laid a **f**,
2 Tim 2:19 But God's firm **f** stands,
Heb 6: 1 and not laying again the **f:**

FOUNTAIN

Ps 36: 9 For with you is the **f** of life;
Prov 5:18 Let your **f** be blessed,
Jer 9: 1 and my eyes a **f** of tears,
Zech 13: 1 On that day a **f** shall be

FREE

Ex 21: 2 he shall go out a **f** person,
Lk 13:12 you are set **f** from your
Jn 8:32 the truth will make you **f**.
Rom 5:15 But the **f** gift is not like the
1 Cor 9:21 I am not **f** from God's law but
Gal 3:28 is no longer slave or **f**,
Heb 13: 5 **f** from the love of money

FRIEND

Ex 33:11 as one speaks to a **f**.
2 Sam 16:17 this your loyalty to your **f**?
2 Chr 20: 7 of your **f** Abraham?
Ps 41: 9 Even my bosom **f** in whom I
Prov 17:17 A **f** loves at all times,
Song 5:16 beloved and this is my **f**,
Mt 11:19 a **f** of tax collectors and
Jn 3:29 The **f** of the bridegroom,
Jas 2:23 he was called the **f** of God.

FRUIT

Gen 1:11 and **f** trees of every kind
Deut 28: 4 and the **f** of your livestock,
Ps 1: 3 yield their **f** in its season,

Prov 8:19 My **f** is better than gold,
Isa 27: 6 fill the whole world with **f**.
Ezek 47:12 will not wither nor their **f** fail,
Hos 9:10 Like the first **f** on the fig tree,
Am 8: 1 a basket of summer **f**.
Mt 3: 8 Bear **f** worthy of repentance.
7:17 every good tree bears good **f**,
Lk 6:44 is known by its own **f**.
Jn 15: 2 to make it bear more **f**.
Acts 14:17 from heaven and **f** seasons,
Eph 5: 9 the **f** of the light is found
Heb 13:15 the **f** of lips that confess his
Rev 22: 2 with its twelve kinds of **f**,

FULFILL

Gen 26: 3 and I will **f** the oath that I
2 Chr 10:15 the LORD might **f** his word,
Ps 20: 5 May the LORD **f** all your
Jer 33:14 when I will **f** the promise I
11:14 in order to **f** the vision,
Mt 1:22 to **f** what had been spoken by
8:17 This was to **f** what had been
Jn 12:38 This was to **f** the word spoken
15:25 It was to **f** the word
Gal 6: 2 you will **f** the law of Christ.
Jas 2: 8 if you really **f** the royal law

FULL (NESS)

Ruth 1:21 I went away **f**,
2 Chr 24:10 the chest until it was **f**.
Job 14: 1 few of days and **f** of trouble,
Ps 33: 5 the earth is **f** of the steadfast
Sir 42:16 work of the Lord is **f** of his
Isa 1:15 your hands are **f** of blood.
Mal 3:10 Bring the **f** tithe into the
Mt 6:22 your whole body will be **f** of
Jn 1:14 **f** of grace and truth.
Acts 6: 3 **f** of the Spirit and of
Eph 1:10 as a plan for the **f** of time,
Jas 3:17 **f** of mercy and good fruits
Rev 4: 6 **f** of eyes in front and

FUTURE

Ex 13:14 When in the **f** your child asks
Ps 22:30 **f** generations will be told
Jer 29:11 to give you a **f** with hope.
1 Cor 3:22 or the present or the **f**

G

GAIN

Gen 24:60 your offspring **g** possession
1 Sam 8: 3 but turned aside after **g**;
Prov 1: 5 the wise also hear and **g** in
28:16 hates unjust **g** will enjoy a
Ezek 28:22 and I will **g** glory in your
Mk 8:36 profit them to **g** the whole
Lk 9:25 if they **g** the whole world,
1 Cor 13: 3 do not have love, I **g** nothing.
Phil 1:21 is Christ and dying is **g**.
1 Tim 3:13 deacons **g** a good standing
Titus 1: 7 or violent or greedy for **g**;
1 Pet 5: 2 not for sordid **g** but eagerly.

GATE (S)

Gen 24:60 of the **g** of their foes."

Neh 1: 3 and its **g** have been destroyed
Ps 24: 7 Lift up your heads, O **g**!
Isa 60:11 Your **g** shall always be open;
Mt 16:18 and the **g** of Hades will not
Rev 21:12 high wall with twelve **g**,
1 Macc 4:38 profaned, and the **g** burned

GATHER

Ex 16: 4 go out and **g** enough for that
Ruth 2: 7 let me glean and **g** among the
Neh 1: 9 I will **g** them from there and
Ps 106:47 O LORD our God, and **g** us
Isa 11:12 and **g** the dispersed of Judah
Jer 3:17 all nations shall **g** to it,
Joel 3: 2 I will **g** all the nations
Mt 12:30 whoever does not **g** with me
23:37 I desired to **g** your children
Lk 3:17 his threshing floor and to **g**
17:37 there the vultures will **g**.
Jn 11:52 but to **g** into one the dispersed
Rev 14:18 sickle and **g** the clusters of the

GAVE

Gen 2:20 The man **g** names to all cattle,
35:12 The land that I **g** to Abraham
Ex 31:18 he **g** him the two tablets of
Deut 2:12 the land that the LORD **g** them
26: 9 this place and **g** us this land,
Josh 11:23 Joshua **g** it for an inheritance
15:13 he **g** to Caleb son of
1 Sam 1: 5 but to Hannah he **g** a double
2 Sam 8: 6 The LORD **g** victory to David
1 Kings 4:29 God **g** Solomon very great
Neh 9:15 you **g** them bread from heaven,
9:34 and the warnings that you **g**
Job 1:21 I return there; the LORD **g**,
Ps 69:21 They **g** me poison for food,
Ezek 3: 2 and he **g** me the scroll to eat
Dan 1: 7 The palace master **g** them
Mt 25:35 I was hungry and you **g** me
25:42 I was hungry and you **g** me no
Mk 6: 7 out two by two, and **g** them
Jn 1:12 in his name, he **g** power
17: 4 finishing the work that you **g**
19:30 he bowed his head and **g** up
Rom 1:24 Therefore God **g** them up in
1:28 God **g** them up to a debased
2 Cor 8: 3 they voluntarily **g** according to
Eph 4: 8 he **g** gifts to his people."
5: 2 loved us and **g** himself up for
2 Thess 2:16 through grace **g** us eternal
Titus 2:14 He it is who **g** himself for us
1 Jn 5:11 God **g** us eternal life, and this
Rev 11:13 and **g** glory to the God of
16:19 great Babylon and **g**

GENERATION (S)

Gen 7: 1 righteous before me in this **g**.
Ex 1: 6 his brothers, and that whole **g**.
Deut 1:35 —not one of this evil **g**
Tob 13:11 **G** after **g** will give joyful praise
1 Macc 2:61 "And so observe, from **g** to **g**
Ps 48:13 you may tell the next **g**
102:18 this be recorded for a **g** to
Sir 44: 1 our ancestors in their **g**.
Dan 4: 3 his sovereignty is from **g** to **g**.
Joel 1: 3 and their children another **g**.
Mt 12:39 An evil and adulterous **g** asks
23:36 this will come upon this **g**.
Mk 9:19 You faithless **g**, how much

Lk	1:50	who fear him from **g** to **g**.
	21:32	this **g** will not pass away until
Phil	2:15	of a crooked and perverse **g**,

GENEROUS
Tob	9:6	and noble, upright and **g**!
Prov	11:25	A **g** person will be enriched,
Sir	35:10	Be **g** when you worship the
Mt	20:15	you envious because I am **g**?
Rom	10:12	Lord of all and is **g** to all
1 Tim	6:18	be rich in good works, **g**,
Jas	1:17	Every **g** act of giving,

GENTILE (S)
Mt	4:15	the Jordan, Galilee of the **G**
Lk	2:32	light for revelation to the **G**
	21:24	until the times of the **G** are
Acts	9:15	to bring my name before **G**
	18: 6	I will go to the **G**.
Rom	2:14	When **G**, who do not possess
	15: 9	will confess you among the **G**,
1 Cor	1:23	to Jews and foolishness to **G**,
Gal	1:16	proclaim him among the **G**,
Eph	3: 6	the **G** have become fellow
1 Tim	2: 7	teacher of the **G** in faith and

GENTLE
Deut	28:54	refined and **g** of men among
Prov	15: 4	A **g** tongue is a tree of
Mt	11:29	for I am **g** and humble in
1 Tim	3: 3	violent but, not quarrelsome,
Jas	3:17	first pure, then peaceable, **g**,
1 Pet	2:18	those who are kind and **g**

GIFT
Num	18: 7	give your priesthood as a **g**;
Prov	18:16	A **g** opens doors; it gives
Eccl	3:13	it is God's **g** that all should eat
Mt	5:23	when you are offering your **g**
Jn	4:10	If you knew the **g** of God,
Acts	2:38	receive the **g** of the Holy
Rom	1:11	you some spiritual **g**
	5:15	of God and the free **g** in the
1 Cor	7: 7	But each has a particular **g**
2 Cor	8:12	the **g** is acceptable
Eph	2: 8	it is the **g** of God
1 Tim	4:14	Do not neglect the **g** that is in
Heb	6: 4	have tasted the heavenly **g**,
1 Pet	3: 7	also heirs of the gracious **g** of
Rev	21: 6	will give water as a **g** from the

GLAD
Ex	4:14	you his heart will be **g**.
Job	22:19	righteous see it and are **g**;
Ps	9: 2	I will be **g** and exult in you;
	48:11	Let Mount Zion be **g**,
	118:24	let us rejoice and be **g** in it.
Prov	10: 1	A wise child makes a **g** father,
	15:20	A wise child makes a **g** father,
Isa	25: 9	let us be **g** and rejoice
	65:18	But be **g** and rejoice forever
Jer	20:15	a son," making him very **g**.
Joel	2:21	be **g** and rejoice, for the LORD
Zech	10: 7	hearts shall be **g** as with wine.
Mt	5:12	Rejoice and be **g**,
Jn	8:56	he saw it and was **g**."
Acts	2:26	therefore my heart was **g**,
Phil	2:17	I am **g** and rejoice with all of

GLORIFY (GLORIFIED)
Lev	10: 3	I will be **g**.' " And Aaron was
Isa	44:23	Jacob, and will be **g** in Israel.
Mk	2:12	were all amazed and **g** God,
Lk	5:26	all of them, and they **g** God
Jn	7:39	because Jesus was not yet **g**.
	13:31	Son of Man has been **g**,
Rom	8:17	that we may also be **g**
Gal	1:24	And they **g** God because
2 Thess	1:10	he comes to be **g** by his saints
1 Pet	4:11	so that God may be **g** in all

GLORY (GLORIOUS)
Ex	14: 4	so that I will gain **g** for myself
	16:10	and the **g** of the LORD
	33:18	Moses said, "Show me your **g**,
Lev	9: 6	so that the **g** of the LORD may
Num	14:10	Then the **g** of the LORD
	16:42	and the **g** of the LORD
Deut	5:24	God has shown us his **g** and
1 Sam	4:21	"The **g** has departed from
1 Kings	8:11	for the **g** of the LORD filled the
1 Chr	16:10	**G** in his holy name;
2 Chr	5:14	for the **g** of the LORD filled
Tob	12:15	and enter before the **g** of the
Jdt	15:9	"You are the **g** of Jerusalem,
1 Macc	1:40	now grew as great as her **g**
Ps	3: 3	a shield around me, my **g**,
	63: 2	beholding your power and **g**,
	108: 5	let your **g** be over all the earth
Prov	19:11	their **g** to overlook an offense.
	25: 2	It is the **g** of God to conceal
Wis	7:25	emanation of the **g** of the
Isa	2:10	and from the **g** of his majesty.
	48:11	My **g** I will not give to
Ezek	1:28	likeness of the **g** of the LORD.
	8: 4	And the **g** of the God of Israel
	11:23	the **g** of the LORD ascended
Dan	2:37	power, the might, and the **g**,
Hab	2:14	of the **g** of the LORD.
Zech	2: 5	and I will be the **g** within it."
Mal	2: 2	heart to give **g** to my name,
Mt	16:27	angels in the **g** of his Father,
	25:31	on the throne of his **g**.
Mk	8:38	he comes in the **g** of his Father
Lk	2: 9	and the **g** of the Lord shone
	9:32	they saw his **g** and the two
Jn	1:14	and we have seen his **g**,
	8:50	do not seek my own **g**;
	17: 5	with the **g** that I had in your
Acts	7:55	saw the **g** of God and Jesus
Rom	1:23	exchanged the **g** of the
	16:27	to whom be the **g** forever!
1 Cor	2: 7	before the ages for our **g**.
	10:31	everything for the **g** of God.
2 Cor	1:20	say the "Amen," to the **g** of
	4:17	for an eternal weight of **g**
Eph	1:12	for the praise of his **g**.
	3:21	to him be **g** in the church
Phil	1:11	for the **g** and praise of God.
	3:19	and their **g** is in their shame;
Col	1:27	are the riches of the **g** of this
1 Thess	2:12	into his own kingdom and **g**.
2 Thess	2:14	the **g** of our Lord Jesus Christ
1 Tim	1:11	that conforms to the **g** gospel
2 Tim	2:10	in Christ Jesus, with eternal **g**.
Heb	1: 3	He is the reflection of God's **g**
	3: 3	Jesus is worthy of more **g** than
1 Pet	1: 7	to result in praise and **g** and
	4:11	To him belong the **g** and the

2 Pet	1: 3	called us by his own **g** and
Rev	1: 6	to him be **g** and dominion
	19: 7	and give him the **g**,

GODLY
Ps	12: 1	no longer anyone who is **g**;
Mal	2:15	**G** offspring. So look to
2 Cor	1:12	with frankness and **g** sincerity,
	7:11	what earnestness this **g** grief
Titus	2:12	self-controlled, upright, and **g**,

GODS
Gen	31:19	stole her father's household **g**.
Ex	12:12	animals; on all the **g** of Egypt
Deut	5: 7	you shall have no other **g**
Josh	24:14	the **g** that your ancestors
1 Sam	17:43	cursed David by his **g**.
1 Kings	20:23	"Their **g** are **g** of the hills
2 Kings	17: 7	They had worshiped other **g**
1 Chr	16:26	For all the **g** of the peoples are
2 Chr	2: 5	God is greater than other **g**.
Jdt	3:8	to destroy all the **g** of the land,
1 Macc	5:68	images of their **g** he burned
Ps	82: 6	You are **g**, children of the
Wis	12:24	accepting as **g** those animals
Jer	2:11	Has a nation changed its **g**,
Zeph	2:11	he will shrivel all the **g** of the
Jn	10:34	your law, 'I said, you are **g**?
1 Cor	8: 5	there may be so-called **g**

OLD
Ex	3:22	jewelry of silver and of **g**,
	20:23	make for yourselves gods of **g**.
Josh	7:21	bar of **g** weighing fifty shekels,
1 Sam	6: 4	Five **g** tumors and five **g** mice
1 Kings	6:21	of the house with pure **g**.
2 Chr	9:13	The weight of **g** that came to
Ezra	1: 6	with silver vessels, with **g**,
Job	22:25	if the Almighty is your **g**
	28:15	It cannot be gotten for **g**,
Ps	19:10	be desired are they than **g**,
Prov	3:14	and her revenue better than **g**.
Isa	60:17	of bronze I will bring **g**,
Dan	2:32	that statue was of fine **g**,
Zech	4: 2	see a lampstand all of **g**,
Mt	2:11	they offered him gifts of **g**,
Rev	3:18	**g** refined by fire so that
	21:18	while the city is pure **g**,

GOOD
Gen	1: 4	saw that the light was **g**;
	3: 5	knowing **g** and evil."
	41:26	The seven **g** cows are seven
Ex	3: 8	of that land to a **g** and broad
Num	10:29	LORD has promised **g** to Israel."
Josh	21:45	the **g** promises that the LORD
2 Sam	14:17	discerning **g** and evil.
1 Kings	8:56	has failed of all his **g** promise,
2 Chr	7: 3	For he is **g**, for his steadfast
Neh	2:18	themselves to the common **g**.
Job	2:10	Shall we receive the **g** at the
Ps	14: 1	is no one who does **g**.
	73: 1	Truly God is **g** to the upright,
	147: 1	How **g** it is to sing praises
Prov	3: 4	will find favor and **g** repute
	19: 2	without knowledge is not **g**,
Isa	5:20	you who call evil **g** and **g** evil,
Jer	6:16	ancient paths, where the **g** way
	24: 2	One basket had very **g** figs,
Am	5:14	Seek **g** and not evil,

Nah	1:15	who brings **g** tidings,
Zech	8:15	days to do **g** to Jerusalem
Mt	5:13	It is no longer **g** for anything,
	25:21	Well done, **g** and trustworthy
Mk	1:15	and believe in the **g** news."
	4:8	Other seed fell into **g** soil
Lk	2:10	I am bringing you **g** news of
	8:8	Some fell into **g** soil,
Jn	1:46	**g** come out of Nazareth?"
	10:11	"I am the **g** shepherd.
Acts	8:12	was proclaiming the **g** news
Rom	7:12	is holy and just and **g**.
	16:19	be wise in what is **g**
2 Cor	9:8	share abundantly in every **g**
Gal	6:10	let us work for the **g** of all,
Eph	2:10	in Christ Jesus for **g** works,
Phil	1:6	the one who began a **g** work
1 Thess	5:21	hold fast to what is **g**;
1 Tim	1:5	a **g** conscience, and sincere
	6:18	They are to do **g**,
2 Tim	2:3	in suffering like a **g** soldier
	4:7	I have fought the **g** fight,
Titus	2:3	are to teach what is **g**,
	2:7	respects a model of **g** works,
Heb	5:14	to distinguish **g** from evil.
	13:16	Do not neglect to do **g**
1 Pet	2:3	tasted that the Lord is **g**.
3 Jn	1:2	that you may be in **g** health,

GOSPEL
Mk	8:35	for the sake of the **g**,
Rom	1:1	set apart for the **g** of God,
	1:16	am not ashamed of the **g**;
1 Cor	1:17	baptize but to proclaim the **g**,
	9:14	get their living by the **g**.
Gal	1:6	are turning to a different **g**
Eph	1:13	the **g** of your salvation,
Phil	1:5	of your sharing in the **g**
Col	1:23	hope promised by the **g** that
2 Thess	1:8	do not obey the **g** of our Lord
Philem	1:13	my imprisonment for the **g**;
1 Pet	4:6	reason the **g** was proclaimed
Rev	14:6	with an eternal **g** to proclaim

GOSSIP
Prov	11:13	A **g** goes about telling secrets,
Sir	19:6	one who hates **g** has less evil
2 Cor	12:20	selfishness, slander, **g**, conceit,

GRACE
Ps	45:2	**g** is poured upon your lips
Zech	4:7	**g** to it!' "
Jn	1:14	full of **g** and truth.
Acts	4:33	great **g** was upon them all.
	15:11	through the **g** of the Lord.
Rom	1:5	whom we have received **g**
	5:21	so **g** might also exercise
1 Cor	1:3	**G** to you and peace from
	3:10	According to the **g** of God
2 Cor	1:2	**G** to you and peace from
	9:14	of the surpassing **g** of God
Gal	1:3	**G** to you and peace from
	1:15	called me through his **g**,
Eph	1:2	**G** to you and peace
	3:2	of the commission of God's **g**
Phil	1:2	**G** to you and peace
Col	1:2	**G** to you and peace
1 Thess	1:1	**G** to you and peace.
2 Thess	1:2	**G** to you and peace
	2:16	through **g** gave us eternal

1 Tim	1:2	**G**, mercy, and peace from God
2 Tim	1:2	**G**, mercy, and peace from God
	2:1	be strong in the **g** that is in
Titus	1:4	**G** and peace from God
	3:15	**G** be with all of you
Philem	1:3	**G** to you and peace from
Heb	2:9	so that by the **g** of God
	13:25	**G** be with all of you
Jas	4:6	he gives all the more **g**;
1 Pet	1:2	May **g** and peace be yours in
	5:12	that this is the true **g** of God.
2 Pet	1:2	May **g** and peace be yours
Jude	1:4	who pervert the **g** of our God
Rev	1:4	**G** to you and peace from

GRACIOUS
Ex	33:19	'The LORD'; and I will be **g** to
2 Sam	12:22	The LORD may be **g** to me,
2 Chr	30:9	the LORD your God is **g** and
Ezra	7:9	for the **g** hand of his God was
Neh	2:8	for the **g** hand of my God was
	9:17	**g** and merciful, slow to anger
Ps	4:1	Be **g** to me, and hear my
	41:4	O LORD, be **g** to me; heal me,
Prov	11:16	A **g** woman gets honor,
Isa	30:18	the LORD waits to be **g** to you;
	33:2	be **g** to us; we wait for
Joel	2:13	he is **g** and merciful, slow to
Jon	4:2	knew that you are a **g** God
Mal	1:9	that he may be **g** to us.
Lk	4:22	were amazed at the **g** words
1 Pet	3:7	are also heirs of the **g** gift of

GRAPES
Gen	40:11	the **g** and pressed them
Ezek	18:2	parents have eaten sour **g**,
Mic	6:15	shall tread **g**, but not drink
Mt	7:16	Are **g** gathered from thorns, or

GREAT (ER) (LY)
Gen	1:16	God made the two **g** lights—
	18:20	How **g** is the outcry against
Ex	32:10	you I will make a **g** nation."
Deut	4:32	has anything so **g** as this ever
	10:17	the **g** God, mighty and
Judg	16:5	what makes his strength so **g**,
2 Sam	7:9	of the **g** ones of the earth.
	22:36	your help has made me **g**.
1 Chr	16:25	For **g** is the LORD, and **g**
Neh	1:5	the **g** and awesome God who
Ps	18:35	your help has made me **g**.
	77:13	What god is so **g** as our God?
Jer	10:6	you are **g**, and your name is **g**
	32:19	**g** in counsel and mighty in
Lam	3:23	**g** is your faithfulness.
Dan	2:31	there was a **g** statue.
	7:3	and four **g** beasts came up
Joel	2:11	day of the LORD is **g**,
Zeph	1:14	The **g** day of the LORD is
Mal	1:11	is **g** among the nations,
	4:5	Elijah before the **g** and terrible
Mt	4:16	have seen a **g** light,
	20:26	whoever wishes to be **g** among
Lk	2:10	bringing you good news of **g**
	6:35	Your reward will be **g**,
Eph	1:19	to the working of his **g** power.
1 Tim	3:16	mystery of our religion is **g**:
Heb	2:3	if we neglect so **g** a salvation?
	12:1	by so **g** a cloud of witnesses,
Jude	1:6	for the judgment of the **g** Day.

Rev	6:17	for the **g** day of their wrath
	20:11	Then I saw a **g** white throne

GREED (Y)
Prov	15:27	Those who are **g** for unjust
Sir	14:9	eye of the **g** person is not
1 Cor	5:11	who is sexually immoral or **g**,
Eph	4:19	to licentiousness, **g**
Titus	1:7	wine or violent or **g** for gain;

GREEK
2 Macc	4:10	over to the **G** way of life.
Jn	19:20	Hebrew, in Latin, and in **G**.
Acts	16:1	but his father was a **G**.
Gal	3:28	is no longer Jew or **G**,

GUARD
Gen	3:24	flaming and turning to **g**
Neh	4:9	and set a **g** as a protection
Ps	17:8	**G** me as the apple of
	91:11	angels concerning you to **g**
Prov	2:11	and understanding will **g** you.
Mt	27:66	So they went with the **g**
Phil	4:7	will **g** your hearts
1 Tim	6:20	**g** what has been entrusted to
2 Tim	1:12	that he is able to **g**
2 Jn	1:8	Be on your **g**,

GUIDE
Ps	31:3	name's sake lead me and **g** me,
	67:4	**g** the nations upon earth.
Isa	58:11	The LORD will **g** you
Lk	1:79	to **g** our feet into the way
Rev	7:17	and he will **g** them to

GUILT
Gen	44:16	out the **g** of your servants;
Lev	4:3	thus bringing **g** on the people,
	5:15	as your **g** offering to the LORD,
Ezra	9:6	and our **g** has mounted up to
Ps	32:5	and you forgave the **g** of my
Prov	14:9	Fools mock at the **g** offering,
Jer	2:22	stain of your **g** is still before
Hos	5:5	Ephraim stumbles in his **g**;
Zech	3:9	I will remove the **g** of this land

H

HADES
Mt	16:18	gates of **H** will not prevail
Rev	1:18	keys of Death and of **H**.
	20:13	Death and **H** gave up the dead

HAND
Gen	3:22	he might reach out his **h**
	16:12	with his **h** against everyone,
Ex	3:19	compelled by a mighty **h**.
	33:22	cover you with my **h** until I
Deut	4:34	by a mighty **h** and an
Josh	8:7	will give it into your **h**.
1 Sam	17:50	no sword in David's **h**.
2 Sam	1:14	your **h** to destroy the LORD's
1 Kings	8:24	this day fulfilled with your **h**.
	13:4	Jeroboam stretched out his **h**
1 Chr	21:17	Let your **h**, I pray,
2 Chr	6:15	day have fulfilled with your **h**.

Neh	2: 8	for the gracious **h** of my God
Ps	10:12	lift up your **h**; do not forget
	32: 4	your **h** was heavy upon me;
	110: 1	"Sit at my right **h**
Prov	3:16	life is in her right **h**;
	21: 1	of water in the **h** of the LORD;
Eccl	2:24	I saw, is from the **h** of God;
	9:10	Whatever your **h** finds to do,
Isa	1:25	I will turn my **h** against you;
	11: 8	put its **h** on the adder's den.
Jer	22:24	signet ring on my right **h**,
Ezek	1: 3	and the **h** of the LORD was on
Dan	3:17	fire and out of your **h**,
Jon	4:11	their right **h** from their left,
Hab	2:16	The cup in the LORD's right **h**
Mt	3:12	winnowing fork is in his **h**,
	22:44	"Sit at my right **h**,
Mk	1:31	and took her by the **h**
	5:41	He took her by the **h**
Lk	5:13	Then Jesus stretched out his **h**,
	22:69	right **h** of the power of God
Jn	10:28	snatch them out of my **h**.
Acts	2:34	"Sit at my right **h**,
Rom	8:34	who is at the right **h** of God,
Eph	1:20	seated him at his right **h**
Heb	1:13	"Sit at my right **h** until I
Jas	4: 8	Cleanse your **h**, you sinners,
1 Pet	3:22	and is at the right **h** of God,
Rev	1:16	In his right **h** he held seven

HAPPY

Gen	30:13	And Leah said, "**H** am I!
1 Kings	4:20	ate and drank and were **h**.
Job	5:17	"How **h** is the one whom God
Ps	1: 1	**H** are those who do not
	32: 1	**H** are those whose
	112: 1	**H** are those who fear the
Prov	3:13	**H** are those who find wisdom
	31:28	rise up and call her **h**;
Eccl	3:12	for them than to be **h**
Sir	14:20	**H** is the person who meditates
Bar	4:4	**H** are we, O Israel, for we
Jon	4: 6	Jonah was very **h** about the

HARM

Gen	31: 7	did not permit him to **h** me.
	48:16	has redeemed me from all **h**,
1 Sam	26:21	for I will never **h** you again,
Neh	6: 2	they intended to do me **h**.
Prov	3:29	Do not plan **h** against your
	13:20	companion of fools suffers **h**.
Am	9: 4	for **h** and not for good.
Lk	6: 9	to do **h** on the sabbath,
Rev	9:19	and with them they inflict **h**.

HATE

Ex	18:21	and **h** dishonest gain;
2 Chr	18: 7	I **h** him, for he never
Ps	5: 5	you **h** all evildoers.
	97:10	LORD loves those who **h** evil;
	139:21	Do I not **h** those who **h** you,
Prov	1:22	and fools **h** knowledge;
	9: 8	is rebuked will only **h** you;
Isa	61: 8	I **h** robbery and wrongdoing;
Jer	44: 4	abominable thing that I **h**!"
Ezek	35: 6	you did not **h** bloodshed,
Mal	2:16	For I **h** divorce, says the LORD,
Mt	5:43	neighbor and **h** your enemy.'
Lk	6:22	are you when people **h** you,
	14:26	and does not **h** father and

Jn	7: 7	The world cannot **h** you,
Rom	7:15	do the very thing I **h**.

HEAD

Gen	3:15	he will strike your **h**,
Num	6: 5	razor shall come upon the **h**;
1 Sam	1:11	no razor shall touch his **h**."
Ps	23: 5	you anoint my **h** with oil;
Prov	1: 9	a fair garland for your **h**,
Isa	59:17	helmet of salvation on his **h**;
Ezek	8: 3	by a lock of my **h**;
Dan	2:32	The **h** of that statue was of
Mt	8:20	has nowhere to lay his **h**."
1 Cor	11: 3	Christ is the **h** of every man,
	11: 5	**h** unveiled disgraces her **h**—
Eph	1:22	and has made him the **h** over
Rev	1:14	His **h** and his hair were white

HEAL (ED) (ING)

Num	12:13	"O God, please **h** her."
Deut	32:39	I wound and I **h**; and no
2 Kings	20: 8	that the LORD will **h** me,
Ps	6: 2	O LORD, **h** me, for my
	30: 2	and you have **h** me.
Wis	16:10	came to their help and **h** them
Sir	38:9	pray to the Lord, and he will **h**
Isa	19:22	striking and **h**; they will return
Jer	3:22	I will **h** your faithlessness.
	30:17	and your wounds I will **h**,
Lam	2:13	is your ruin; who can **h** you?
Ezek	30:21	not been bound up for **h**
	34: 4	the weak, you have not **h**
Hos	5:13	or **h** your wound.
	7: 1	when I would **h** Israel,
Lk	5:17	Lord was with him to **h**.
Jn	4:47	to come down and **h** his son,
Acts	4:30	stretch out your hand to **h**,

HEAR

Num	14:13	"Then the Egyptians will **h**
Deut	1:17	**h** out the small and the
	20: 3	say to them: "**H**, O Israel!
1 Kings	8:30	O **h** in heaven your dwelling
2 Kings	19:16	O LORD, and **h**; open your
2 Chr	7:14	then I will **h** from heaven,
Job	5:27	**H**, and know it for yourself
	26:14	a whisper do we **h** of him!
Ps	30:10	**H**, O LORD, and be gracious
	94: 9	the ear, does he not **h**?
Eccl	7:21	may **h** your servant cursing
Sir	5:11	Be quick to **h**, but deliberate in
Isa	1:10	**H** the word of the LORD
	21: 3	I cannot **h**, I am dismayed
	65:24	are yet speaking I will **h**.
Bar	1: 3	who came to **h** the book,
Ezek	33: 7	you **h** a word from my mouth
Mt	11: 5	the deaf **h**, the dead are raised,
Jn	5:25	when the dead will **h** the voice
Acts	13: 7	wanted to **h** the word of God.
Heb	3: 7	"Today, if you **h** his voice,
Rev	1: 3	blessed are those who **h**

HEART

Gen	6: 6	it grieved him to his **h**.
Ex	4:21	but I will harden his **h**,
	10:27	LORD hardened Pharaoh's **h**,
Deut	4:29	him with all your **h** and soul.
	10:12	your God with all your **h** and
	30: 6	your God with all your **h** and
1 Sam	10: 9	God gave him another **h**;

1 Sam	12:24	him faithfully with all your **h**;
1 Kings	2: 4	with all their **h** and
	11: 4	and his **h** was not true to the
2 Kings	22:19	because your **h** was penitent,
2 Chr	6:38	they repent with all their **h**
	17: 6	His **h** was courageous in the
Tob	1:12	mindful of God with all my **h**,
1 Macc	2:24	and his **h** was stirred.
Job	19:27	My **h** faints within me!
	31: 7	and my **h** has followed my
Ps	7:10	who saves the upright in **h**.
	37: 4	you the desires of your **h**.
	86:11	give me an undivided **h** to
	119:111	are the joy of my **h**.
Prov	2: 2	and inclining your **h** to
	13:12	Hope deferred makes the **h**
	23:17	Do not let your **h** envy
Eccl	2:10	I kept my **h** from no pleasure,
	7: 7	and a bribe corrupts the **h**.
Song	4: 9	You have ravished my **h**,
Sir	2:2	Set your **h** right and be
Isa	57:15	revive the **h** of the contrite.
Jer	3:10	to me with her whole **h**,
	17: 9	**h** is devious above all else¬
	29:13	seek me with all your **h**,
Bar	2:31	I will give them a **h** that obeys
Ezek	36:26	the **h** of stone and give you
Joel	2:12	with all your **h**, with fasting,
Mal	2: 2	do not lay it to **h**.
Mt	5: 8	"Blessed are the pure in **h**,
	15:19	For out of the **h** come evil
Lk	2:19	and pondered them in her **h**.
	24:25	and how slow of **h** to believe
Acts	1:24	"Lord, you know everyone's **h**.
	28:27	with their **h** and turn—
Rom	2:29	is a matter of the **h**—
2 Cor	2: 4	distress and anguish of **h**
Eph	1:18	eyes of your **h** enlightened,
Phil	1: 7	you hold me in your **h**,
1 Tim	1: 5	that comes from a pure **h**,
2 Tim	2:22	the Lord from a pure **h**.
Heb	3:12	unbelieving **h** that turns away
	10:22	with a true **h** in full assurance
Rev	18: 7	Since in her **h** she says,

HEAVEN

Gen	14:19	maker of **h** and earth;
	22:11	LORD called to him from **h**,
Ex	16: 4	to rain bread from **h** for you,
Deut	3:24	what god in **h** or on earth can
	26:15	from **h**, and bless your people
1 Kings	8:23	no God like you in **h** above
	8:30	O hear in **h** your dwelling
2 Kings	1:10	let fire come down from **h**
2 Chr	6:14	in **h** or on earth, keeping
Job	16:19	my witness is in **h**,
Ps	73:25	Whom have I in **h** but you?
Isa	66: 1	**H** is my throne and the
Dan	2:19	Daniel blessed the God of **h**.
Mt	3: 2	for the kingdom of **h**
	7:21	will of my Father in **h**.
Mk	8:11	him for a sign from **h**,
	13:31	**H** and earth will pass away
Lk	3:21	the **h** was opened,
	12:33	an unfailing treasure in **h**,
	19:38	and glory in the highest **h**!"
Jn	3:13	No one has ascended into **h**
	12:28	Then a voice came from **h**,
Acts	2: 2	And suddenly from **h**
	11:10	was pulled up again to **h**.

Phil	2:10	in **h** and on earth and under
	3:14	for the prize of the **h** call
Col	1: 5	laid up for you in **h**.
1 Thess	1:10	wait for his Son from **h**,
Heb	1:10	the **h** are the work of your
	12:26	the earth but also the **h**."
1 Pet	1: 4	unfading, kept in **h** for you,
Rev	4: 1	there in **h** a door stood open!
	12: 3	portent appeared in **h**:

HELL

Mt	5:22	will be liable to the **h** of fire.
	23:33	escape being sentenced to **h**?
Mk	9:43	hands and to go to **h**,
2 Pet	2: 4	into **h** and committed them to

HELP

Gen	4: 1	with the **h** of the LORD."
Ex	2:23	cry for **h** rose up to God.
1 Chr	12:22	David to **h** him, until there
2 Chr	16:12	but sought **h** from physicians.
Neh	6:16	with the **h** of our God.
Ps	18: 6	my God I cried for **h**.
	115:11	He is their **h** and their shield.
Lam	1: 7	there was no one to **h** her,
Acts	16: 9	over to Macedonia and **h** us."
1 Thess	5:14	**h** the weak, be patient with
Heb	2:18	he is able to **h** those who are

HID

Gen	4:14	I shall be **h** from your face;
Josh	2: 6	and **h** them with the stalks of
1 Sam	10:22	"See, he has **h** himself among
2 Kings	11: 3	in the house of the
Job	28:11	**h** things they bring to light
Ps	19:12	Clear me from **h** faults.
	142: 3	they have **h** a trap for me.
Prov	2: 4	search for it as for **h** treasures—
Isa	40:27	"My way is **h** from the LORD,
Dan	2:22	He reveals deep and **h** things;
Mt	13:35	**h** from the foundation of the
Lk	10:21	because you have **h** these
1 Cor	2: 7	secret and **h**, which God
Eph	3: 9	the mystery **h** for ages in God
Col	1:26	the mystery that has been **h**
Heb	4:13	before him no creature is **h**,
Rev	2:17	give some of the **h** manna,

HIGH

Gen	14:18	was priest of God Most **H**.
1 Kings	3: 2	sacrificing at the **h** places,
Ps	7: 7	it take your seat on **h**.
	91: 1	the shelter of the Most **H**,
	113: 5	God, who is seated on **h**,
Prov	24: 7	Wisdom is too **h** for fools;
Eccl	10: 6	folly is set in many **h** places,
Jer	2:20	On every **h** hill
Dan	4:17	that the Most **H** is sovereign
Mt	4: 8	took him to a very **h** mountain
Mk	5: 7	Son of the Most **H** God?
Jn	18:22	how you answer the **h** priest?"
Acts	23: 4	dare to insult God's **h** priest?"
Eph	4: 8	"When he ascended on **h** he

HOLY

Ex	3: 5	you are standing is **h** ground."
	40: 9	so that it shall become **h**.
Lev	11:44	and be **h**, for I am **h**.
Num	4:15	they must not touch the **h**
Deut	5:12	sabbath day and keep it **h**,

Deut	26:19	you to be a people **h**
Josh	5:15	place where you stand is **h**."
1 Sam	2: 2	"There is no **H** One like the
2 Kings	4: 9	our way is a **h** man of God.
1 Chr	6:49	the work of the most **h** place,
2 Chr	3: 8	He made the most **h** place;
Ezra	9: 2	Thus the **h** seed has mixed
Tob	11:14	and blessed be all his **h** angels
1 Macc	1:15	abandoned the **h** covenant
Job	6:10	denied the words of the **H**
Ps	2: 6	my king on Zion, my **h** hill."
	77:13	Your way, O God, is **h**.
	89:18	king to the **H** One of Israel.
Prov	9:10	knowledge of the **H** One is
Isa	1: 4	who have despised the **H** One
	58:13	the **h** day of the LORD
Jer	2: 3	Israel was **h** to the Lord,
Ezek	22:26	have profaned my **h** things;
Dan	4:13	and there was a **h** watcher,
	9:24	your people and your **h** city:
Jon	2: 4	again upon your **h** temple?'
Zech	8: 3	be called the **h** mountain.
	14:20	the LORD shall be as **h**
Mt	1:18	with child from the **H** Spirit.
	28:19	the Son and of the **H** Spirit,
Mk	1:24	are, the **H** One of God."
Lk	1:15	will be filled with the **H** Spirit.
	3:22	the **H** Spirit descended upon
	11:13	Father give the **H** Spirit to
Jn	6:69	you are the **H** One of God."
	20:22	"Receive the **H** Spirit.
Acts	1: 5	be baptized with the **H** Spirit
	13:35	let your **H** One experience
	19: 2	heard that there is a **H** Spirit."
Rom	1: 2	prophets in the **h** scriptures,
	12: 1	sacrifice, **h** and acceptable
1 Cor	7:14	husband is made **h**
Eph	1: 4	to be **h** and blameless before
	4:30	not grieve the **H** Spirit of God,
Col	1:22	present you **h** and blameless
1 Tim	2: 8	lifting up **h** hands without
2 Tim	1: 9	called us with a **h** calling,
Titus	3: 5	renewal by the **H** Spirit.
Heb	2: 4	and by gifts of the **H** Spirit,
Heb	9: 2	this is called the **H** Place.
1 Pet	1:15	he who called you is **h**,
	3: 5	the **h** women who hoped in
1 Jn	2:20	been anointed by the **H** One,
Rev	3: 7	are the words of the **h** one,
	21: 2	the **h** city, the new Jerusalem,

HOME (LESS)

Isa	58: 7	the **h** poor into your house;

HONEY

Ex	3: 8	flowing with milk and **h**,
Judg	14: 8	body of the lion, and **h**.
Ps	19:10	sweeter also than **h**,
Prov	5: 3	of a loose woman drip **h**,
Isa	7:15	He shall eat curds and **h**
Mt	3: 4	food was locusts and wild **h**.

HONOR

Ex	20:12	**H** your father and your
1 Sam	2: 8	and inherit a seat of **h**.
2 Chr	1:11	for possessions, wealth, **h**,
Ps	8: 5	them with glory and **h**,
Prov	3: 9	**H** the LORD with your
	15:33	and humility goes before **h**.
	29:23	lowly in spirit will obtain **h**.

Isa	29:13	and **h** me with their lips,
Mt	13:57	"Prophets are not without **h**
	19:19	**H** your father and mother;
Lk	14: 8	at the place of **h**, in case
Jn	4:44	a prophet has no **h** in the
Rom	12:10	one another in showing **h**.
Eph	6: 2	**H** your father and mother"—
Heb	2: 7	them with glory and **h**,
2 Pet	1:17	For he received **h** and glory
Rev	4: 9	give glory and **h** and thanks

HOPE

Ruth	1:12	I thought there was **h** for me,
Ezra	10: 2	even now there is **h** for Israel
Jdt	9:11	savior of those without **h**.
Esth	9: 1	enemies of the Jews **h**
Job	13:15	I have no **h**; but I will
Ps	9:18	nor the **h** of the poor
	39: 7	My **h** is in you.
	130: 7	**h** in the LORD!
Prov	11: 7	their **h** perishes,
	24:14	your **h** will not be cut off
Sir	34:15	their **h** is in him who saves
Isa	8:17	and I will **h** in him.
Jer	14: 8	O **h** of Israel,
Ezek	37:11	and our **h** is lost;
Mt	12:21	his name the Gentiles will **h**."
Jn	5:45	whom you have set your **h**.
Acts	2:26	my flesh will live in **h**.
Rom	4:18	Hoping against **h**, he believed
	15:13	that you may abound in **h**
1 Cor	13:13	**h**, and love abide,
2 Cor	1:10	our **h** that he will rescue us
Eph	1:12	to set our **h** on Christ,
Col	1: 5	because of the **h** laid up
1 Thess	1: 3	steadfastness of **h** in our Lord
1 Tim	1: 1	and of Christ Jesus our **h**,
Titus	1: 2	in the **h** of eternal life
Heb	3: 6	the pride that belong to **h**.
1 Pet	1: 3	a living **h** through the
1 Jn	3: 3	And all who have this **h** in

HORN (S)

Gen	22:13	in a thicket by its **h**.
Josh	6: 4	seven trumpets of rams' **h**
Dan	7: 7	and it had ten **h**.
Zech	1:18	looked up and saw four **h**.
Rev	5: 6	having seven **h** and seven eyes,

HOSPITABLE

1 Tim	3: 2	respectable, **h**, an apt teacher,
Titus	1: 8	but he must be **h**, a lover
1 Pet	4: 9	Be **h** to one another

HOUR

Mt	6:27	add a single **h** to your span
Mk	14:35	the **h** might pass from him.
Jn	2: 4	My **h** has not yet come."
	12:23	"The **h** has come for the Son
1 Jn	2:18	Children, it is the last **h**!
Rev	3:10	will keep you from the **h**

HOUSE

Gen	19: 2	turn aside to your servant's **h**
Ex	12:22	door of your **h** until morning.
Num	12: 7	is entrusted with all my **h**.
Josh	2: 1	entered the **h** of a prostitute
1 Sam	1: 7	went up to the **h** of the LORD.
2 Sam	2:10	But the **h** of Judah followed
	7:11	LORD will make you a **h**.

1 Kings 8:43 has been invoked on this **h**
1 Chr 22: 1 Here shall be the **h** of the LORD
Ezra 1: 5 rebuild the **h** of the LORD
Jdt 9:13 and against your sacred **h**,
1 Macc 7:37 "You chose this **h** to be called
Ps 23: 6 dwell in the **h** of the LORD
    69: 9 zeal for your **h** that has
Prov 7:27 Her **h** is the way to Sheol
    14:11 The **h** of the wicked is
Eccl 10:18 through indolence the **h** leaks.
Jer 18: 2 go down to the potter's **h**,
    32:34 the **h** that bears my name,
Joel 3:18 forth from the **h** of the LORD
Hag 1: 4 while this **h** lies in ruins?
Mt 7:24 built his **h** on rock.
    13:57 country and in their own **h**."
Mk 3:25 that **h** will not be able
Lk 6:48 like a man building a **h**,
    19: 9 salvation has come to this **h**,
Jn 2:16 my Father's **h** a marketplace!"
Rom 16: 5 church in their **h**.
Heb 3: 2 was faithful in all God's **h**.
2 Jn 1:10 receive into the **h** or welcome

HUMAN (KIND)

Gen 1:26 "Let us make **h** in our image,
    6: 7 from the earth the **h** beings
Num 19:16 or a **h** bone, or a grave,
1 Kings 13: 2 and **h** bones shall be burned
Ps 8: 4 what are **h** beings that
    33:13 from heaven; he sees all **h**.
Dan 2:34 , not by **h** hands, and it struck
    8:25 broken, and not by **h** hands.
Hos 11: 4 with cords of **h** kindness,
Mt 9: 8 such authority to **h** beings.
Lk 20: 6 'Of **h** origin,' all the people
Jn 5:34 I accept such **h** testimony,
Acts 5:29 obey God rather than any **h**
1 Cor 1:26 wise by **h** standards,
Phil 2: 7 being born in **h** likeness.
1 Thess 2: 3 not **h** authority but God,
Heb 12: 9 we had **h** parents to discipline
Rev 4: 7 with a face like a **h** face,

HUMBLE

Ex 10: 3 refuse to **h** yourself before me?
Deut 8: 2 in order to **h** you, testing you
2 Sam 22:28 You deliver a **h** people,
2 Chr 7:14 by my name **h** themselves,
Job 22:29 pride; for he saves the **h**.
Ps 18:27 For you deliver a **h** people,
    55:19 hear, and will **h** them—
Prov 3:34 but to the **h** he shows favor.
Isa 57:15 those who are contrite and **h**
Zeph 3: 2 all you **h** of the land,
Mt 11:29 for I am gentle and **h** in heart,
2 Cor 12:21 my God may **h** me before you,
Jas 4: 6 but gives grace to the **h**."
1 Pet 3: 8 a tender heart, and a **h** mind.

HUNGER (HUNGRY)

Ex 16: 3 this whole assembly with **h**."
Deut 8: 3 humbled you by letting you **h**,
Neh 9:15 their **h** you gave them bread
Ps 50:12 "If I were **h**, I would not tell
Prov 10: 3 the righteous go **h**, but he
Isa 29:8 as when a **h** person dreams
Mt 12: 1 his disciples were **h**, and they
    25:42 for I was **h** and you gave me
Mk 11:12 came from Bethany, he was **h**.

Rom 12:20 "if your enemies are **h**,
1 Cor 4:11 present hour we are **h** and

HUSBAND (S)

Gen 3: 6 also gave some to her **h**,
Num 30: 6 time that her **h** hears of it,
Deut 24: 4 her first **h**, who sent her away,
Prov 7:19 For my **h** is not at home;
    31:28 call her happy; her **h** too,
Isa 54: 5 your Maker is your **h**, the
Jer 3:20 faithless wife leaves her **h**,
Mt 1:19 Her **h** Joseph, being a
Jn 4:17 "I have no **h**." Jesus said to
Rom 7: 2 by the law to her **h** as long
1 Cor 7: 2 and each woman her own **h**.
    7:39 bound as long as her **h** lives.
2 Cor 11: 2 you in marriage to one **h**,
Eph 5:22 subject to your **h** as you are
    5:23 For the **h** is the head of the
Rev 21: 2 a bride adorned for her **h**.

HYPOCRISY

Mt 23:28 are full of **h** and lawlessness.
Lk 12: 1 Pharisees, that is, their **h**.
Jas 3:17 a trace of partiality or **h**.

HYPOCRITE (S)

Ps 26: 4 nor do I consort with **h**;
Mt 6: 2 as the **h** do in the synagogues
    15: 7 You **h**! Isaiah prophesied
    23:27 and Pharisees, **h**! For you are
Mk 7: 6 rightly about you **h**,
Lk 12:56 You **h**! You know how to

I

IDOL (S)

Ex 34:17 You shall not make cast **i**.
Deut 7: 5 and burn their **i** with fire.
2 Kings 17:15 They went after false **i** and
Ps 31: 6 who pay regard to worthless **i**,
Isa 2: 8 Their land is full of **i**,
Ezek 14: 3 taken their **i** into their hearts,
Acts 15:20 from things polluted by **i** and
1 Cor 8: 1 food sacrificed to **i**:
1 Jn 5:21 keep yourselves from **i**.
Rev 9:20 and **i** of gold and silver and

IMAGE

Gen 1:26 us make humankind in our **i**,
Ex 32: 4 and cast an **i** of a calf;
Ps 106:19 Horeb and worshiped a cast **i**.
Wis 2:23 us in the **i** of his own eternity,
Sir 17: 3 and made them in his own **i**.
Rom 8:29 conformed to the **i** of his Son,
1 Cor 11: 7 the **i** and reflection of God;
Col 1:15 the **i** of the invisible God,
Rev 13:14 them to make an **i** for the

IMMANUEL (EMMANUEL)

Isa 7:14 son, and shall name him **I**.

IMMORALITY

Sir 41:17 Be ashamed of sexual **i**,
1 Cor 5: 1 there is sexual **i** among you,
Jude 1: 7 indulged in sexual **i** and

IMPOSSIBLE

Gen 11: 6 to do will now be **i** for them.
Zech 8: 6 Even though it seems **i** to
Mt 17:20 and nothing will be **i** for you."
Heb 6: 4 For it is **i** to restore again

IMPURE (IMPURITY)

Zech 13: 1 cleanse them from sin and **i**.
Rom 1:24 lusts of their hearts to **i**,
Eph 4:19 to practice every kind of **i**.
Col 3: 5 fornication, **i**, passion, evil

INHERIT (ANCE)

Lev 20:24 You shall **i** their land, and I
Deut 10: 9 no allotment or **i** with his
2 Kings 2: 9 Please let me **i** a double share
Ps 37:11 But the meek shall **i** the land,
Prov 13:22 good leave an **i** to their
Eccl 7:11 is as good as an **i**,
Mt 5: 5 for they will **i** the earth.
Lk 10:25 "what must I do to **i** eternal
1 Cor 6: 9 not **i** the kingdom of God?
Heb 1:14 who are to **i** salvation?
Rev 21: 7 who conquer will **i** these

INNOCENT

Ex 23: 7 and do not kill the **i** and
Deut 19:10 blood of an **i** person may not
1 Macc 1:37 they shed **i** blood;
Job 34: 5 'I am **i**, and God has taken
Ps 19:13 and **i** of great transgression.
Prov 6:17 and hands that shed **i** blood,
Mt 10:16 be wise as serpents and **i** as
Lk 23:47 "Certainly this man was **i**."
Phil 2:15 blameless and **i**, children of

ISRAEL

Gen 49:24 the Shepherd, the Rock of **I**,
Ex 28:11 names of the sons of **I**;
Num 19:13 shall be cut off from **I**.
Deut 10:12 O **I**, what does the LORD your
Judg 17: 6 there was no king in **I**; all
Ruth 4:14 his name be renowned in **I**!
1 Sam 3:20 And all **I** from Dan to
    18:16 all **I** and Judah loved David;
2 Sam 5: 2 who shall be ruler over **I**."
    14:25 in all **I** there was no one
1 Kings 1:35 to be ruler over **I** and
    19:18 leave seven thousand in **I**,
2 Kings 5: 8 king of **I** had torn his clothes,
1 Chr 17:22 made your people **I** to be your
Ps 22: 3 enthroned on the praises of **I**.
    125: 5 evildoers. Peace be upon **I**!
Isa 1: 3 master's crib; but **I** does not
    44:21 you are my servant; O **I**,
Jer 2: 3 **I** was holy to the LORD
    31:31 covenant with the house of **I**
Ezek 34: 2 shepherds of **I** who have
    37:28 that I the LORD sanctify **I**,
Dan 9:20 the sin of my people **I**,
Hos 11: 1 When **I** was a child,
Mic 5: 2 who is to rule in **I**,
Mal 1: 5 beyond the borders of **I**!"
Mt 2: 6 shepherd my people **I**.' "
Mk 12:29 'Hear, O **I**: the Lord our God,
Lk 22:30 judging the twelve tribes of **I**.
Acts 9:15 and before the people of **I**;
Rom 11: 7 **I** failed to obtain what it
Eph 2:12 commonwealth of **I**, and
Rev 7: 4 tribe of the people of **I**:

J

JEALOUS (JEALOUSY)
Gen	37:11	his brothers were **j** of him,
Ex	20: 5	LORD your God am a **j** God,
Num	5:14	a spirit of **j** comes on him,
	5:30	and he is **j** of his wife;
Deut	4:24	is a devouring fire, a **j** God.
1 Kings	14:22	provoked him to **j** with their
Prov	6:34	For **j** arouses a husband's fury,
	27: 4	is able to stand before **j**?
Ezek	36: 6	I am speaking in my **j** wrath,
	39:25	I will be **j** for my holy name.
Joel	2:18	the LORD became **j** for his land,
Mt	27:18	out of **j** that they had handed
1 Cor	3: 3	there is **j** and quarreling
	10:22	provoking the Lord to **j**?
2 Cor	11: 2	I feel a divine **j** for you,
Gal	5:20	enmities, strife, **j**, anger,

JERUSALEM
Josh	10: 1	**J** heard how Joshua had taken
Judg	1: 8	fought against **J** and took it.
1 Sam	17:54	Philistine and brought it to **J**;
2 Sam	11: 1	But David remained at **J**.
	15:29	the ark of God back to **J**,
1 Kings	9:19	desired to build, in **J**,
	11:13	sake of **J**, which I have chosen.
2 Kings	19:31	from **J** a remnant shall go out
	25:10	down the walls around **J**.
1 Chr	6:15	LORD sent Judah and **J** into
	21:15	sent an angel to **J** to destroy it;
2 Chr	6: 6	I have chosen **J** in order that
	20:27	returned to **J** with joy,
Ezra	1: 2	build him a house at **J**
	10: 7	that they should assemble at **J**,
Neh	2:17	rebuild the wall of **J**, so that
	12:27	dedication of the wall of **J**
Tob	13:8	and acknowledge him in **J**.
Jdt	15:9	"You are the glory of **J**.
Esth	2: 6	had been carried away from **J**
1 Macc	6:7	had erected on the altar in **J**;
Ps	79: 1	they have laid **J** in ruins.
	147:12	Praise the LORD, O **J**!
Eccl	1:16	surpassing all who were over **J**
Isa	52: 2	rise up, O captive **J**;
	62: 7	no rest until he establishes **J**
Jer	3:17	**J** shall be called the throne
	4:14	O **J**, wash your heart clean of
	13:27	Woe to you, O **J**! How long
Lam	1: 8	**J** sinned grievously, so she has
Ezek	14:21	send upon **J** my four deadly
Dan	5: 3	the house of God in **J**,
	9:12	what has been done against **J**
Joel	3:17	And **J** shall be holy, and
Am	2: 5	devour the strongholds of **J**.
Ob	1:11	gates and cast lots for **J**,
Mic	4: 2	word of the LORD from **J**.
Zeph	3:16	said to **J**: Do not fear, O Zion
Zech	1:14	I am very jealous for **J** and for
	14: 2	the nations against **J** to battle,
Mal	3: 4	offering of Judah and **J** will be
Mt	21:10	When he entered **J**, the whole
Lk	4: 9	the devil took him to **J**,
	23:28	"Daughters of **J**, do not weep
Jn	5: 1	and Jesus went up to **J**.
	10:22	the Dedication took place in **J**.

Acts	1: 8	witnesses in **J**, in all Judea
	6: 7	increased greatly in **J**, and
Rom	15:19	so that from **J** and as far
1 Cor	16: 3	to take your gift to **J**.
Heb	12:22	the living God, the heavenly **J**,
Rev	3:12	the new **J** that comes down

JEW(S)
Ezra	5: 5	upon the elders of the **J**, and
Neh	4: 1	enraged, and he mocked the **J**.
Esth	3:13	to annihilate all **J**, young and
	4:14	deliverance will rise for the **J**
Dan	3: 8	forward and denounced the **J**.
Zech	8:23	take hold of a **J**, grasping
Mt	2: 2	been born king of the **J**?
	27:37	Jesus, the King of the **J**."
Jn	4:22	for salvation is from the **J**.
Acts	13:43	many **J** and devout converts
	20:21	both **J** and Greeks about
Rom	3:29	is God the God of **J** only?
1 Cor	9:20	To the **J** I became as a **J**
Gal	1:13	of my earlier life in **J**.
	3:28	There is no longer **J** or Greek,

JOY (FUL)
Judg	19: 3	and came with **j** to meet him.
1 Sam	18: 6	tambourines, with songs of **j**,
1 Kings	1:40	great **j**, so that the earth
1 Chr	16:27	strength and **j** are in his place.
2 Chr	30:26	There was great **j** in Jerusalem,
Ezra	6:22	the LORD had made them **j**,
Neh	8:10	not be grieved, for the **j** of the
Tob	13:17	Jerusalem will sing hymns of **j**,
Esth	8:17	there was gladness and **j**
1 Macc	4:58	very great **j** among the people,
Job	8:21	your lips with shouts of **j**.
	33:26	into his presence with **j**,
Ps	51:12	Restore to me the **j** of your
	71:23	My lips will shout for **j** when I
	98: 4	Make a **j** noise to the LORD,
	119:111	they are the **j** of my heart.
Prov	12:20	who counsel peace have **j**.
	15:23	an apt answer is a **j** to anyone,
Eccl	5:20	occupied with the **j** of their
Sir	26:2	loyal wife brings **j** to her
Isa	29:19	The meek shall obtain fresh **j**
	55:12	you shall go out in **j**, and be
	61: 7	everlasting **j** shall be theirs.
Jer	31:13	turn their mourning into **j**,
	33: 9	a name of **j**, a praise and a
Lam	5:15	The **j** of our hearts has ceased
Bar	5:9	For God will lead Israel with **j**,
Ezek	24:25	their **j** and glory, the delight of
Joel	1:12	surely, **j** withers away among
Mt	13:44	in his **j** he goes and sells all
	28: 8	with fear and great **j**, and ran
Mk	4:16	immediately receive it with **j**.
Lk	1:44	in my womb leaped for **j**.
	2:10	good news of great **j** for all
	24:41	in their **j** they were
Jn	3:29	my **j** has been fulfilled.
	15:11	that your **j** may be complete.
	16:20	your pain will turn into **j**.
Acts	8: 8	So there was great **j** in that
	13:52	the disciples were filled with **j**
Rom	14:17	righteousness and peace and **j**
	15:13	fill you with all **j** and peace
2 Cor	2: 3	my **j** would be the **j** of all of
Gal	5:22	love, **j**, peace, patience,
Phil	1: 4	constantly praying with **j** in

Phil	4: 1	my **j** and crown,
1 Thess	1: 6	you received the word with **j**
	2:19	what is our hope or **j** or crown
2 Tim	1: 4	I may be filled with **j**.
Philem	1: 7	I have indeed received much **j**
Heb	13:17	Let them do this with **j** and
Jas	1: 2	consider it nothing but **j**,
1 Pet	1: 8	indescribable and glorious **j**,
1 Jn	1: 4	our **j** may be complete.
2 Jn	1:12	so that our **j** may be complete.
3 Jn	1: 4	I have no greater **j** than this,

JUDEA
Mt	2: 1	was born in Bethlehem of **J**,
Lk	7:17	him spread throughout **J**
Jn	7: 3	"Leave here and go to **J**
Acts	9:31	the church throughout **J**,
Rom	15:31	from the unbelievers in **J**,
Gal	1:22	churches of **J** that are in

JUDGE (D) (S)
Gen	16: 5	May the LORD **j** between you
	18:25	Shall not the **J** of all the earth
Ex	18:26	they **j** the people at all times
Lev	19:15	with justice you shall **j** your
Num	35:24	then the congregation shall **j**
Deut	1:16	**j** rightly between one person
Judg	2:16	Then the LORD raised up **j**
	11:27	Let the LORD, who is **j**, decide
Ruth	1: 1	In the days when the **j** ruled,
1 Sam	2:10	LORD will **j** the ends of the
1 Chr	16:33	for he comes to **j** the earth.
Job	21:22	he **j** those that are on high
	31:28	to be punished by the **j**,
Ps	7:11	God is a righteous **j**,
	75: 2	I will **j** with equity.
Prov	31: 9	Speak out, **j** righteously,
Eccl	3:17	God will **j** the righteous and
Isa	11: 3	He shall not **j** by what his eyes
	33:22	For the LORD is our **j**,
Jer	11:20	of hosts, who **j** righteously,
Ezek	7: 3	will **j** you according to your
	33:20	house of Israel, I will **j** all
Joel	3:12	there I will sit to **j** all
Mic	4: 3	He shall **j** between many
Lk	6:37	"Do not **j**, and you will not be
	19:22	'I will **j** you by your own
Jn	7:24	Do not **j** by appearances, but **j**
	12:47	for I came not to **j** the world,
Acts	10:42	ordained by God as **j** of the
Rom	2:16	through Jesus Christ, will **j**
	3: 6	then how could God **j** the
1 Cor	4: 4	It is the Lord who **j** me.
	11:31	But if we **j** ourselves, we would
1 Tim	1:12	he **j** me faithful and appointed
2 Tim	4: 8	the Lord, the righteous **j**,
Heb	10:30	"The Lord will **j** his people."
	13: 4	for God will **j** fornicators and
Jas	4:12	are you to **j** your neighbor?
1 Pet	4: 5	who stands ready to **j** the
Rev	20: 4	were given authority to **j**.

JUDGMENT (S)
Ex	6: 6	and with mighty acts of **j**.
Deut	1:17	for the **j** is God's.
1 Chr	16:14	his **j** are in all the earth
Ps	76: 8	the heavens you uttered **j**;
	119:66	me good **j** and knowledge,
Prov	18: 1	for all who have sound **j**.
Eccl	11: 9	God will bring you into **j**.

Wis 12:12 Or will resist your **j**?
Sir 6:23 my child, and accept my **j**;
Isa 66:16 by fire will the LORD execute **j**,
Jer 25:31 he is entering into **j** with all
Ezek 20:35 I will enter into **j** with you
Dan 7:22 then **j** was given for the holy
Joel 3: 2 I will enter into **j** with them
Hab 1:12 you have marked them for **j**;
Zeph 3: 5 morning he renders his **j**,
Mal 3: 5 draw near to you for **j**;
Mt 5:22 you will be liable to **j**; and if
 12:36 day of **j** you will have to give
Jn 5:30 and my **j** is just, because I seek
 12:31 Now is the **j** of this world;
Rom 11:33 How unsearchable are his **j**
 14:13 no longer pass **j** on one
1 Cor 7:40 in my **j** she is more blessed if
2 Cor 5:10 before the **j** seat of Christ,
2 Thess 1: 5 of the righteous **j** of God,
Heb 10:27 but a fearful prospect of **j**,
Jas 2:13 mercy triumphs over **j**.
1 Pet 4:17 the time has come for **j**
2 Pet 3: 7 the day of **j** and destruction
1 Jn 4:17 boldness on the day of **j**,
Jude 1: 6 in deepest darkness for the **j**
Rev 14: 7 for the hour of his **j** has come;
 16: 7 your **j** are true and just!"

JUST (ICE)

Ex 23: 6 You shall not pervert the **j** due
Deut 16:19 You must not distort **j**; you
 32: 4 and all his ways are **j**.
1 Sam 8: 3 took bribes and perverted **j**.
2 Sam 15: 4 and I would give them **j**."
2 Chr 9: 8 execute **j** and righteousness."
Neh 9:33 You have been **j** in all that has
Tob 3: 2 and all your deeds are **j**;
Job 9:19 it is a matter of **j**,
 19: 7 but there is no **j**.
 34:12 the Almighty will not pervert **j**.
Ps 82: 3 Give **j** to the weak and the
 119:121 I have done what is **j** and
 145:17 The LORD is **j** in all his ways,
Prov 12: 5 thoughts of the righteous are **j**;
 28: 5 The evil do not understand **j**,
Eccl 3:16 the place of **j**, wickedness was
Sir 18: 2 the Lord alone is **j**.
Isa 1:17 learn to do good; seek **j**,
 26: 7 O **J** One, you make smooth
 59: 9 Therefore **j** is far from us, and
Jer 9:24 I act with steadfast love, **j**,
Ezek 45: 9 and do what is **j** and right.
Hos 12: 6 hold fast to love and **j**, and
Am 5: 7 Ah, you that turn **j** to
 5:24 But let **j** roll down like waters,
Mic 3: 1 Israel! Should you not know **j**?
Hab 1: 4 law becomes slack and **j** never
Mal 2:17 "Where is the God of **j**?"
Mt 12:18 will proclaim **j** to the Gentiles.
Lk 11:42 and neglect **j** and the love of
 18: 7 will not God grant **j** to his
Jn 5:30 I judge; and my judgment is **j**,
Acts 8:33 In his humiliation **j** was
2 Thess 1: 6 it is indeed **j** of God to repay
Heb 11:33 administered **j**, obtained
1 Jn 1: 9 he who is faithful and **j** will
Rev 16: 7 judgments are true and just!"

JUSTIFY (JUSTIFIED) (JUSTIFICATION)

Job 32: 2 he **j** himself rather than God;

Ps 51: 4 so that you are **j** in your
Sir 23:11 false oath, he will not be **j**,
Mt 12:37 your words you will be **j**,
Lk 10:29 But wanting to **j** himself, he
Lk 16:15 "You are those who **j**
Rom 5:18 act of righteousness leads to **j**
 8:30 whom he called he also **j**;
1 Cor 6:11 were **j** in the name of the Lord
2 Cor 3: 9 more does the ministry of **j**
Gal 2:16 a person is **j** not by the works
 2:21 for if **j** comes through the law,
Titus 3: 7 having been **j** by his grace,

K

KEEP (S) (KEPT) (KEEPER)

Gen 4: 9 am I my brother's **k**?"
 17: 9 you shall **k** my covenant,
Ex 19: 5 voice and **k** my covenant,
 20: 6 those who love me and **k** my
Num 6:24 The LORD bless you and **k** you;
Deut 6:17 diligently **k** the
 7: 8 the Lord loved you and **k** the
Josh 6:18 **k** away from the things
 14:10 the LORD has **k** me alive,
2 Sam 22:22 For I have **k** the ways of the
2 Kings 17:19 Judah also did not **k** the
1 Chr 29:18 **k** forever such purposes and
Neh 1: 5 those who love him and **k** his
Job 14:16 you would not **k** watch over
Ps 37:28 The righteous shall be **k** safe
 103: 9 nor will he **k** his anger forever.
Prov 7: 5 may **k** you from the loose
Eccl 3: 6 a time to **k**, and a time to
Mt 19:20 "I have **k** all these; what do I
Mk 7: 9 in order to **k** your tradition!
Lk 17:33 who lose their life will **k** it.
Jn 8:51 whoever **k** my word will never
Rom 16:17 to **k** an eye on those who
1 Cor 16:13 **K** alert, stand firm in your
2 Cor 12: 7 to **k** me from being too elated
2 Thess 3: 6 to **k** away from believers who
1 Tim 5:22 **k** yourself pure.
2 Tim 4: 7 I have **k** the faith.
Heb 13: 5 **K** your lives free from the love
Jas 2:10 whoever **k** the whole law but
1 Pet 3:10 let them **k** their tongues from
2 Pet 1: 8 they **k** you from being
1 Jn 5:21 **k** yourselves from idols
Jude 1:24 who is able to **k** you from
Rev 3:10 Because you have **k** my word

KEY (S)

Isa 22:22 on his shoulder the **k** of the
Mt 16:19 you the **k** of the kingdom
Lk 11:52 taken away the **k** of knowledge;
Rev 1:18 and I have the **k** of Death and
 20: 1 the **k** to the bottomless pit

KILL (ED)

Gen 4:14 who meets me may **k** me."
 37:18 they conspired to **k** him.
Ex 2:15 he sought to **k** Moses. But
 4:23 I will **k** your firstborn son.' "
1 Kings 11:40 sought therefore to **k**
1 Macc 2:24 he ran and **k** him on the altar

Eccl 3: 3 a time to **k**, and a time to heal
Mt 10:28 Do not fear those who **k** the
 17:23 they will **k** him, and on the
Mk 14: 1 arrest Jesus by stealth and **k**
Jn 10:10 comes only to steal and **k** and

KIND (NESS)

Gen 1:24 living creatures of every **k**:
Ruth 2:20 whose **k** has not forsaken
2 Sam 9: 3 I may show the **k** of God?"
2 Chr 10: 7 "If you will be **k** to this people
Ps 145:17 and **k** in all his doings.
Prov 11:17 Those who are **k** reward
 31:26 teaching of **k** is on her tongue.
Hos 11: 4 with cords of human **k**, with
Lk 6:35 for he is **k** to the ungrateful
Jn 21:19 the **k** of death by which he
Rom 11:22 Note then the **k** and the
1 Cor 13: 4 Love is patient; love is **k**;
2 Cor 6: 6 knowledge, patience, **k**,
Gal 5:22 love, joy, peace, patience, **k**,
Eph 2: 7 riches of his grace in **k**
 4:32 and be **k** to one another,
Col 3:12 with compassion, **k**, humility,
Titus 3: 4 goodness and loving **k** of God
Sir 3:14 **k** to a father will not be

KING (S) ('S)

Gen 35:11 and **k** shall spring from you.
Ex 1: 8 Now a new **k** arose over Egypt,
Num 23:21 acclaimed as a **k** among them.
Deut 17:14 "I will set a **k** over me, like all
Judg 9: 8 to anoint a **k** over themselves.
 17: 6 there was no **k** in Israel;
1 Sam 11:15 made Saul **k** before the LORD
 12:12 LORD your God was your **k**.
2 Sam 2: 4 they anointed David **k**
1 Kings 1:30 shall succeed me as **k**,
Tob 10:13 Lord of heaven and earth, **K**
Jdt 9:12 **K** of all your creation,
Ps 33:16 A **k** is not saved by his
 44: 4 You are my **K** and my God;
Prov 21: 1 The **k** heart is a stream of
Eccl 8: 2 Keep the **k** command because
Sir 51:12 to the **K** of the kings of kings,
Isa 6: 5 my eyes have seen the **K**, the
 32: 1 a **k** will reign in righteousness,
Jer 10:10 God and the everlasting **K**.
Ezek 37:24 My servant David shall be **k**
Mic 2:13 Their **k** will pass on before
Zeph 3:15 The **k** of Israel, the LORD, is
Zech 9: 9 Lo, your **k** comes to you;
 14: 9 the LORD will become **k** over
Mal 1:14 for I am a great **K**, says the
Mt 2: 2 child who has been born **k** of
 27:37 "This is Jesus, the **K** of the
Mk 15:32 Let the Messiah, the **K** of
Lk 19:38 "Blessed is the **k** who comes
 23: 3 "Are you the **k** of the Jews?"
Jn 1:49 You are the **K** of Israel!"
 19:15 "We have no **k** but the
Acts 17: 7 another **k** named Jesus."
1 Tim 1:17 To the **K** of the ages,
Rev 15: 3 true are your ways, **K** of the
 19:16 "King of **k** and Lord of lords."

KINGDOM

Ex 19: 6 a priestly **k** and a holy nation.
Deut 17:18 taken the throne of his **k**,
1 Sam 13:14 now your **k** will not continue;

2 Sam 7:12 and I will establish his **k**.
1 Kings 11:31 tear the **k** from the hand of
1 Chr 29:11 yours is the **k**, O LORD, and
Ps 145:13 Your **k** is an everlasting **k**, and
Wis 10:10 she showed him the **k** of God,
Isa 9: 7 throne of David and his **k**.
Jer 18: 7 concerning a nation or a **k**,
Ezek 29:14 they shall be a lowly **k**.
Dan 2:39 After you shall arise another **k**
4: 3 His **k** is an everlasting **k**, and
Mt 5: 3 for theirs is the **k** of heaven.
6:33 But strive first for the **k** of God
25:34 inherit the **k** prepared for you
Mk 1:15 the **k** of God has come near
3:24 If a **k** is divided against itself,
10:15 whoever does not receive the **k**
12:34 are not far from the **k** of God."
Lk 7:28 the least in the **k** of God is
13:18 "What is the **k** of God like?
17:21 the **k** of God is among you
23:42 when you come into your **k**."
Jn 3: 3 no one can see the **k** of God
18:36 "My **k** is not from this world
Acts 1: 6 will restore the **k** to Israel?"
14:22 we must enter the **k** of God."
19: 8 persuasively about the **k**
Rom 14:17 For the **k** of God is not food
1 Cor 4:20 For the **k** of God depends
6: 9 will not inherit the **k** of God?
Eph 5: 5 inheritance in the **k** of Christ
Col 1:13 transferred us into the **k** of his
4:11 co-workers for the **k** of God,
1 Thess 2:12 calls you into his own **k**
2 Thess 1: 5 you worthy of the **k** of God,
2 Tim 4:18 save me for his heavenly **k**.
Heb 12:28 a **k** that cannot be shaken,
Jas 2: 5 heirs of the **k** that he has
2 Pet 1:11 entry into the eternal **k** of
Rev 1: 6 made us to be a **k**, priests
11:15 has become the **k** of our Lord

KISS (ED)

Gen 27:26 "Come near and **k** me, my
45:15 he **k** all his brothers and wept
Ex 18: 7 he bowed down and **k** him;
Ruth 1: 9 Then she **k** them, and they
1 Kings 19:20 "Let me **k** my father and my
Job 31:27 my mouth has **k** my hand;
Ps 85:10 righteousness and peace will **k**
Prov 24:26 An honest answer gives a **k** on
Song 1: 2 Let him **k** me with the kisses
Mt 26:48 "The one I will **k** is the man;
Lk 7:45 gave me no **k**, but from the
22:48 "Judas, is it with a **k** that you
Acts 20:37 they embraced Paul and **k**
Rom 16:16 one another with a holy **k**.
1 Cor 16:20 one another with a holy **k**.
1 Thess 5:26 and sisters with a holy **k**.
1 Pet 5:14 Greet one another with a **k**

KNOW (ING) (KNEW)

Gen 3: 5 be like God, **k** good and evil."
22:12 for now I **k** that you fear God,
Ex 6: 7 You shall **k** that I am the LORD
33:12 'I **k** you by name, and you
Num 16:28 "This is how you shall **k** that
Deut 7: 9 **K** therefore that the LORD your
8: 2 testing you to **k** what was in
Josh 3: 7 so that they may **k** that I will
23:14 you **k** in your hearts and souls

1 Sam 17:46 earth may **k** that there is a
1 Kings 8:39 **k** what is in every human
2 Chr 33:13 Then Manasseh **k** that the
Job 19:25 For I **k** that my Redeemer
42: 2 "I **k** that you can do all
Ps 36:10 steadfast love to those who **k**
46:10 "Be still, and **k** that I am God!
139:23 Search me, O God, and **k** my
Prov 27: 1 you do not **k** what a day may
Eccl 8:16 I applied my mind to **k**
Sir 5:10 Stand firm for what you **k**,
Isa 44: 8 no other rock; I **k** not one.
Jer 1: 5 in the womb I **k** you, and
29:11 surely I **k** the plans I have for
Ezek 6:10 they shall **k** that I am the LORD
Mt 7:23 'I never **k** you; go away from
12:25 He **k** what they were thinking
24:42 not **k** on what day your Lord
Mk 12:24 you **k** neither the scriptures
Lk 1: 4 so that you may **k** the truth
4:41 they **k** that he was the Messiah
23:34 do not **k** what they are doing."
Jn 10:14 I **k** my own and my own **k**
13: 1 Jesus **k** that his hour had
21:15 "Yes, Lord; you **k** that I love
Acts 1: 7 is not for you to **k** the times
1:24 "Lord, you **k** everyone's heart.
Rom 6: 6 We **k** that our old self was
8:28 We **k** that all things work
1 Cor 1:21 world did not **k** God through
3:16 **k** that you are God's temple
13:12 then I will **k** fully, even as I
2 Cor 4:14 we **k** that the one who raised
8: 9 For you **k** the generous act of
Eph 1:17 as you come to **k** him,
3:19 and to **k** the love of Christ
Phil 3:10 I want to **k** Christ and the
4:12 I **k** what it is to have little
Col 4: 1 **k** that you also have a Master
1 Thess 5: 2 For you yourselves **k** very well
2 Thess 1: 8 on those who do not **k** God
1 Tim 3:15 you may **k** how one ought to
2 Tim 1:12 am not ashamed, for I **k** the
Titus 1:16 profess to **k** God, but they
Heb 8:11 '**K** the Lord,' for they shall all **k**
Jas 1: 3 because you **k** that the testing
4: 4 Do you not **k** that friendship
1 Pet 1:18 You **k** that you were ransomed
2 Pet 1:12 though you **k** them already
1 Jn 2: 3 we **k** him, if we obey his
3:24 by this we **k** that he abides
5:13 may **k** that you have eternal
3 Jn 1:12 **k** that our testimony is true
Rev 2: 2 "I **k** your works, your toil and
3: 3 you will not **k** at what hour I

KNOWLEDGE

Gen 2: 9 tree of the **k** of good and evil.
Num 24:16 and knows the **k** of the Most
2 Chr 1:10 Give me now wisdom and **k**
Job 21:22 Will any teach God **k**,
Ps 119:66 good judgment and **k**,
139: 6 Such **k** is too wonderful
Prov 1: 7 LORD is the beginning of **k**;
15: 7 lips of the wise spread **k**;
18:15 intelligent mind acquires **k**,
Eccl 2:26 God gives wisdom and **k** and
7:12 the advantage of **k** is that
Sir 6:33 love to listen you will gain **k**
Isa 11: 9 full of the **k** of the LORD

53:11 find satisfaction through his **k**.
Jer 3:15 with **k** and understanding.
Dan 1:17 God gave **k** and skill in every
Hos 4: 6 are destroyed for lack of **k**;
Hab 2:14 will be filled with the **k** of the
Mal 2: 7 a priest should guard **k**,
Lk 1:77 give **k** of salvation to his
Rom 11:33 riches and wisdom and **k** of
15:14 filled with all **k**, and able to
1 Cor 8: 1 **K** puffs up, but love
2 Cor 8: 7 in faith, in speech, in **k**,
11: 6 in speech, but not in **k**;
Eph 3:19 love of Christ that surpasses **k**,
Phil 1: 9 more and more with **k**
Col 1:10 as you grow in the **k** of God.
2: 3 the treasures of wisdom and **k**.
1 Tim 2: 4 and to come to the **k** of the
Heb 10:26 sin after having received the **k**
2 Pet 1: 3 the **k** of him who called us
3:18 grow in the grace and **k** of
1 Jn 2:20 and all of you have **k**.

L

LABOR (ER)

Ex 20: 9 Six days you shall **l** and do all
Lev 19:13 the wages of a **l** until morning.
Judg 1:28 put the Canaanites to forced **l**,
Ps 107:12 were bowed down with hard **l**;
127: 1 those who build it **l** in vain.
Prov 12:24 will be put to forced **l**.
Isa 55: 2 **l** for that which does not
Hab 2:13 **l** only to feed the flames
Lk 10: 7 for the **l** deserves to be paid.
1 Cor 3: 8 wages according to the **l**
15:58 in the Lord your **l** is not in
Phil 2:16 not run in vain or **l** in vain.
1 Thess 1: 3 your work of faith and **l** of

LAMB (S) ('S)

Gen 22: 8 himself will provide the **l**
Ex 12:21 and slaughter the passover **l**.
2 Sam 12: 6 he shall restore the **l** fourfold,
Sir 13:17 have in common with a **l**?
Isa 40:11 he will gather the **l** in his
65:25 wolf and the **l** shall feed
Jer 11:19 a gentle **l** led to the slaughter.
Mk 14:12 when the Passover **l** is
Lk 10: 3 sending you out like **l** into
Jn 1:29 "Here is the **L** of God who
21:15 "Feed my **l**."
1 Cor 5: 7 our paschal **l**, Christ, has been
1 Pet 1:19 like that of a **l** without defect
Rev 5:12 "Worthy is the **L** that was
21:27 written in the **L** book of life.

LAMP (S)

1 Sam 3: 3 the **l** of God had not yet
2 Sam 22:29 Indeed, you are my **l**, O LORD,
1 Kings 15: 4 his God gave him a **l** in
2 Kings 8:19 had promised to give a **l** to
Ps 18:28 you who light my **l**; the LORD,
119:105 Your word is a **l** to my feet
Prov 6:23 For the commandment is a **l**
Prov 20:27 human spirit is the **l** of the
Mt 5:15 No one after lighting a **l** puts it

Mt	6:22	"The eye is the **l** of the body.
Lk	12:35	and have your **l** lit;
Jn	5:35	was a burning and shining **l**,
Rev	18:23	the light of a **l** will shine in
	22: 5	they need no light of **l** or sun,

LAND

Gen	1:10	God called the dry **l** Earth,
	13:15	the **l** that you see I will give
Ex	3: 8	a **l** flowing with milk and
	8:22	the LORD am in this **l**.
Num	13: 2	to spy out the **l** of Canaan,
	35:33	shall not pollute the **l** in
Deut	8: 7	bringing you into a good **l**,
	29:24	LORD done thus to this **l**?
Josh	2: 1	"Go, view the **l**, especially
	11:23	So Joshua took the whole **l**,
Judg	1:27	continued to live in that **l**.
Ruth	1: 1	was a famine in the **l**,
2 Sam	21:14	heeded supplications for the **l**.
1 Kings	8:34	bring them again to the **l** that
2 Kings	17: 5	of Assyria invaded all the **l**
2 Chr	7:14	their sin and heal their **l**.
Neh	10:31	if the peoples of the **l** bring
Tob	14:7	forever in the **l** of Abraham
1 Macc	14:11	He established peace in the **l**,
Ps	25:13	children shall possess the **l**;
	37:11	the meek shall inherit the **l**,
Prov	12:11	Those who till their **l** will have
Sir	46:8	the **l** flowing with milk and
Isa	2: 8	Their **l** is filled with idols;
	53: 8	cut off from the **l** of the living,
Jer	2: 7	you entered you defiled my **l**,
	22:29	O **l**, **l**, **l**, hear the word
Ezek	7:23	For the **l** is full of bloody
Dan	11:41	shall come into the beautiful **l**,
Zech	3: 9	remove the guilt of this **l**
Mal	4: 6	come and strike the **l** with a
Mk	15:33	came over the whole **l**
Rev	10: 2	his left foot on the **l**,

LAST

Ruth	3:10	this **l** instance of your loyalty
2 Sam	23: 1	these are the **l** words of David:
Isa	41: 4	and will be with the **l**.
	48:12	I am the first, and I am the **l**.
Mt	19:30	first will be **l**, and the **l**
	27:64	and the **l** deception would be
Mk	9:35	to be first must be **l** of all
	15:37	loud cry and breathed his **l**.
Jn	6:40	raise them up on the **l** day."
	15:16	bear fruit, fruit that will **l**,
Acts	2:17	'In the **l** days it will be,
1 Cor	15:26	The **l** enemy to be destroyed is
	15:45	the **l** Adam became a
2 Tim	3: 1	in the **l** days distressing times
Heb	1: 2	in these **l** days he has spoken
Jas	5: 3	laid up treasure for the **l** days.
1 Pet	1: 5	to be revealed in the **l** time.
2 Pet	2:20	the **l** state has become worse
1 Jn	2:18	Children, it is the **l** hour!
Jude	1:18	"In the **l** time there will be
Rev	1:17	I am the first and the **l**,
	21: 9	bowls full of the seven **l**

LAUGH (INGSTOCK) (LAUGHTER)

Gen	21: 6	who hears will **l** with me."
Job	12: 4	I am a **l** to my friends;
Ps	59: 8	But you **l** at them, O LORD;
	126: 2	our mouth was filled with **l**,

Prov	14:13	Even in **l** the heart is sad,
Eccl	3: 4	time to weep, and a time to **l**;
	7: 3	Sorrow is better than **l**,
Lam	3:14	I have become the **l** of all my
Lk	6:21	weep now, for you will **l**.

LAY (LAID)

Gen	22:12	"Do not **l** your hand on the
Ex	7: 4	I will **l** my hand upon Egypt
Num	27:18	and **l** your hand upon him;
Deut	9:25	I **l** prostrate before the LORD
	34: 9	Moses had **l** his hands on
Job	38: 4	"Where were you when I **l** the
Ps	139: 5	and **l** your hand upon me.
Prov	10:14	The wise **l** up knowledge, but
Mt	8:20	Man has nowhere to **l** his
	28: 6	see the place where he **l**.
Mk	6:29	took his body, and **l** it in a
Lk	6:48	and **l** the foundation on rock;
Jn	10:15	I **l** down my life for the sheep.
	13:37	I will **l** down my life for you
Acts	6: 6	prayed and **l** their hands on
	8:19	on whom I **l** my hands may
1 Cor	3:11	no one can **l** any foundation
Col	1: 5	the hope **l** up for you in
Heb	4:13	all are naked and **l** bare to the
	12: 1	let us also **l** aside every weight
1 Jn	3:16	we ought to **l** down our lives

LAW (FUL)

Num	5:29	is the **l** in cases of jealousy,
Deut	17:18	have a copy of this **l** written
	27:26	uphold the words of this **l** by
Josh	1: 8	book of the **l** shall not depart
2 Kings	22: 8	found the book of the **l**
2 Chr	6:16	to walk in my **l** as you have
	17: 9	the book of the **l** of the LORD
Ezra	7: 6	a scribe skilled in the **l** of
Neh	8: 2	Ezra brought the **l** before the
Ps	1: 2	on his **l** they meditate day and
	40: 8	your **l** is within my heart."
	119:142	and your **l** is the truth.
Prov	28: 9	will not listen to the **l**,
	29:18	are those who keep the **l**.
Jer	8: 8	and the **l** of the LORD is
	31:33	I will put my **l** within them,
Dan	9:11	Israel has transgressed your **l**
Hos	4: 6	you have forgotten the **l** of
Hab	1: 4	the **l** becomes slack and justice
Zech	7:12	not to hear the **l** and the
Mt	5:17	have come to abolish the **l**
	19: 3	"Is it **l** for a man to divorce
Lk	14: 3	"Is it **l** to cure people on the
	20:22	Is it **l** for us to pay taxes
Jn	7:19	none of you keeps the **l**.
	18:31	him according to your **l**."
Acts	6:13	this holy place and the **l**;
	13:39	you could not be freed by the **l**
Rom	6:14	not under **l** but under grace.
	7: 4	you have died to the **l** through
	8: 4	that **l** might be fulfilled in us
1 Cor	9:20	I might win those under the **l**.
	10:23	"All things are **l**," but not all
Gal	2:19	through the **l** I died to the **l**
	3:11	justified before God by the **l**;
Eph	2:15	He has abolished the **l**
Phil	3: 9	own that comes from the **l**,
1 Tim	1: 8	Now we know that the **l** is
Titus	3: 9	and quarrels about the **l**,
Heb	7:19	(for the **l** made nothing

Heb	10: 1	Since the **l** has only a shadow of
Jas	1:25	who look into the perfect **l**,
	2:10	whoever keeps the whole **l** but

LEAD (S) (ER) (ERS)

Ex	15:10	they sank like **l** in the mighty
	32:34	**l** the people to the place
1 Chr	28: 4	for he chose Judah as **l**,
Ps	23: 2	he **l** me beside still waters;
	139:24	and **l** me in the way
Prov	2:18	for her way **l** down to death,
	21: 5	plans of the diligent **l** surely
Eccl	5: 6	Do not let your mouth **l** you
Sir	19:2	and women **l** intelligent men
	20:26	A liar's way **l** to disgrace
Isa	11: 6	and a little child shall **l** them.
Jer	31: 9	I will **l** them back,
Dan	12: 3	those who **l** many to
Mt	7:14	the road is hard that **l** to life,
Mk	13:22	signs and omens, to **l** astray,
Lk	19:47	the **l** of the people kept
	23:35	but the **l** scoffed at him,
Jn	11: 4	"This illness does not **l** to
Rom	2: 4	God's kindness is meant to **l**
	6:16	either of sin, which **l** to death,
1 Cor	7:17	let each of you **l** the life that
2 Cor	2:14	in Christ always **l** us in
	7:10	a repentance that **l** to salvation
Col	1:10	**l** lives worthy of the Lord
1 Tim	2: 2	so that we may **l** a quiet and

LEARN (ED) (ING)

Deut	5: 1	you shall **l** them and observe
	18: 9	you must not **l** to imitate the
Ps	119:152	Long ago I **l** from your decrees
Prov	1: 2	**l** about wisdom and
	9: 9	and they will gain in **l**.
Isa	1:17	**l** to do good; seek justice
Jer	35:13	Can you not **l** a lesson and
Bar	3:9	give ear, and **l** wisdom!
Mt	11:29	my yoke upon you, and **l** from
Mk	13:28	"From the fig tree **l** its lesson:
Jn	6:45	Everyone who has heard and **l**
Eph	4:20	That is not the way you **l**
Phil	4: 9	the things that you have **l**
	4:11	for I have **l** to be content with
1 Tim	5: 4	first **l** their religious duty
2 Tim	3:14	you have **l** and firmly
Titus	3:14	let people **l** to devote
Rev	14: 3	No one could **l** that song

LEFT (LEAVE)

Gen	7:23	Only Noah was **l**,
Ex	11: 8	'**L** us, you and all the people
Num	10:31	"Do not **l** us, for you know
	11:20	'Why did we ever **l** Egypt?' "
Deut	28:14	either to the right or to the **l**,
Prov	14: 7	**L** the presence of a fool
Isa	30:21	when you turn to the **l**, your
Joel	2:14	and **l** a blessing behind him,
Mt	5:24	**l** your gift there before the
	6: 3	do not let your **l** hand know
Mk	8: 8	took up the broken pieces **l**
	10:28	"Look, we have **l** everything
	17:34	will be taken and the other **l**.
Jn	14:18	"I will not **l** you orphaned;
	14:27	Peace I **l** with you;
Eph	5:31	a man will **l** his father and
2 Pet	2:15	They have **l** the straight road
Jude	1: 6	but **l** their proper dwelling,

LIAR (LIE) (LYING)

Gen 19:32 drink wine, and we will l with
Deut 6: 7 when you l down and when
Ruth 3: 4 uncover his feet and l down;
2 Kings 9:12 They said, "L! Come on, tell
Job 24:25 who will prove me a l, and
Ps 23: 2 me l down in green pastures;
120: 2 "Deliver me, O Lord, from l
Prov 12:22 L lips are an abomination to
14: 5 A faithful witness does not l,
Hos 4: 2 Swearing, l, and murder,
Mk 7:30 found the child l on the bed,
Lk 2:12 of cloth and l in a manger."
Jn 5: 6 Jesus saw him l there and
8:44 for he is a l and the father of
Acts 5: 3 Satan filled your heart to l
Rom 3: 4 Although everyone is a l, let
Col 3: 9 Do not l to one another,
1 Jn 1: 6 we l and do not do what is
2:21 no l comes from the truth.

LIFE (LIVE)

Gen 2: 7 his nostrils the breath of l;
3:22 of life, and eat, and l forever"
Ex 21: 6 he shall serve him for l.
33:20 no one shall see me and l."
Num 35:31 accept no ransom for the l of a
Deut 8: 3 one does not l by bread alone,
30:19 Choose l so that you and your
1 Sam 19: 5 for he took his l in his hand
Neh 9: 6 all of them you give l,
Jdt 13:20 because you risked your own l
Job 10: 1 "I loathe my l; I will give
14:14 If mortals die, will they l again?
Ps 16:11 show me the path of l.
63: 3 steadfast love is better than l,
119:175 Let me l that I may praise you
Prov 8:35 For whoever finds me finds l
16:22 Wisdom is a fountain of l to
Eccl 2:17 So I hated l, because what is
7:12 is that wisdom gives l
Sir 30:22 A joyful hart is l itself.
Isa 11: 6 The wolf shall l with the lamb,
53:10 When you make his l an
Lam 3:58 Lord, you have redeemed my l.
Ezek 18:27 they shall save their l.
Jon 2: 6 you brought up my l from the
Mal 2: 5 a covenant of l and well-
Mt 6:25 do not worry about your l,
19:29 and will inherit eternal l.
20:28 to give his l a ransom for
Mk 9:43 for you to enter l maimed
10:30 the age to come eternal l.
Lk 6: 9 to save l or to destroy it?"
10:28 do this, and you will l."
Jn 10:10 I came that they may have l,
12:25 Those who love their l lose it,
14: 6 way, and the truth, and the l.
20:31 believing you may have l
Acts 2:28 known to me the ways of l;
11:18 the repentance that leads to l."
Rom 6:23 God is eternal l in Christ
8:38 neither death, nor l, nor
14: 8 If we l, we l to the Lord
1 Cor 15:19 If for this l only we have
2 Cor 3: 6 but the Spirit gives l.
6:16 "I will l in them and walk
Gal 2:20 no longer I who l, but it is
5:25 If we l by the Spirit, let us
Eph 4: 1 to lead a l worthy of the

Eph 5: 8 L as children of light
Phil 1:20 whether by l or by death.
2:16 to the word of l that I can
Col 3: 3 your l is hidden with Christ
1 Tim 1:16 believe in him for eternal l.
4: 8 for both the present l and the l
2 Tim 3:12 all who want to l a godly life
Titus 1: 2 in the hope of eternal l that
Heb 7:16 power of an indestructible l.
10:38 my righteous one will l by
Jas 1:12 will receive the crown of l
3:13 Show by your good l that your
1 Pet 3: 7 heirs of the gracious gift of l
2 Pet 1: 3 needed for l and godliness,
1 Jn 2:17 who do the will of God l
3:16 that he laid down his l for us
Rev 2:10 give you the crown of l.
20: 4 They came to l and reigned

LIKE (NESS)

Gen 1:26 our image, according to our l;
3: 5 you will be l God, knowing
28:14 your offspring shall be l the
Ex 8:10 no one l the LORD our God,
24:17 glory of the LORD was l
Num 11: 7 the manna was l coriander
Deut 18:15 prophet l me from among
32:31 their rock is not l our Rock;
1 Sam 2: 2 "There is no Holy One l the
2 Sam 7:22 for there is no one l you,
1 Kings 22:13 let your word be l the word of
1 Chr 17:21 Who is l your people Israel,
Job 40: 9 Have you an arm l God, and
Ps 1: 3 They are l trees planted by
90: 4 years in your sight are l
103:15 mortals, their days are l grass;
Prov 7:22 he follows her, and goes l
25:11 A word fitly spoken is l apples
Eccl 2:16 can the wise die just l fools?
Isa 1:18 though your sins are l scarlet,
40: 6 their constancy is l the flower
53: 6 All we l sheep have gone
64: 6 our righteous deeds are l a
Jer 23:29 Is not my word l fire,
Lam 1:12 if there is any sorrow l my
2: 5 The Lord has become l an
Ezek 1: 4 something l gleaming amber.
Dan 7: 4 l a lion and had eagles' wings
10: 6 His body was l beryl, his face l
Hos 6: 4 Your love is l a morning cloud,
14: 5 I will be l the dew to Israel;
Mic 7:18 Who is a God l you, pardoning
Nah 1: 6 His wrath is poured out l fire,
Zech 1: 4 Do not be l your ancestors,
Mt 10:16 I am sending you out l sheep
Lk 6:48 l a man building a house
Rom 5:15 free gift is not l the trespass.
Phil 2: 7 being born in human l.
Jas 1:24 forget what they were l.
3: 9 who are made in the l of God.
1 Pet 1:24 "All flesh is l grass and all its
2 Pet 3:10 the Lord will come l a thief,
Rev 4: 7 first living creature l a lion,
10: 1 his face l the sun,

LION ('S) (S)

Gen 49: 9 he stretches out like a l,
Judg 14: 6 he tore the l apart barehanded
1 Sam 17:34 and whenever a l or a bear
Ps 91:13 You will tread on the l and

Song 4: 8 from the dens of l,
Sir 27:28 lies in wait for them like a l.
Isa 11: 7 L and the l shall eat straw like
Jer 25:38 Like a l he has left his covert
Ezek 1:10 the face of a l on the right
Dan 6:20 to deliver you from the l?"
7: 4 like a l and had eagles' wings.
Hos 13: 7 I will become like a l to them,
2 Tim 4:17 I was rescued from the l
1 Pet 5: 8 Like a roaring l your adversary
Rev 4: 7 first living creature like a l,

LIPS

Deut 23:23 Whatever your l utter you
Job 27: 4 my l will not speak falsehood,
Ps 12: 3 LORD cut off all flattering l,
40: 9 I have not restrained my l,
63: 3 my l will praise you.
Prov 10:21 The l of the righteous feed
12:22 Lying l are an abomination to
15: 7 l of the wise spread knowledge
Eccl 10:12 the l of fools consume them.
Song 4:11 Your l distill nectar, my bride;
Isa 6: 5 I am a man of unclean l,
29:13 honor me with their l, while
Hos 14: 2 offer the fruit of our l.
Mal 2: 7 For the l of a priest should
Mt 15: 8 honors me with their l, but
Rom 3:13 of vipers is under their l."
1 Cor 14:21 the l of foreigners I will speak
Heb 13:15 fruit of l that confess his
1 Pet 3:10 and their l from speaking

LISTEN (S)

Ex 6:30 why would Pharaoh l to me?"
23:22 if you l attentively to his voice
2 Kings 17:40 They would not l, however,
Ps 5: 2 L to the sound of my cry,
34:11 Come, O children, l to me;
Prov 4: 1 L, children, to a father's
8:34 Happy is the one who l to me,
Eccl 5: 1 to draw near to l is better than
Song 5: 2 L! my beloved is knocking.
Sir 11:8 Do not answer before you l,
Isa 1:10 l to the teaching of our God,
Mt 12:42 l to the wisdom of Solomon
Mk 4:23 anyone with ears to hear l!"
9: 7 my Son, the Beloved; l to
Lk 10:16 "Whoever l to you l to me
16:31 'If they do not l to Moses and
Jn 10:16 and they will l to my voice.
Acts 3:22 You must l to whatever he tells
Jas 1:19 let everyone be quick to l,
1 Jn 4: 6 Whoever knows God l to us,
Rev 2: 7 anyone who has an ear l to

LITTLE

Ex 16:18 who gathered l had no
23:30 L by l I will drive
1 Kings 17:12 and a l oil in a jug;
Ps 8: 5 them a l lower than God,
Prov 6:10 A l sleep, a l slumber,
16: 8 Better is a l with righteousness
Eccl 10: 1 l folly outweighs wisdom and
Sir 51:28 Hear but a l of my instruction,
Isa 11: 6 and a l child shall lead them.
Mt 14:31 "You of l faith, why did you
19:14 "Let the l children come to
Lk 7:47 to whom l is forgiven, loves l."
18:17 kingdom of God as a l child

1 Cor	5: 6	a **l** yeast leavens the whole
2 Cor	8:15	who had **l** did not have too **l**
Gal	5: 9	A **l** yeast leavens the whole
1 Tim	5:23	but take a **l** wine for the sake
Heb	2: 7	made them for a **l** while lower
1 Pet	5:10	you have suffered for a **l** while,
1 Jn	4: 4	**L** children, you are from God
Rev	3: 8	know that you have but **l**

LIVING

Gen	2: 7	and the man became a **l** being.
Deut	5:26	heard the voice of the **l** God
Josh	3:10	among you is the **l** God who
1 Sam	17:26	defy the armies of the **l** God?"
2 Kings	19: 4	has sent to mock the **l** God,
Ps	84: 2	sing for joy to the **l** God.
Eccl	9: 4	is joined with all the **l** has
Isa	53: 8	from the land of the **l**,
Jer	10:10	he is the **l** God and the
	17:13	forsaken the fountain of **l**
Ezek	1: 5	something like four **l**
	10:17	for the spirit of the **l** creatures
Dan	6:26	he is the **l** God, enduring
Hos	1:10	"Children of the **l** God."
Zech	14: 8	On that day **l** waters shall flow
Mt	16:16	the Song of the **l** God."
	22:32	not of the dead, but of the **l**."
Jn	4:10	would have given you **l** water."
	6:51	I am the **l** bread that came
Rom	9:26	called children of the **l** God."
	12: 1	present your bodies as a **l**
1 Cor	9:14	get their **l** by the gospel.
2 Cor	6:16	are the temple of the **l** God;
1 Tim	4:10	our hope set on the **l** God,
2 Tim	4: 1	to judge the **l** and the dead,
Heb	4:12	word of God is **l** and active,
	10:20	new and **l** way that he opened
1 Pet	1:23	**l** and enduring word of God
	2: 4	Come to him, a **l** stone,
Rev	1:18	and the **l** one. I was dead,
	4: 6	are four **l** creatures, full of eyes

LOOK (ED) (S)

Gen	15: 5	"**L** toward heaven and count
	19:17	do not **l** back or stop
Ex	3: 6	for he was afraid to **l** at God.
Num	21: 8	who is bitten shall **l** at it
Deut	3:27	**L** well, for you shall not
	26:15	**L** down from your holy
1 Sam	16: 7	"Do not **l** on his appearance
Ps	14: 2	The LORD **l** down from heaven
	123: 2	eyes **l** to the LORD our God
Prov	4:25	Let your eyes **l** directly
	31:27	She **l** well to the ways of
Isa	3: 9	**l** on their faces bears witness
	17: 7	eyes will **l** to the Holy One
Jer	6:16	Stand at the crossroads, and **l**,
Hab	1:13	you cannot **l** on wrongdoing;
Zech	12:10	they **l** on the one whom they
Mal	2:15	So **l** to yourselves, and do not
Mt	5:28	who **l** at a woman with lust
	23:27	on the outside **l** beautiful, but
Mk	13:21	'**L**! Here is the Messiah!'
	16: 6	**L**, there is the place they laid
Lk	9:16	he **l** up to heaven, and blessed
	24:39	**L** at my hands and my feet;
Jn	4:35	I tell you, **l** around you, and
	13:33	You will **l** for me;
Phil	2: 4	Let each of you **l** not to your
1 Pet	1:12	into which angels long to **l**!

1 Jn	1: 1	what we have **l** at and touched
Rev	5:11	I **l**, and I heard the voice
	14: 1	I **l**, and there was the Lamb

LOSE (LOSS) (LOST)

Num	17:12	we are **l**, all of us are **l**
Ps	119:176	have gone astray like a **l** sheep;
Sir	9:6	or you may **l** your inheritance.
Jer	50: 6	My people have been **l** sheep;
Ezek	34:16	I will seek the **l**, and I will
Mk	8:35	to save their life will **l** it,
Lk	15:24	he was **l** and is found!'
	19:10	to seek out and to save the **l**."
Jn	6:39	that I should **l** nothing of all
	12:25	Those who love their life **l** it,
1 Cor	3:15	the builder will suffer **l**;
2 Cor	4: 1	we do not **l** heart.
Phil	3: 8	I regard everything as **l**
Heb	12: 3	may not grow weary or **l** heart.
	12: 5	**l** heart when you are punished
2 Pet	3:17	and **l** your own stability.
2 Jn	1: 8	do not **l** what we have worked

LOVE (D) (S)

Gen	24:67	became his wife; and he **l** her.
Ex	15:13	"In your steadfast **l** you led the
Lev	19:18	**l** your neighbor as yourself:
Num	14:18	abounding in steadfast **l**,
Deut	5:10	who **l** me and keep my
	6: 5	You shall **l** the LORD your God
Josh	22: 5	to **l** the LORD your God,
Judg	16:15	"How can you say, 'I **l** you,'
Ru	4:15	for your daughter-in-law **l** you
1 Sam	16:21	Saul **l** him greatly, and he
	20:14	the faithful **l** of the LORD;
2 Sam	1:26	your **l** to me was wonderful,
	22:51	steadfast **l** to his anointed,
1 Kings	3: 3	Solomon **l** the LORD, walking
	11: 2	Solomon clung to these in **l**.
1 Chr	16:34	his steadfast **l** endures forever.
2 Chr	6:14	keeping covenant in steadfast **l**
Ezra	3:11	steadfast **l** endures forever
Tob	14:7	sincerely **l** God will rejoice
Esth	2:17	the king **l** Esther more than all
1 Macc	4:33	the sword of those who **l** you,
Job	10:12	granted me life and steadfast **l**,
	37:13	or for **l**, he causes it to happen
Ps	33: 5	He **l** righteousness and justice;
	69:36	who **l** his name shall live
	97:10	**l** those who hate evil;
	119:97	Oh, how I **l** your law!
Prov	7:18	let us delight ourselves with **l**.
	10:12	but **l** covers all offenses.
	13: 1	A wise child **l** discipline,
	19: 8	To get wisdom is to **l** oneself;
Eccl	3: 8	a time to **l**, and a time to hate
Song	3: 5	not stir up or awaken **l** until it
	8: 6	for **l** is strong as death,
Wis	6:18	of her is the keeping of her
Sir	7:30	all your might **l** your Maker,
Isa	54:10	I shall not depart from you
	61: 8	For I the LORD **l** justice, I hate
Jer	9:24	I act with steadfast **l**, justice,
	31: 3	I **l** you with an everlasting **l**;
Lam	3:22	The steadfast **l** of the LORD
Ezek	33:32	are like a singer of **l** songs,
Dan	9: 4	covenant and steadfast **l**
Hos	3: 1	"Go, **l** a woman who has a
	14: 4	I will **l** them freely, for my
Joel	2:13	and abounding in steadfast **l**,

Am	5:15	Hate evil and **l** good,
Jon	4: 2	and abounding in steadfast **l**,
Mic	6: 8	to **l** kindness, and to walk
Zeph	3:17	will renew you in his **l**;
Zech	8:17	and I **l** no false oath;
Mal	1: 2	I have **l** you, says the LORD.
Mt	5:44	**L** your enemies and pray for
	22:37	" 'You shall **l** the Lord your
Mk	10:21	Jesus, looking at him, **l** him
Lk	7:42	of them will **l** him more?"
	16:13	hate the one and **l** the other,
Jn	3:16	"For God so **l** the world that
	15:13	No one has greater **l** than this,
	21:15	do you **l** me more than these?"
Rom	5: 8	God proves his **l** for us in that
	8:28	for good for those who **l** God,
	8:35	us from the **l** of Christ?
1 Cor	13: 4	**L** is patient; **l** is kind;
	14: 1	Pursue **l** and strive for the
2 Cor	5:14	For the **l** of Christ urges us on
	9: 7	for God **l** a cheerful giver.
Gal	2:20	who **l** me and give himself
	5:22	fruit of the Spirit is **l**, joy,
Eph	3:17	rooted and grounded in **l**.
	5: 2	as Christ **l** us and gave himself
Phil	1: 9	that your **l** may overflow more
	2: 2	same **l**, being in full accord
Col	2: 2	be encouraged and united in **l**,
	3:14	clothe yourselves with **l**,
1 Thess	3:12	increase and abound in **l** for
	5: 8	the breastplate of faith and **l**,
2 Thess	2:10	they refused to **l** the truth
	3: 5	your hearts to the **l** of God
1 Tim	1: 5	**l** that comes from a pure
	6:10	For the **l** of money is a root
2 Tim	3: 4	of pleasure rather than **l** of
Titus	2: 4	the young women to **l**
Philem	1: 7	encouragement from your **l**,
Heb	13: 1	Let mutual **l** continue.
	13: 5	free from the **l** of money,
Jas	1:12	promised to those who **l** him.
1 Pet	1: 8	have not seen him, you **l** him;
	2:17	**L** the family of believers.
2 Pet	1: 7	and mutual affection with **l**.
1 Jn	2:15	Do not **l** the world or the
	4:16	God is **l**, and those who
	5: 2	**l** God and obey his
2 Jn	1: 5	let us **l** one another.
3 Jn	1: 6	they have testified to your **l**
Jude	1: 2	May mercy, peace, and **l** be
Rev	2: 4	you have abandoned the **l** you
	3:19	and discipline those whom I **l**.

LOW (ER) (LY)

Deut	28:43	you shall descend **l** and **l**.
Job	5:11	on high those who are **l**,
Ps	8: 5	made them a little **l** than God,
	116: 6	I was brought **l**, he saved me.
Prov	16:19	better to be of a **l** spirit
	29:23	who is **l** in spirit will obtain
Isa	40: 4	mountain and hill be made **l**;
Lk	1:52	and lifted up the **l**;
Rom	12:16	but associate with the **l**;
Eph	4: 9	descended into the **l** parts of
Heb	2: 7	a little while **l** than the angels;
Jas	1:10	the rich in being brought **l**,

LUST (S)

Ezek	23: 8	poured out their **l** upon her.
Mt	5:28	looks at a woman with **l** has

Rom	1:24	in the **l** of their hearts
Eph	4:22	corrupt and deluded by its **l**,
2 Pet	3: 3	and indulging their own **l**

M

MADE
Gen	1:31	saw everything that he had **m**,
	6: 6	sorry that he had **m**
	45: 9	God has **m** me lord of all
Ex	1:14	**m** their lives bitter with hard
Ex	15:25	the LORD **m** for them a statute
	36: 8	the workers **m** the tabernacle
Num	14:36	**m** all the congregation
	21: 2	Israel **m** a vow to the LORD
Deut	5: 2	LORD our God **m** a covenant
	32: 6	you and established you?
Josh	24:25	So Joshua **m** a covenant with
Judg	11:30	And Jephthah **m** a vow to the
1 Sam	15:11	"I regret that I **m** Saul king,
	20:16	Jonathan **m** a covenant with
2 Sam	23: 5	he has **m** with me an
1 Kings	12:28	the king took counsel, and **m**
2 Kings	18: 4	serpent that Moses had **m**,
	19:15	you have **m** heaven and earth.
2 Chr	3:10	holy place he **m** two carved
	4:19	Solomon **m** all the things that
Neh	9:10	You **m** a name for yourself,
	12:43	God had **m** them rejoice with
Tob	8:6	You **m** Adam, and for him
1 Macc	4:49	They **m** new holy vessels,
Job	7:20	Why have you **m** me your
	33: 4	The spirit of God has **m** me,
Ps	73:28	I have **m** the Lord GOD my
	100: 3	It is he that **m** us, and we are
	118:24	the day that the LORD has **m**;
	139:14	fearfully and wonder-fully **m**.
Prov	8:26	when he had not yet **m** earth
Eccl	3:11	He has **m** everything suitable
	7:13	what he has **m** crooked?
Sir	43:33	For the God has **m** all things,
Wis	14:8	the idol **m** with hands is
Isa	66: 2	these things my hand has **m**,
Jer	10:12	It is he who **m** the earth
	31:32	covenant that I **m** with their
Ezek	3:17	Mortal, I have **m** you a
Dan	3: 1	King Nebuchadnezzar **m** a
Am	5: 8	**m** the Pleiades and Orion,
Jon	1: 9	God of heaven, who **m** the sea
Mt	5:33	vows you have **m** to the Lord.'
Mk	2:27	"The sabbath was **m** for
	15: 5	But Jesus no further reply,
Lk	17:19	your faith has **m** you well."
	19:46	you have **m** it a den of robbers
Jn	1:18	who has **m** him known.
	9: 6	and **m** mud with the saliva
Acts	2:36	**m** him both Lord and Messiah
	10:15	"What God has **m** clean, you
1 Cor	1:20	Has not God **m** foolish the
	15:22	so all will be **m** alive in Christ.
2 Cor	5:21	our sake he **m** him to be sin
	12: 9	is **m** perfect in weakness."
Eph	2: 5	**m** us alive together with Christ
	2:14	he has **m** both groups into
Heb	2: 7	have **m** them for a little while
Heb	8: 9	like the covenant that I **m** with

Jas	3: 9	**m** in the likeness of God
Rev	5:10	have **m** them to be a kingdom
	14: 7	worship him who **m** heaven

MAJESTY (MAJESTIC)
Ex	15: 7	In the greatness of your **m** you
1 Chr	16:27	Honor and **m** are before him;
Esth	1: 4	splendor and pomp of his **m**
Job	37:22	around God is awesome **m**.
	40:10	yourself with **m** and dignity;
Ps	96: 6	Honor and **m** are before him;
	145: 5	glorious splendor of your **m**
Isa	26:10	do not see the **m** of the LORD.
	53: 2	he had no form or **m** that we
Dan	4:30	power and for my glorious **m**?"
Mic	5: 4	in the **m** of the name of the
Acts	19:27	will be deprived of her **m** that
Heb	1: 3	right hand of the **M** on high,
2 Pet	1:16	been eyewitnesses of his **m**.
Jude	1:25	our Lord, be glory, **m**, power,

MAKE (R)
Gen	1:26	"Let us **m** humankind in our
	24:40	and **m** your way successful.
Ex	6: 3	I did not **m** myself known to
	20: 4	not **m** for yourself an idol,
	32: 1	"Come, **m** gods for us, who
Num	6:25	LORD **m** his face to shine upon
	21: 8	"**M** a poisonous serpent,
Deut	7: 2	**M** no covenant with them and
	30: 9	**m** you abundantly prosperous
Josh	9: 7	can we **m** a treaty with you?"
2 Sam	7: 9	I will **m** for you a great name
Ezra	10: 3	us **m** a covenant with our God
	10:11	Now **m** confession to the LORD
Job	7:17	that you **m** so much of them,
	35:10	'Where is God my **M**, who
Ps	4: 8	O LORD, **m** me lie down in
	95: 6	kneel before the LORD, our **M**!
	110: 1	**m** your enemies your
Prov	3: 6	he will **m** straight your paths.
	22: 2	the LORD is the **m** of them all.
Eccl	5: 4	When you **m** a vow to God, do
Isa	29:16	say of its **m**, "He did not
Isa	40: 3	**m** straight in the desert a
	44: 9	All who **m** idols are nothing,
Jer	16:20	mortals **m** for themselves gods?
	30:10	no one shall **m** him afraid.
Ezek	37:26	I will **m** a covenant of peace
	39: 7	My holy name I will **m** known
Hos	2:18	I will **m** for you a covenant on
	8:14	Israel has forgotten his **M**,
Hab	2:18	idol once its **m** has shaped it
Mt	27:65	go, **m** it as secure as you
	28:19	**m** disciples of all nations,
Mk	1:17	I will **m** you fish for people."
Lk	1:17	to **m** ready a people prepared
Jn	1:23	'**M** straight the way of the
Acts	2:35	**m** your enemies your
Rom	14: 4	Lord is able to **m** them stand.
2 Cor	5: 9	we **m** it our aim to please
Heb	2:17	to **m** a sacrifice of atonement
	4:11	Let us therefore **m** every effort
2 Pet	1: 5	you must **m** every effort to
1 Jn	1:10	we **m** him a liar, and his
Rev	17:14	they will **m** war on the Lamb,
	19:19	gathered to **m** war against the

MAN ('S) (MEN)
Gen	2: 7	God formed **m** from the dust

	32:24	a **m** wrestled with him until
Lev	20:10	If a **m** commits adultery with
Num	13: 2	"Send **m** to spy out the land
Deut	22: 5	shall not wear a **m** apparel,
Judg	8:21	as the **m** is, so is his strength
	15:15	it he killed a thousand **m**.
1 Sam	13:14	a **m** after his own heart;
1 Kings	12:10	The young **m** who had grown
Esth	6: 7	"For the **m** whom the king
Job	38: 3	Gird up your loins like a **m**,
Ps	90: 1	A Prayer of Moses, the **m** of
	127: 5	is the **m** who has his quiver
Prov	30:19	and the way of a **m** with a girl.
Sir	25:8	**m** who lives with a sensible
Isa	53: 3	**m** of suffering and acquainted
Jer	30: 6	see every **m** with his hands
Dan	1:17	four young **m** God gave
Zech	6:12	is a **m** whose name is Branch:
Mt	9: 6	the Son of **M** has authority
	19: 5	a **m** shall leave his father and
Lk	6: 5	Son of **M** is lord of the
	9:30	saw two **m**, Moses and Elijah,
Jn	3:14	so must the Son of **M** be lifted
	9:35	believe in the Son of **M**?"
Acts	4:13	uneducated and ordinary **m**,
	7:56	Son of **M** standing at the
Rom	1:27	**M** committed shameless acts
	5:12	into the world through one **m**,
1 Cor	7: 2	should have his own wife
	11:14	that if a **m** wears long hair,
Eph	5:31	"For this reason a **m** will leave
1 Tim	2: 8	**m** should pray, lifting up holy
Titus	2: 2	Tell the older **m** to be
	2: 6	urge the younger **m** to be
Rev	14:14	the Son of **M**, with a golden

MANNA
Ex	16:31	house of Israel called it **m**;
Num	11: 6	nothing at all but this **m**
Deut	8:16	in the wilderness with **m** that
Josh	5:12	The **m** ceased on the day they
Ps	78:24	rained down on them **m** to eat,
Jn	6:49	ate the **m** in the wilderness,
Heb	9: 4	a golden urn holding the **m**,
Rev	2:17	give some of the hidden **m**,

MARRIAGE (MARRIED) (MARRIES)
Gen	20: 3	for she is a **m** woman."
Deut	24: 5	When a man is newly **m**, he
Sir	23:18	who sins against his **m** bed
Isa	62: 4	and your land shall be **m**.
Mt	5:32	whoever **m** a divorced woman
	19: 9	**m** another commits adultery."
Mk	12:23	For the seven had her."
Lk	17:27	marrying and being given in **m**,
Rom	7: 2	Thus a **m** woman is bound by
1 Cor	7:10	To the **m** I give this command
	7:38	who **m** his fiancee does well;
Gal	4:27	of the one who is **m**."
1 Tim	3:12	Let deacons be **m** only once,
Titus	1: 6	is blameless, **m** only once,
Heb	13: 4	Let **m** be held in honor by
Rev	19: 7	the **m** of the Lamb has come

MASTER (S)
Gen	4: 7	but you must **m** it."
Ex	21: 5	"I love my **m**, my wife, and my
Ps	12: 4	who is our **m**?"
Prov	25:13	refresh the spirit of their **m**.
Eccl	2:19	Yet they will be **m** of all

Mal 1: 6 And if I am a **m**, where is the
Mt 6:24 "No one can serve two **m**;
25:23 **m** said to him, 'Well done,
Lk 16:13 No slave can serve two **m**;
Jn 13:16 are not greater than their **m**,
Eph 6: 5 obey your earthly **m** with fear
6: 9 And, **m**, do the same to them
Col 3:22 obey your earthly **m** in
4: 1 you also have a **M** in heaven.
1 Tim 6: 1 regard their **m** as worthy of all
Titus 2: 9 to be submissive to their **m**
1 Pet 2:18 accept the authority of your **m**
2 Pet 2: 1 even deny the **M** who bought

MATURE (MATURITY)

1 Macc 16:3 Heaven's mercy are **m** in years.
Lk 8:14 and their fruit does not **m**.
1 Cor 2: 6 the **m** we do speak wisdom,
Eph 4:13 to **m**, to the measure
Phil 3:15 are **m** be of the same mind
Col 1:28 present everyone **m** in Christ.
4:12 may stand **m** and fully assured
Heb 5:14 solid food is for the **m**,
Jas 1: 4 you may be **m** and complete,

MEDITATE (MEDITATION)

Josh 1: 8 you shall **m** on it day and
Job 15: 4 and hindering **m** before God.
Ps 1: 2 his law they **m** day and night.
19:14 **m** of my heart be acceptable
143: 5 I **m** on the works of your

MEEK (NESS)

Ps 10:17 hear the desire of the **m**;
37:11 the **m** shall inherit the land,
Isa 29:19 The **m** shall obtain fresh joy in
Mt 5: 5 "Blessed are the **m**, for they
2 Cor 10: 1 the **m** and gentleness of Christ
Col 3:12 kindness, humility, **m**, and
Jas 1:21 with **m** the implanted word

MERCY (MERCIES) (MERCIFUL)

Gen 19:16 the LORD being **m** to him,
43:14 God Almighty grant you **m**
Ex 25:17 make a **m** seat of pure gold;
33:19 show **m** on whom I will show
Deut 4:31 LORD your God is a **m** God,
Josh 11:20 might receive no **m**, but be
1 Kings 20:31 house of Israel are **m** kings;
1 Chr 21:13 LORD, for his **m** is very great;
Neh 9:19 your great **m** did not forsake
9:31 you are a gracious and **m** God.
Job 9:15 I must appeal for **m** to my
Ps 51: 1 Have **m** on me, O God,
119:156 Great is your **m**, O LORD;
145: 8 The LORD is gracious and **m**,
Prov 12:10 the **m** of the wicked is cruel
21:10 find no **m** in their eyes.
Isa 47: 6 you showed them no **m**;
55: 7 that he may have **m** on them,
Jer 3:12 for I am **m**, says the LORD;
50:42 are cruel and have no **m**.
Dan 2:18 told them to seek **m** from the
9: 9 God belong **m** and forgiveness,
Hab 1:17 destroying nations without **m**?
3: 2 wrath may you remember **m**.
Zech 1:12 how long will you withhold **m**
7: 9 kindness and **m** to one another;
Mt 5: 7 "Blessed are the **m**, for they
9:13 'I desire **m**, not sacrifice.'

Mk 5:19 what **m** he has shown you."
10:47 Son of David, have **m** on
Lk 1:50 His **m** is for those who fear
6:36 Be **m**, just as your Father is
18:13 'God, be **m** to me, a sinner!'
Rom 9:15 have **m** on whom I have **m**
11:32 so that he may be **m** to all.
1 Cor 7:25 by the Lord's **m** is trustworthy.
2 Cor 1: 3 the Father of **m** and the God
4: 1 since it is by God's **m** that we
Eph 2: 4 God, who is rich in **m**, out of
Phil 2:27 But God had **m** on him,
1 Tim 1:13 I received **m** because I had
2 Tim 1:18 grant that he will find **m**
Titus 3: 5 according to his **m**,
Heb 2:17 he might be a **m** and faithful
4:16 we may receive **m** and find
Jas 2:13 **m** triumphs over judgment.
3:17 full of **m** and good fruits,
1 Pet 1: 3 By his great **m** he has given
2 Jn 1: 3 Grace, **m**, and peace will be
Jude 1:21 the **m** of our Lord Jesus Christ

MESSAGE (MESSENGER)

Judg 3:20 "I have a **m** from God for
Prov 26: 6 to send a **m** by a fool.
Isa 28: 9 whom will he explain the **m**?
Hag 1:13 Haggai, the **m** of the LORD,
Mal 2: 7 he is the **m** of the LORD of
3: 1 See, I am sending my **m** to
Mt 11:10 'See, I am sending my **m**
Jn 12:38 who has believed our **m**,
Acts 2:41 welcomed his **m** were baptized,
10:36 You know the **m** he sent to
Rom 10:16 who has believed our **m**?"
1 Cor 1:18 **m** about the cross is foolishness
2 Cor 5:19 the **m** of reconciliation
12: 7 a **m** of Satan to torment me
Heb 4: 2 **m** they heard did not benefit
1 Jn 1: 5 **m** we have heard from him

MESSIAH

Mt 1: 1 the genealogy of Jesus the **M**,
16:16 Peter answered, "You are the **M**,
Mk 13:21 'Look! Here is the **M**!'
Lk 2:11 Savior, who is the **M**, the Lord.
23:35 is the **M** of God, his chosen
Jn 1:41 "We have found the **M**"
10:24 If you are the **M**, tell us
Acts 2:36 made him both Lord and **M**,
3:20 may send the **M** appointed for
Rom 9: 5 the **M**, who is over all,
Rev 11:15 our Lord and of his **M**,

MIGHT (Y)

Gen 10: 9 a **m** hunter before the LORD."
49:24 hands of the **M** One of Jacob,
Ex 6: 1 by a **m** hand he will let them
Deut 7: 8 you out with a **m** hand,
10:17 great God, **m** and awesome,
Judg 16:30 He strained with all his **m**;
2 Sam 1:19 How the **m** have fallen!
6: 5 the LORD with all their **m**,
2 Chr 6:41 and the ark of your **m**.
2 Chr 14:11 helping the **m** and the weak.
Neh 9:32 great and **m** and awesome God,
Job 36: 5 "Surely God is **m** and does not
Ps 71:16 come praising the **m** deeds
89: 8 who is as **m** as you, O LORD?
150: 1 him in his **m** firmament!

Sir 15:8 is **m** in power and sees
Isa 9: 6 Wonderful Counselor, **M** God,
Jer 32:19 in counsel and **m** in deed;
Bar 2:11 Egypt with a **m** hand and with
Ezek 20:33 **m** hand and an outstretched
Dan 4: 3 how **m** his wonders!
Mic 3: 8 with justice and **m**, to declare
Zech 4: 6 Not by **m**, nor by power,
Mt 13:15 they **m** not look with their
Mk 14:35 the hour **m** pass from him.
Lk 1:49 **M** One has done great things
22: 4 about how he **m** betray him to
Jn 1: 7 that all **m** believe through him.
Acts 28:27 they **m** not look with their
1 Cor 9:22 I **m** by all means save some
10: 6 so that we **m** not desire evil
2 Cor 8: 9 his poverty you **m** become rich.
1 Pet 2:24 we **m** live for righteousness;
1 Jn 4: 9 that we **m** live through him.
Rev 18: 8 for **m** is the Lord God who

MIND (FUL) (S)

Gen 37:11 father kept the matter in **m**.
Num 23:19 that he should change his **m**.
Deut 29: 4 given you a **m** to understand,
1 Sam 15:29 not recant or change his **m**.
1 Chr 28: 9 for the LORD searches every **m**,
29: 9 with single **m** they had offered
Ps 7: 9 you who test the **m** and hearts,
110: 4 and will not change his **m**,
Eccl 2: 3 my **m** still guiding me with
3:11 past and future into their **m**,
Isa 26: 3 steadfast **m** you keep in peace
Jer 17:10 I the LORD test the **m** and
23:16 speak visions of their own **m**,
Lam 3:21 But this I call to **m**,
Ezek 28: 2 compare your **m** with the **m** of
Dan 4:16 Let his **m** be changed from
Jon 3: 9 may relent and change his **m**;
Mt 22:37 soul, and with all your **m**.'
Mk 3:21 has gone out of his **m**."
5:15 clothed and in his right **m**,
Lk 10:27 and with all your **m**;
24:45 opened their **m** to understand
Rom 8: 5 set their **m** on the things of
11:34 has known the **m** of the Lord?
1 Cor 1:10 united in the same **m** and the
2:16 But we have the **m** of Christ.
2 Cor 3:14 But their **m** were hardened.
4: 4 world has blinded the **m** of
Eph 4:23 in the spirit of your **m**,
Phil 2: 5 Let the same **m** be in you that
4: 7 guard your hearts and your **m**
Col 3: 2 Set your **m** on things that are
1 Thess 4:11 live quietly, to **m** your own
2 Tim 3: 8 corrupt **m** and counterfeit
Heb 8:10 my laws in their **m**, and write
1 Pet 1:13 prepare your **m** for action;
Rev 2:23 who searches **m** and hearts,
17: 9 calls for a **m** that has wisdom:

MINISTRY

Acts 1:17 allotted his share in this **m**."
Rom 11:13 to the Gentiles, I glorify my **m**
2 Cor 4: 1 we are engaged in this **m**,
5:18 the **m** of reconciliation;
Eph 4:12 for the work of **m**, for building
2 Tim 4: 5 carry out your **m** fully.
Heb 8: 6 obtained a more excellent **m**,

MIRACLES

1 Chr	16:12	works he has done, his **m**, and
Ps	78:11	the **m** that he had shown them
	105: 5	works he has done, his **m**, and
Acts	8:13	signs and great **m** that took
	19:11	extraordinary **m** through Paul,
1 Cor	12:10	to another the working of **m**,
Gal	3: 5	work **m** among you by your
Heb	2: 4	and wonders and various **m**,

MONEY

Ex	22:25	If you lend **m** to my people,
	30:16	take the atonement **m** from
2 Kings	12: 4	**m** offered as sacred donations
Ps	15: 5	who do not lend **m** at interest,
Eccl	5:10	lover of **m** will not be satisfied
	10:19	and **m** meets every need.
Isa	55: 1	buy wine and milk without **m**
Mic	3:11	its prophets give oracles for **m**;
Mk	11:15	the tables of the **m** changers
Lk	3:14	"Do not extort **m** from anyone
	9: 3	nor bag, nor bread, nor **m**
Jn	2:14	**m** changers seated at their
1 Tim	3: 3	and not a lover of **m**.
	6:10	For the love of **m** is a root of
2 Tim	3: 2	of themselves, lovers of **m**,
Heb	13: 5	free from the love of **m**,

MOON (S)

Gen	37: 9	sun, the **m**, and eleven stars
Deut	17: 3	the sun or the **m** or any
Josh	10:13	stood still, and the **m** stopped,
2 Chr	8:13	for the sabbaths, the new **m**,
Ps	8: 3	**m** and the stars that you have
	148: 3	Praise him, sun and **m**; praise
Song	6:10	fair as the **m**, bright as the sun,
Isa	13:10	the **m** will not shed its light
Jer	31:35	order of the **m** and the stars
Ezek	32: 7	the **m** shall not give its light
Joel	2:31	darkness, and the **m** to blood,
Hab	3:11	the **m** stood still in its exalted
Mt	24:29	the **m** will not give its light
Acts	2:20	darkness and the **m** to blood,
1 Cor	15:41	and another glory of the **m**,
Col	2:16	observing festivals, new **m**, or
Rev	6:12	the full **m** became like blood,
	21:23	no need of sun or **m** to shine

MORNING

Gen	1: 5	and there was **m**, the first day.
Ex	12:10	that remains until the **m**
	16:12	the **m** you shall have your fill
Deut	28:67	shall say, "If only it were **m**!"
2 Sam	23: 4	like the light of **m**, like the sun
Job	38: 7	the **m** stars sang together
Ps	5: 3	LORD, in the **m** you hear my
	30: 5	but joy comes with the **m**.
Prov	27:14	early in the **m**, will be counted
Eccl	11: 6	In the **m** sow your seed,
Isa	50: 4	**M** by **m** he wakens
Lam	3:23	they are new every **m**; great is
Hos	6: 4	Your love is like a **m** cloud,
	13: 3	like the **m** mist or like the dew
Zeph	3: 5	**m** he renders his judgment,
Lk	24:22	at the tomb early this **m**,
Acts	2:15	is only nine o'clock in the **m**.
2 Pet	1:19	day dawns and the **m** star rises
Rev	2:28	I will also give the **m** star.
	22:16	the bright **m** star."

MORTAL (S)

Num	23:19	or a **m**, that he should change
1 Sam	15:29	**m**, that he should change his
Job	9: 2	can a **m** be just before God?
	22: 2	"Can a **m** be of use to God
Ps	56:11	What can a mere **m** do to me?
Sir	35:24	repays **m** according to their
Isa	51:12	afraid of a mere **m** who must
Rom	1:23	resembling a **m** human being
	8:11	will give life to your **m** bodies
2 Cor	5: 4	what is **m** may be swallowed
1 Jn	5:16	There is sin that is **m**;
Rev	13: 3	its **m** wound had been healed.

MOTHER ('S) (S)

Gen	2:24	leaves his father and his **m**
	3:20	she was the **m** of all living.
Ex	20:12	your father and your **m**,
	21:15	Whoever strikes father or **m**
Deut	5:16	your father and your **m**,
	27:16	who dishonors father or **m**."
Judg	5: 7	Deborah, arose as a **m** in
1 Sam	2:19	His **m** used to make for him
2 Sam	20:19	a city that is a **m** in Israel;
1 Kings	19:20	kiss my father and my **m**,
Job	1:21	"Naked I came from my **m**
Ps	27:10	If my father and **m** forsake me,
	51: 5	a sinner when my **m**
Prov	1: 8	do not reject your **m** teaching;
	23:25	Let your father and **m** be glad;
Song	6: 9	darling of her **m**, flawless to
Isa	66:13	As a **m** comforts her child, so I
Jer	20:17	**m** would have been my grave
Hos	2: 2	Plead with your **m**, plead
	10:14	when **m** were dashed in pieces
Mic	7: 6	rises up against her **m**,
Mt	10:37	Whoever loves father or **m**
	12:48	Jesus replied, "Who is my **m**,
Mk	7:10	your father and your **m**;
Lk	14:26	not hate father and **m**, wife
Jn	3: 4	time into the **m** womb and
	19:27	disciple, "Here is your **m**."
Eph	5:31	leave his father and **m** and
1 Tim	5: 2	older women as **m**, to younger
Heb	7: 3	Without father, without **m**,
Rev	17: 5	"Babylon the great, **m** of

MOUNT (AIN) (AINS)

Gen	7:20	waters swelled above the **m**,
	8: 4	to rest on the **m** of Ararat.
Ex	3: 1	came to Horeb, the **m** of God.
Deut	5: 4	face to face at the **m**,
Job	14:18	the **m** falls and crumbles away,
Ps	36: 6	is like the mighty **m**,
	90: 2	Before the **m** were brought
Isa	40: 4	every **m** and hill be made low
	52: 7	beautiful upon the **m** are the
Ezek	34: 6	all the **m** and on every high
	39: 4	shall fall upon the **m** of Israel;
Dan	2:45	stone was cut from the **m**
Hos	10: 8	shall say to the **m**, Cover us,
Nah	1:15	Look! On the **m** the feet of
Mt	4: 8	very high **m** and showed him
	17:20	say to this **m**, 'Move from here
Mk	13:14	Judea must flee to the **m**;
Lk	3: 5	every **m** and hill shall be made
	23:30	say to the **m**, 'Fall on us';
Jn	4:21	neither on this **m** nor in
1 Cor	13: 2	remove **m**, but do not have love
2 Pet	1:18	with him on the holy **m**.

Rev	16:20	and no **m** were to be found;

MOURN (ING)

Gen	23: 2	Abraham went in to **m** for
Neh	8: 9	do not **m** or weep."
Esth	4: 3	was great **m** among the Jews,
	9:22	and from **m** into a holiday;
1 Macc	1:39	her feasts were turned into **m**,
Ps	30:11	You have turned my **m** into
Eccl	3: 4	time to **m**, and a time to dance
Sir	7:34	but **m** with those who **m**.
Isa	61: 2	to comfort all who **m**;
Jer	6:26	make **m** as for an only child
	31:13	I will turn their **m** into joy,
Lam	5:15	dancing has been turned to **m**.
Zech	12:10	they shall **m** for him,
Mt	5: 4	"Blessed are those who **m**,
	9:15	wedding guests cannot **m** as
Lk	6:25	for you will **m** and weep.
1 Cor	7:30	who **m** as though they were
Rev	21: 4	**m** and crying and pain will

MOUTH (S)

Ex	4:12	will be with your **m** and teach
Num	16:30	ground opens its **m** and
	22:38	word God puts in my **m**.
Deut	8: 3	comes from the **m** of the LORD.
	30:14	in your **m** and in your heart
Josh	1: 8	not depart out of your **m**;
2 Kings	4:34	putting his **m** upon his **m**,
Job	23:12	my bosom the words of his **m**.
	40: 4	lay my hand on my **m**.
Ps	19:14	Let the words of my **m** and the
	119:103	sweeter than honey to my **m**!
	141: 3	Set a guard over my **m**, O LORD;
Prov	8: 7	for my **m** will utter truth;
	15: 2	the **m** of fools pour out folly
	26:28	a flattering **m** works ruin.
Eccl	5: 2	Never be rash with your **m**,
Song	1: 2	with the kisses of his **m**!
Wis	1:11	lying **m** destroys the soul.
Sir	28:25	and a bolt for your **m**.
Isa	40: 5	the **m** of the LORD has spoken
	49: 2	my **m** like a sharp sword,
	53: 7	he did not open his **m**.
Jer	1: 9	put my words in your **m**.
Ezek	3: 2	So I opened my **m**, and he
Dan	6:22	and shut the lions' **m**
	7: 8	and a **m** speaking arrogantly.
Hos	6: 5	them by the words of my **m**,
Mal	2: 7	seek instruction from his **m**,
Mt	4: 4	comes from the **m** of God.' "
Lk	6:45	of the heart that the **m** speaks.
Acts	8:32	he does not open his **m**.
Rom	3:14	"Their **m** are full of cursing
Eph	4:29	evil talk come out of your **m**,
2 Thess	2: 8	with the breath of his **m**,
Heb	11:33	shut the **m** of lions,
Jas	3:10	same **m** come blessing and
1 Pet	2:22	deceit was found in his **m**."
Rev	3:16	spit you out of my **m**.
	10:10	sweet as honey in my **m**,

MURDER (ER) (ERS)

Ex	20:13	You shall not **m**.
Num	35:31	a **m** must be put to death
Deut	5:17	You shall not **m**.
Hos	4: 2	Swearing, lying, and **m**, and
Mt	5:21	'You shall not **m**;
	15:19	evil intentions, **m**, adultery,

Mk	10:19	'You shall not **m**; You shall not
Lk	23:25	prison for insurrection and **m**,
Jn	8:44	was a **m** from the beginning
Acts	3:14	asked to have a **m** given to
Rom	1:29	Full of envy, **m**, strife, deceit,
Jas	2:11	"You shall not **m**."
1 Jn	3:12	And why did he **m** him?
Rev	21:8	faithless, the polluted, the **m**,

MYSTERY

Dan	2:19	the **m** was revealed to Daniel
	4:9	no **m** is too difficult for you
Rom	16:25	of the **m** that was kept secret
1 Cor	2:1	proclaiming the **m** of God
	15:51	I will tell you a **m**!
Eph	1:9	known to us the **m** of his will,
	6:19	boldness the **m** of the gospel,
Col	1:26	the **m** that has been hidden
	2:2	the knowledge of God's **m**,
	4:3	may declare the **m** of Christ,
2 Thess	2:7	the **m** of lawlessness is already
1 Tim	3:9	hold fast to the **m** of the faith
	3:16	the **m** of our religion is great
Rev	1:20	As for the **m** of the seven stars
	10:7	the **m** of God will be fulfilled

N

NAKED

Gen	2:25	man and his wife were both **n**,
Job	1:21	**N** I came from my mother's

NAME

Gen	2:19	living creature, that was its **n**.
Num	17:2	Write each man's **n** on his
Judg	13:17	the the LORD, "What is your **n**,
2 Sam	7:9	I will make for you a great **n**,
1 Kings	8:29	My **n** shall be there,'
Ezra	6:12	God who has established his **n**
Prov	10:7	the **n** of the wicked will rot
Eccl	7:1	A good **n** is better than
Song	1:3	your **n** is perfume poured out;
Lam	3:55	I called on your **n**, O LORD,
Ezek	20:9	acted for the sake of my **n**,
Dan	2:20	Blessed be the **n** of God from
Joel	2:32	who calls on the **n** of the LORD
Mic	5:4	majesty of the **n** of the LORD
Zech	13:9	my **n**, and I will answer them
Mal	1:6	O priests, who despise my **n**.
Mt	6:9	heaven, hallowed be your **n**.
Mk	11:9	comes in the **n** of the Lord!
Lk	1:31	and you will **n** him Jesus.
Jn	1:12	him, who believed in his **n**,
Acts	2:21	who calls on the **n** of the Lord
1 Cor	6:11	you were justified in the **n** of
Phil	2:9	the **n** that is above every **n**
Col	3:17	do everything in the **n** of the
Heb	1:4	**n** he has inherited is more
Jas	5:14	them with oil in the **n** of

NATION (S)

Ex	34:24	I will cast out **n** before you,
Deut	15:6	you will lend to many **n**, but
1 Kings	4:34	from all the **n** to hear the
Ps	2:1	Why do the **n** conspire, and
Joel	3:2	I will gather all the **n** and

Zeph	3:8	for my decision is to gather **n**,
Hag	2:7	I will shake all the **n**,
Mal	3:12	Then all **n** will count you
Mt	24:9	hated by all **n** because of my
Mk	11:17	a house of prayer for all the **n**?
Rev	2:26	I will give authority over the **n**;

NEAR

Deut	30:14	No, the word is very **n** to you;
Ps	69:18	Draw **n** to me, redeem me,
Isa	55:6	call upon him while he is **n**;
Joel	1:15	for the day of the LORD is **n**,
Mal	3:5	I will draw **n** to you for
Mk	1:15	kingdom of God has come **n**;
Rom	10:8	The word is **n** you, on your
Jas	4:8	**n** to God, and he will draw **n**
Rev	1:3	written in it; for the time is **n**.

NEED (Y)

1 Sam	2:8	lifts the **n** from the ash heap,
Ps	9:18	For the **n** shall not always be
Prov	14:31	are kind to the **n** honor him.
Sir	4:3	or delay giving to the **n**.

NEIGHBOR

Ex	3:22	each woman shall ask her **n**
Deut	5:20	false witness against your **n**.
Prov	24:28	against your **n** without cause
Isa	19:2	against the other, **n** against **n**,
Mt	19:19	shall love your **n** as yourself."
Lk	10:29	Jesus, "And who is my **n**?"

NEVER

Gen	8:21	I will **n** again curse the ground
2 Chr	18:7	he **n** prophesies anything
Prov	10:30	righteous will **n** be removed,
Isa	51:6	deliverance will **n** be ended.
Jer	33:17	David shall **n** lack a man to sit
Dan	6:26	kingdom shall **n** be destroyed,
Joel	2:26	people shall **n** again be put to
Mt	7:23	declare to them, 'I **n** knew
Mk	3:29	the Holy Spirit can **n** have
Jn	6:35	comes to me will **n** be hungry,
1 Cor	13:8	**n** ends. But as for prophecies
Heb	13:5	I will **n** leave you or forsake
1 Pet	5:4	crown of glory that **n** fades

NEW

Ex	1:8	a **n** king arose over Egypt,
Jdt	16:1	Raise to him a **n** psalm;
1 Macc	4:47	built a **n** altar like the former
Ps	33:3	Sing to him a **n** song;
Eccl	1:9	is nothing **n** under the sun.
Sir	9:10	for **n** ones cannot equal them.
Jer	31:31	I will make a **n** covenant with
Lam	3:23	they are **n** every morning;
Mt	9:17	**n** wine put into old wineskins
Mk	1:27	A **n** teaching—with authority!
Lk	22:20	is the **n** covenant in my blood.
Jn	13:34	I give you a **n** commandment,
Acts	17:19	know what this **n** teaching
1 Cor	11:25	This cup is the **n** covenant in
2 Cor	5:17	Christ, there is a **n** creation:
1 Pet	1:3	he has given us a **n** birth into
2 Pet	3:13	we wait for **n** heavens and a **n**

NIGHT

Gen	1:5	and the darkness he called **N**.
Ex	13:21	a pillar of fire by **n**, to give
Josh	1:8	shall meditate on it day and **n**,

Mt	24:43	**n** the thief was coming,
Lk	6:12	spent the **n** in prayer to God.
Jn	3:2	He came to Jesus by **n** and
1 Cor	11:23	Lord Jesus on the **n** when he
1 Thess	5:2	like a thief in the **n**.
Rev	20:10	tormented day and **n** forever

NOTHING

2 Sam	24:24	Lord my God that cost me **n**.
2 Chr	9:2	was **n** hidden from Solomon
Job	1:9	Does Job fear God for **n**?
Ps	73:25	there is **n** on earth that I desire
Prov	13:4	the lazy craves, and gets **n**,
Eccl	1:9	there is **n** new under the sun.
Sir	39:20	**n** is too marvelous for him.
Isa	53:2	**n** in his appearance that we
Mt	17:20	**n** will be impossible for you
Lk	1:37	**n** will be impossible with God
Jn	5:30	I can do **n** on my own.
Rom	7:18	For I know that **n** good dwells
1 Cor	13:2	but do not have love, I am **n**.

NUMEROUS

Gen	17:2	will make you exceedingly **n**."
Ex	1:9	Israelite people are more **n**
Zech	10:8	be as **n** as they were before.

O

OBEY

Ex	19:5	if you **o** my voice and keep my
Deut	12:28	Be careful to **o** all these words
Josh	24:24	will serve, and him we will **o**."
1 Sam	15:22	to **o** is better than sacrifice,
Mt	8:27	the winds and the sea **o** him?'
Lk	11:28	the word of God and **o** it!"
Acts	5:29	**o** God rather than any human
2 Cor	10:5	thought captive to **o** Christ.
Eph	6:1	Children, **o** your parents in
Col	3:22	Slaves, **o** your earthly masters
Heb	13:17	**O** your leaders and submit to
1 Jn	3:24	All who **o** his commandments

OFFER (ING) (INGS)

Gen	22:2	**o** him there as a burnt **o**
Ex	29:38	what you shall **o** on the altar:
Deut	12:14	you shall **o** your burnt **o**
Ps	4:5	**O** right sacrifices,
Hos	14:2	we will **o** the fruit of our lips
Mt	5:24	then come and **o** your gift.
Heb	9:25	Nor was it to **o** himself again

OIL

Ex	29:7	You shall take the anointing **o**,
1 Sam	16:13	Samuel took the horn of **o**,
1 Kings	17:16	neither did the jug of **o** fail,
2 Kings	4:6	Then the **o** stopped flowing.
Ps	23:5	you anoint my head with **o**;
Prov	5:3	her speech is smoother than **o**;
Mt	25:3	they took no **o** with them;
Jas	5:14	anointing them with **o** in the

OLD

Gen	17:12	when he is eight days **o**,
Num	1:3	twenty years **o** and upward,
Deut	32:7	Remember the days of **o**,

Ps	74:12	Yet God my King is from of **o**,
Sir	9:10	Do not abandon **o** friends,
Joel	2:28	**o** men shall dream dreams,
Mk	2:22	new wine into **o** wineskins;
Jn	3: 4	be born after having grown **o**?
Acts	2:17	**o** men shall dream dreams.
1 Cor	5: 7	Clean out the **o** yeast
2 Cor	5:17	everything **o** has passed away;

ONE

Gen	2:24	and they become **o** flesh.
Ps	14: 3	there is no **o** who does good,
Eccl	4: 9	Two are better than **o**,
Sir	1:8	There is but **o** who is wise,
Ezek	37:22	I will make them **o** nation
Mal	2:10	Have we not all **o** father?
Mk	10: 8	the two shall become **o** flesh.'
Lk	10:42	there is need of only **o** thing.
Jn	1:18	No **o** has ever seen God.
Rom	3:10	There is no **o** who is righteous,
1 Cor	8: 4	there is no God but **o**."
Eph	4: 5	**o** Lord, **o** faith, **o** baptism
1 Tim	2: 5	**o** God; there is also **o** mediator
2 Pet	3: 8	But do not ignore this **o** fact,

ONLY

Gen	7:23	**O** Noah was left,
Num	11: 4	If **o** we had meat to eat
Deut	15: 5	if **o** you will obey the LORD
1 Kings	18:22	I, even I **o**, am left a prophet
Ps	37: 8	Do not fret—it leads **o** to evil.
Mt	4:10	Lord your God, and serve **o**
Mk	13:32	Son, but **o** the Father.
Jn	1:18	It is God the **o** Son,
Rom	3:29	Or is God the God of Jews **o**?
1 Tim	1:17	the **o** God, be honor and glory
1 Jn	4: 9	God sent his **o** Son into the

OPEN (ED)

Deut	28:12	The LORD will **o** for you his
1 Macc	3:48	they **o** the book of the law
Ps	78: 2	I will **o** my mouth in a parable
Song	5: 2	**O** to me, my sister, my love
Isa	53: 7	yet he did not **o** his mouth
Mt	13:35	I will **o** my mouth to speak in

OPPRESS (OPPRESSED)

Ex	22:21	shall not wrong or **o** a resident
Ps	105:14	he allowed no one to **o** them
Sir	4:9	Rescue the **o** from the
Zech	7:10	not **o** the widow, the orphan
Jas	2: 6	is it not the rich who **o** you?
Jdt	9:11	of the lowly, helper of the **o**,

ORPHAN

Ex	22:22	not abuse any widow or **o**.
Isa	1:17	defend the **o**, plead for the
Hos	14: 3	In you the **o** finds mercy."

OTHER (S)

Ex	20: 3	you shall have no **o** gods
Deut	4:35	there is no **o** besides him.
Judg	2:19	following **o** gods,
1 Sam	8:20	we also may be like **o** nations,
2 Kings	17: 7	They had worshiped **o** gods
2 Chr	2: 5	God is greater than **o** gods.
Sir	1:4	was created before all **o**
Isa	44: 8	There is no **o** rock
Dan	3:29	**o** god who is able to deliver
Mt	6:24	to the one and love the **o**,

Lk	17:34	will be taken and the **o** left.
Jn	20:30	Now Jesus did many **o** signs

OX

Deut	25: 4	You shall not muzzle an **o**
1 Cor	9: 9	You shall not muzzle an **o**

P

PAIN

Gen	3:16	**p** you shall bring forth children
Job	33:19	chastened with **p** upon their
Jer	15:18	Why is my **p** unceasing,
Jn	16:21	woman is in labor, she has **p**,
1 Pet	2:19	endure **p** while suffering
Rev	21: 4	crying and **p** will be no more,

PARABLE (S)

Ps	78: 2	I will open my mouth in a **p**;
Sir	39:2	penetrates the subtleties of **p**;
Mt	13:18	Hear then the **p** of the sower.
Lk	20:19	had told this **p** against them,

PARADISE

Lk	23:43	you will be with me in **P**."
Rev	2: 7	of life that is in the **p** of God.

PARENT

Deut	8: 5	that as a **p** disciplines a child
Ezek	18:20	nor a **p** suffer for the iniquity

PARTIALITY

Deut	16:19	you must not show **p**
Job	13: 8	Will you show **p** toward him,
Prov	28:21	To show **p** is not good
Sir	35:15	and with him there is no **p**.
Mt	22:16	do not regard people with **p**.
Rom	2:11	For God shows no **p**.
Eph	6: 9	with him there is no **p**.
Jas	3:17	a trace of **p** or hypocrisy.

PASSOVER

Ex	12:11	It is the **p** of the LORD.
Num	9: 2	Let the Israelites keep the **p**
Josh	5:10	**p** in the evening on the
2 Kings	23:21	Keep the **p** to the LORD your
Ezra	6:19	the returned exiles kept the **p**
Mk	14:12	when the **P** lamb is sacrificed,
Lk	22: 8	Go and prepare the **P** meal for
Heb	11:28	By faith he kept the **P**

PATH

Ps	16:11	You show me the **p** of life.
Prov	12:28	the **p** of righteousness there is
Mt	13: 4	some seeds fell on the **p**,

PATIENT

Neh	9:30	years you were **p** with them,
Job	6:11	is my end, that I should be **p**?
Wis	15:1	our God, are kind and true, **p**,
Sir	1:23	Those who are **p** stay calm
Lk	8:15	bear fruit with **p** endurance.
Rom	12:12	in hope, be **p** in suffering,
1 Cor	13: 4	Love is **p**; love is kind;
1 Thess	5:14	help the weak, be **p** with all of
Jas	5: 7	Be **p**, therefore, beloved

PAY

Lev	25:51	shall **p** for their redemption
Num	16:15	**P** no attention to their
Deut	24:15	You shall **p** them their wages
1 Macc	2:68	**P** back the Gentiles in full,
Prov	19:19	tempered person will **p** the
Mt	22:17	to **p** taxes to the emperor,
Lk	19: 8	I will **p** back four times as
Rom	13: 7	**P** to all what is due

PEACE

Lev	26: 6	And I will grant **p** in the land,
Num	6:26	upon you, and give you **p**.
1 Sam	1:17	Then Eli answered, "Go in **p**;
1 Kings	2:33	shall be **p** from the LORD
1 Chr	19:19	they made **p** with David,
Job	22:21	Agree with God, and be at **p**
Ps	34:14	evil, and do good; seek **p**,
Prov	12:20	those who counsel **p** have joy.
Eccl	3: 8	time for war, and a time for **p**
Isa	9: 6	Everlasting Father, Prince of **P**.
Jer	6:14	"**P**, **p**," when there is no **p**
Lam	3:17	my soul is bereft of **p**
Zech	8:19	therefore love truth and **p**.
Mt	10:34	I have come to bring **p** to the
Mk	9:50	and be at **p** with one another."
Lk	2:14	on earth **p** among those
Jn	14:27	**P** I leave with you
Gal	5:22	of the Spirit is love, joy, **p**,
Phil	4: 7	the **p** of God, which surpasses
Col	3:15	And let the **p** of Christ rule in
1 Thess	5: 3	say, "There is **p** and security,"
2 Thess	3:16	Lord of **p** himself give you **p**
2 Tim	2:22	righteousness, faith, love, and **p**
Heb	12:14	Pursue **p** with everyone,
1 Pet	3:11	let them seek **p** and pursue it.

PEOPLE

Gen	11: 6	Look, they are one **p**
Ex	5: 1	the God of Israel, 'Let my **p** go
Num	14:11	How long will this **p** despise
Deut	4:20	to become a **p** of his very own
Josh	3:16	Then the **p** crossed over
Ruth	1:16	your **p** shall be my **p**
2 Kings	23: 3	**p** joined in the covenant.
1 Chr	29:17	and now I have seen your **p**,
2 Chr	7: 5	**p** dedicated the house of God
Ezra	3: 1	the **p** gathered together in
Neh	4: 6	for the **p** had a mind to work
Jdt	13:17	the enemies of your **p**."
Esth	3: 6	been told who Mordecai's **p**
1 Macc	3:43	us restore the ruins of our **p**,
Ps	29:11	LORD give strength to his **p**!
Isa	1: 3	my **p** do not understand.
Ezek	13:23	I will save my **p** from your
Zech	8: 7	I will save my **p** from the east
Mt	1:21	will save his **p** from their sins."
Mk	8:27	Who do **p** say that I am?"
Lk	1:17	a **p** prepared for the Lord."
Jn	18:14	have one person die for the **p**.
Acts	3:22	your own **p** a prophet like me.
Rom	9:25	were not my **p** I will call 'my **p**,'
2 Cor	6:16	and they shall be my **p**.
Titus	1:10	also many rebellious **p**,
1 Pet	2:10	Once you were not a **p**,
Rev	18: 4	Come out of her, my **p**,

PERFECT

2 Sam	22:31	This God—his way is **p**;
Ps	19: 7	law of the LORD is **p**,

Perfect — Proclaim

Song	6: 9	My dove, my **p** one,
Wis	6:15	thought on her is **p**
Ezek	27: 3	said, "I am **p** in beauty."
Mt	5:48	Be **p**, therefore, as your
2 Cor	12: 9	for power is made **p** in
Col	3:14	everything together in **p**
1 Jn	4:18	but **p** love casts out fear;

PERISH

Lev	26:38	You shall **p** among the nations,
Esth	4:16	and if I **p**, I **p**."
Ps	37:20	But the wicked **p**,
Prov	11:10	when the wicked **p**, there is
Lk	13: 3	you will all **p** as they did.
Jn	10:28	never **p**. No one will snatch
Acts	8:20	May your silver **p** with you,
Heb	1:11	they will **p**, but you remain;
2 Pet	3: 9	not wanting any to **p**,

PERSECUTE (D)

Ps	119:84	will you judge those who **p** me?
Mt	5:44	and pray for those who **p** you,
Lk	21:12	they will arrest you and **p** you;
Jn	15:20	they **p** me, they will **p** you;
Acts	9: 4	Saul, Saul, why do you **p** me?"
Rom	12:14	Bless those who **p** you;

PHARAOH

Gen	41:14	Then **P** sent for Joseph,
Ex	1:22	Then **P** commanded all his
Rom	9:17	For the scripture says to **P**,

PHARISEE (S)

Lk	11:37	a **P** invited him to dine with
Jn	3: 1	was a **P** named Nicodemus,
Acts	23: 6	Brothers, I am a **P**, a son of **P**.

PHILISTINE (S)

Gen	21:34	in the land of the **P**.
1 Sam	14: 1	let us go over to the **P** garrison

PIERCED

Zech	12:10	the one whom they have **p**,
Rev	1: 7	even those who **p** him;

PILLAR

Gen	19:26	and she became a **p** of salt.
Ex	13:21	in a **p** of cloud by day,
Rev	3:12	I will make you a **p** in the

PLAGUE

Ex	11: 1	one more **p** upon Pharaoh
Num	14:37	died by a **p** before the LORD.
Rev	16:21	cursed God for the **p** of the

PLANT

Gen	1:29	given you every **p** yielding
Eccl	3: 2	a time to die; a time to **p**,
Am	9:15	I will **p** them upon their land,
Mt	15:13	Every **p** that my heavenly

PLEASE (D) (PLEASING)

Ps	69:31	This will **p** the LORD more
Sir	44:16	Enoch **p** the Lord and was
Rom	8: 8	are in the flesh cannot **p** God.
1 Thess	2: 4	not to **p** mortals, but to **p** God
1 Tim	5: 4	for this is **p** in God's sight.
Heb	11: 6	faith it is impossible to **p** God,

PLEASURE

Prov	18: 2	takes no **p** in understanding,
Eccl	2: 2	and of **p**, "What use is it?"
Ezek	18:32	For I have no **p** in the death of
2 Tim	3: 4	lovers of **p** rather than lovers

POOR

Deut	15:11	Open your hand to the **p** and
1 Sam	2: 8	He raises up the **p** from the
Job	5:16	So the **p** have hope,
Ps	34: 6	This **p** soul cried, and was
Prov	13: 7	others pretend to be **p**,
Eccl	4:13	Better is a **p** but wise youth
Mt	5: 3	Blessed are the **p** in spirit,
Mk	12:42	A **p** widow came
Lk	4:18	bring good news to the **p**.
Jn	12: 8	You always have the **p** with
2 Cor	8: 9	for your sakes he became **p**,
Jas	2: 5	Has not God chosen the **p** in

POSSESS

Deut	28:21	that you are entering to **p**.
1 Sam	10: 6	spirit of the LORD will **p** you,
Ps	25:13	and their children shall **p** the
Isa	60:21	they shall **p** the land forever.

POUR

Deut	12:16	shall **p** it out on the ground
Ps	62: 8	O people; **p** out your heart
Isa	44: 3	For I will **p** water on the
Joel	2:28	Then afterward I will **p** out my
Acts	2:17	that I will **p** out my Spirit

POWER

Ex	15: 6	O LORD, glorious in **p**
1 Sam	11: 6	God came upon Saul in **p**
Jdt	9:14	the God of all **p** and might,
Job	36:22	God is exalted in his **p**;
Ps	66: 3	Because of your great **p**,
Eccl	8: 8	No one has **p** over the wind
Sir	39:18	can limit his saving **p.**
Isa	40:29	He gives **p** to the faint,
Jer	27: 5	by my great **p** and my
Dan	6:27	from the **p** of the lions."
Zech	4: 6	Not by might, nor by **p**,
Mt	22:29	the scriptures nor the **p** of
Mk	9: 1	God has come with **p**."
Lk	1:17	With the spirit and **p** of Elijah
Jn	19:11	You would have no **p** over me
Acts	1: 8	receive **p** when the Holy Spirit
1 Cor	1:18	being saved it is the **p** of God.
Phil	3:10	know Christ and the **p** of his
2 Pet	1: 3	His divine **p** has given us
Jude	1:25	our Lord, be glory, majesty, **p**,

PRAISE

Ex	15: 2	and I will **p** him,
2 Chr	20:21	sing to the LORD and **p** him
Ps	22:23	You who fear the LORD, **p** him!
Prov	31:31	and let her works **p** her
Isa	38:18	death cannot **p** you;
Mt	21:16	prepared **p** for yourself
Lk	19:37	disciples began to **p** God
Rom	15:11	"**P** the Lord, all you Gentiles
1 Cor	14:15	I will sing **p** with the spirit,
Jas	5:13	They should sing songs of **p**.
Rev	19: 5	"**P** our God, all you his

PRAY

1 Sam	12:23	by ceasing to **p** for you;

1 Kings	8:30	when they **p** toward this place;
Job	42: 8	my servant Job shall **p** for you,
Ps	122: 6	**P** for the peace of Jerusalem
Jer	7:16	do not **p** for this people,
Mt	6: 5	And whenever you **p**,
Lk	6:28	**p** for those who abuse you
1 Thess	5:17	**p** without ceasing,
2 Thess	1:11	To this end we always **p** for
Jas	5:16	**p** for one another,

PRECEPT (S)

Ps	19: 8	the **p** of the LORD are right
Sir	18:14	and who are eager for his **p**
Isa	28:10	For it is **p** upon **p**,

PRECIOUS

1 Sam	26:21	because my life was **p** in your
Ps	116:15	**P** in the sight of the LORD
Prov	3:15	She is more **p** than jewels,
1 Pet	1:19	but with the **p** blood of Christ,

PREPARE

Ps	23: 5	You **p** a table before me
Isa	40: 3	wilderness **p** the way of the
Mal	3: 1	my messenger to **p** the way
Mt	3: 3	**p** the way of the Lord
Jn	14: 2	I go to **p** a place for you?

PRESENCE

1 Sam	2:21	Samuel grew up in the **p** of
Job	1:12	Satan went out from the **p** of
Ps	16:11	In your **p** there is fullness of
Jn	17: 5	me in your own **p** with the
Heb	9:24	to appear in the **p** of God on
Rev	20:11	the heaven fled from his **p**,

PRIDE

2 Chr	32:26	himself for the **p** of his heart,
Ps	20: 7	Some take **p** in chariots,
Prov	11: 2	When **p** comes, then comes
Sir	10:13	For the beginnng of **p** is sin,
Isa	2:11	the **p** of everyone shall be
2 Cor	7: 4	I have great **p** in you;

PRIEST (HOOD)

Gen	14:18	he was **p** of God Most High.
Ex	18: 1	Jethro, the **p** of Midian,
Num	5:10	anyone gives to the **p** shall be
1 Sam	2:11	in the presence of the **p** Eli.
2 Macc	11:3	the high **p** for sale every year.
Ps	110: 4	"You are a **p** forever
Jer	23:11	Both prophet and **p** are
Ezek	1: 3	the Lord came to the **p** Ezekiel
Mk	14:63	high **p** tore his clothes
Heb	3: 1	Jesus, the apostle and high **p**

PRISON

Ps	142: 7	Bring me out of **p**,
Isa	42: 7	**p** those who sit in darkness
Mt	25:36	I was in **p** and you visited me.'
Lk	22:33	I am ready to go with you to **p**
Acts	12: 5	While Peter was kept in **p**,
Heb	13: 3	those who are in **p**,
Rev	20: 7	will be released from his **p**

PROCLAIM (ED)

Deut	32: 3	For I will **p** the name of the
Ps	22:31	and **p** his deliverance to a
Isa	61: 1	to **p** liberty to the captives,
Jon	3: 2	Nineveh, that great city, and **p**

Mt 10:27 **p** from the housetops.
Lk 4:19 to **p** the year of the Lord's favor
1 Cor 11:26 you **p** the Lord's death until he
Phil 1:15 Some **p** Christ from envy and

PROMISE
1 Kings 8:20 Lord has upheld the **p** that he
Neh 9: 8 and you have fulfilled your **p,**
Ps 105:42 For he remembered his holy **p,**
Acts 2:39 For the **p** is for you,
Eph 6: 2 first commandment with a **p:**
2 Pet 3: 9 Lord is not slow about his **p,**

PROPHECY (NOUN)
Prov 29:18 Where there is no **p,**
Acts 21: 9 who had the gift of **p.**
Rev 19:10 Jesus is the spirit of **p."**

PROPHESY (VERB)
Isa 30:10 Do not **p** to us what is right
Jer 5:31 the prophets **p** falsely,
Ezek 13: 2 **p** against the prophets of Israel
Am 7:16 Do not **p** against Israel,
Mt 7:22 Lord, did we not **p** in your
Lk 22:64 **P**! Who is it that struck you?

PROPHET (NOUN)
Ex 7: 1 brother Aaron shall be your **p.**
Deut 18:18 I will raise up for them a **p**
1 Sam 3:20 trustworthy **p** of the LORD.
1 Kings 18:36 the **p** Elijah came near
2 Kings 6:12 It is Elisha, the **p** in Israel,
2 Chr 35:18 since the days of the **p** Samuel;
1 Macc 14:41 until a trustworthy **p** should
Jer 1: 5 appointed you a **p** to the
Ezek 33:33 they shall know that a **p** has
Hos 9: 7 Israel cries, "The **p** is a fool,
Mal 4: 5 I will send you the **p** Elijah
Mt 11: 9 did you go out to see? A **p?**
Lk 4:24 no **p** is accepted in the **p's**
Jn 1:21 Are you the **p?"**

PROSPER
Gen 39:23 the LORD made it **p.**
Ps 1: 3 all that they do, they **p.**
Isa 53:10 the will of the LORD shall **p.**

PROSTITUTE
Deut 23:17 Israel shall be a temple **p;**
Josh 6:25 But Rahab the **p,** with her
Prov 23:27 For a **p** is a deep pit;
1 Cor 6:16 whoever is united to a **p**
Heb 11:31 By faith Rahab the **p** did not

PROUD
2 Chr 32:25 for his heart was **p.**
Ps 94: 2 the **p** what they deserve!
Prov 16:19 divide the spoil with the **p.**
Sir 10:9 How can dust and ashes be **p?**
Ezek 28:17 Your heart was **p** because of
Hos 13: 6 and their heart was **p;**
Ob 1: 3 Your **p** heart has deceived you,
Rom 11:20 So do not become **p,** but
Jas 4: 6 God opposes the **p,** but gives

PROVIDE
Gen 22:14 The LORD will **p";**
1 Cor 10:13 he will also **p** the way out
1 Tim 5: 8 And whoever does not **p** for

PUNISH
Ex 32:34 I will **p** them for their sin."
2 Sam 7:14 I will **p** him with a rod
Isa 13:11 I will **p** the world for its evil
Jer 2:19 Your wickedness will **p** you,

PURE
Ex 25:11 shall overlay it with **p** gold,
2 Sam 22:27 the **p** you show yourself **p,**
Tob 8:15 O God, with every **p** blessing;
Job 4:17 human beings be **p** before
Prov 15:26 but gracious words are **p.**
Wis 7:25 a **p** emanation of the glory
Hab 1:13 Your eyes are too **p** to behold
Mt 5: 8 Blessed are the **p** in heart,
Phil 4: 8 whatever is just, whatever is **p,**
1 Tim 1: 5 that comes from a **p** heart,
Titus 1:15 To the **p** all things are **p,**
Jas 1:27 Religion that is **p** and
Rev 21:18 while the city is **p** gold,

PURPOSE
Ps 138: 8 The LORD will fulfill his **p** for
Prov 19:21 but it is the **p** of the LORD
Rom 8:28 are called according to his **p.**
Jas 1:18 fulfillment of his own **p** he

PURSUE
Ps 34:14 seek peace, and **p** it.
Isa 51: 1 me, you that **p** righteousness,
Rom 14:19 Let us then **p** what makes for
1 Cor 14: 1 **P** love and strive
1 Tim 6:11 **p** righteousness, godliness,
Heb 12:14 **P** peace with everyone,
1 Pet 3:11 let them seek peace and **p** it.

Q

QUESTION
Job 38: 3 I will **q** you,
Sir 19:15 **Q** a friend, for often it is
Mt 22:35 a lawyer, asked him a **q** to test
Mk 11:29 I will ask you one **q;** answer

QUICK
Prov 20: 3 but every fool is **q** to quarrel.
Eccl 7: 9 Do not be **q** to anger,
Jas 1:19 let everyone be **q** to listen,

QUIET
Eccl 9:17 The **q** words of the wise
1 Tim 2: 2 may lead a **q** and peaceable

R

RACE
Eccl 9:11 the **r** is not to the swift
2 Tim 4: 7 I have finished the **r,**
Heb 12: 1 run with perseverance the **r**

1 Pet 2: 9 But you are a chosen **r,**

RAIN
Gen 7: 4 seven days I will send **r**
Ex 16: 4 I am going to **r** bread from
Deut 11:14 he will give the **r** for your land
1 Kings 18: 1 I will send **r** on the earth."
Job 38:28 Has the **r** a father,
Isa 45: 8 skies **r** down righteousness;
Mt 7:25 The **r** fell, the floods came,
Jas 5:17 fervently that it might not **r,**

RAISE (D)
Deut 18:15 your God will **r** up for you a
Judg 2:18 Whenever the LORD **r** up

RANSOM
Ps 49: 8 For the **r** of life is costly,
Hos 13:14 Shall I **r** them from the power
Mk 10:45 to give his life a **r** for many."
1 Tim 2: 6 who gave himself a **r** for all

READ
Deut 17:19 and he shall **r** in it all the days
Josh 8:34 And afterward he **r** all the
Neh 8: 8 So they **r** from the book,
Isa 34:16 Seek and **r** from the book
Jer 36: 6 shall **r** the words of the LORD
Dan 5:16 if you are able to **r** the writing
Mk 12:10 Have you not **r** this scripture?
Lk 4:16 He stood up to **r,**

REAP
Lev 19: 9 When you **r** the harvest of
Ps 126: 5 those who sow in tears **r** with
Hos 8: 7 they shall **r** the whirlwind.
Lk 12:24 they neither sow nor **r,**
Jn 4:38 I sent you to **r** that
2 Cor 9: 6 who sows sparingly will also **r**
Gal 6: 7 for you **r** whatever you sow.
Rev 14:15 Use your sickle and **r,**

REBEL
Num 14: 9 do not **r** against the LORD;
Josh 22:18 If you **r** against the LORD today,

REBUKE
Ps 6: 1 O LORD, do not **r** me in your
Prov 17:10 A **r** strikes deeper
Eccl 7: 5 better to hear the **r** of the wise
Zech 3: 2 The LORD **r** you, O Satan!
Mk 8:32 took him aside and began to **r**
Lk 17: 3 you must **r** the offender.
Titus 1:13 For this reason **r** them sharply,
Jude 1: 9 The Lord **r** you!"

RECEIVE
Deut 9: 9 I went up the mountain to **r**
Ps 24: 5 They will **r** blessing from the
Mt 10:41 a prophet will **r** a prophet's
Mk 10:15 not **r** the kingdom of God
Lk 7:22 the blind **r** their sight,
Jn 16:24 Ask and you will **r,**
Acts 1: 8 But you will **r** power
Rom 11:31 they too may now **r** mercy.
1 Cor 4: 5 will **r** commendation from
Jas 1:12 and will **r** the crown of life
Rev 4:11 to **r** glory and honor and

RECONCILE
Acts	7:26	and tried to **r** them,
Col	1:20	God was pleased to **r** to

REDEEM (ER)
Ex	6: 6	**r** you with an outstretched
Ruth	4: 6	I cannot **r** it for myself
Ps	26:11	**r** me, and be gracious
Sir	51:12	*Give thanks to the r of Israel.*
Hos	13:14	Shall I **r** them from Death?
Lk	24:21	he was the one to **r** Israel.
Titus	2:14	might **r** us from all iniquity

REFINE (S)
Jer	9: 7	I will now **r** and test them,
Zech	13: 9	**r** them as one **r** silver
Mal	3: 3	and **r** them like gold and silver

REFUGE
Num	35:11	to be cities of **r** for you,
Josh	20: 2	Appoint the cities of **r**,
Ruth	2:12	wings you have come for **r**!"
2 Sam	22: 3	in whom I take **r**, my shield
Ps	2:12	Happy are all who take **r** in
Prov	14:32	but the righteous find a **r**
Isa	25: 4	you have been a **r** to the poor,
Jer	16:19	my **r** in the day of trouble
Nah	1: 7	he protects those who take **r**

REIGN
Ex	15:18	The LORD will **r** forever and
Deut	17:20	his descendants may **r** long
1 Sam	8:11	the king who will **r** over you:
Ps	146:10	The LORD will **r** forever,
Prov	8:15	By me kings **r**,
Isa	24:23	LORD of hosts will **r** on Mount
Jer	23: 5	he shall **r** as king and deal
Lam	5:19	But you, O LORD, **r** forever;
Mic	4: 7	LORD will **r** over them in
Lk	1:33	He will **r** over the house of
1 Cor	15:25	For he must **r** until he has
2 Tim	2:12	we will also **r** with him;
Rev	11:15	he will **r** forever and ever."

REJECT (ED)
Ex	20: 5	of those who **r** me,
Isa	30:12	Because you **r** this word,
Hos	4: 6	you have **r** knowledge,

REJOICE
Lev	23:40	shall **r** before the LORD your
1 Chr	16:10	those who seek the LORD **r**.
2 Chr	6:41	let your faithful **r** in your
Neh	12:43	God had made them **r** with
Ps	5:11	who take refuge in you **r**;
Prov	23:25	let her who bore you **r**.
Sir	8: 7	Do not **r** over any one's death;
Isa	35: 1	the desert shall **r** and blossom;
Hab	3:18	yet I will **r** in the LORD;
Zep	3:17	will **r** over you with gladness,
Zech	9: 9	**R** greatly, O daughter Zion!
Lk	6:23	**R** in that day and leap
Rom	12:15	**R** with those who **r**,
Phil	3: 1	**r** in the Lord.
1 Thess	5:16	**R** always,
1 Pet	4:13	**r** insofar as you are sharing
Rev	18:20	**R** over her, O heaven,

RELY
2 Kings	18:20	On whom do you now **r**,

2 Chr	14:11	for we **r** on you,
Prov	3: 5	do not **r** on your own insight.
Rom	2:17	a Jew and **r** on the law
2 Cor	1: 9	we would **r** not on ourselves
Gal	3:10	For all who **r** on the works

REMEMBER
Gen	9:15	I will **r** my covenant
Ex	20: 8	**R** the sabbath day,
Deut	5:15	**R** that you were a slave
Josh	1:13	**R** the word that Moses
1 Chr	16:12	**R** the wonderful works
Neh	13:31	**R** me, O my God,
Job	10: 9	**R** that you fashioned me like
Ps	77:11	I will **r** your wonders of old.
Eccl	12: 1	**R** your creator in the days
Isa	64: 9	and do not **r** iniquity forever.
Jer	31:34	and **r** their sin no more.
Lam	5: 1	**R**, O Lord, what has befallen
Ezek	36:31	Then you shall **r** your evil
Hos	7: 2	I **r** all their wickedness.
Hab	3: 2	in wrath may you **r** mercy.
Mk	8:18	And do you not **r**?
Lk	23:42	Jesus, **r** me when you come
Phil	1: 3	my God every time I **r** you,
2 Tim	2: 8	**R** Jesus Christ,
Heb	8:12	and I will **r** their sins no
Jude	1:17	**r** the predictions of the apostles
Rev	3: 3	**R** then what you received

REMNANT
Gen	45: 7	for you a **r** on earth,
2 Kings	19:31	from Jerusalem a **r** shall go
Ezra	9: 8	who has left us a **r**,
Isa	10:21	A **r** will return,
Jer	23: 3	I myself will gather the **r** of my
Zeph	3:13	the **r** of Israel;
Zech	8:12	I will cause the **r** of this people
Rom	9:27	only a **r** of them will be saved

REPENT
1 Kings	8:47	**r**, and plead with you
Job	42: 6	I despise myself, and **r**
Mt	4:17	**R**, for the kingdom of heaven
Mk	6:12	proclaimed that all should **r**.
Lk	13: 3	unless you **r**, you will all
Acts	2:38	**R**, and be baptized every one
Rev	2:21	time to **r**, but she refuses to **r**

RESCUE (D) (S)
2 Chr	32:17	other lands did not **r** their
1 Macc	2:48	They **r** the law out of the
Ps	31: 2	Incline your ear to me; **r** me
Sir	29:12	it will **r** you from every
Isa	1:17	seek justice, **r** the oppressed,
Ezek	34:10	I will **r** my sheep from their
Mt	6:13	but **r** us from the evil one
Rom	7:24	Who will **r** me from this body
2 Cor	1:10	continue to **r** us;
2 Pet	2: 7	if he **r** Lot, a righteous man

REST
Gen	8: 4	the ark came to **r** on the
Ex	31:15	a sabbath of solemn **r**,
Lev	25: 4	sabbath of complete **r** for the
Num	10:36	And whenever it came to **r**,
Deut	12:10	gives you **r** from your enemies
Josh	11:23	And the land had **r** from war.
2 Sam	7:11	I will give you **r** from all
1 Kings	5: 4	God has given me **r** on every

1 Chr	28: 2	build a house of **r** for the ark
Job	3:17	there the weary are at **r**.
Ps	95:11	They shall not enter my **r**."
Prov	6:10	folding of the hands to **r**,
Isa	11: 2	the LORD shall **r** on him,
Jer	6:16	and find **r** for your souls.
Mt	11:28	and I will give you **r**.
Mk	6:31	by yourselves and **r** a while."
1 Cor	2: 5	so that your faith might **r** not
Gal	3:12	But the law does not **r** on
Heb	3:11	They will not enter my **r**."
Rev	14:13	they will **r** from their labors,

RESTORE
Deut	30: 3	God will **r** your fortunes
2 Chr	24: 4	Joash decided to **r** the house
Neh	4: 2	Will they **r** things?
1 Macc	4:57	they **r** the gates and
Ps	80: 3	**R** us, O God;
Isa	49: 6	**r** the survivors of Israel;
Lam	5:21	**R** us to yourself, O LORD
Dan	9:25	**r** and rebuild Jerusalem
Zech	9:12	I declare that I will **r** to you
Mt	17:11	and will **r** all things;
Acts	1: 6	will **r** the kingdom to Israel?"
1 Pet	5:10	will himself **r**, support,

RESURRECTION
2 Macc	7:14	you there will be no **r** to life!"
Mt	22:28	In the **r**, then, whose wife
Mk	12:18	who say there is no **r**,
Lk	14:14	the **r** of the righteous."
Jn	11:24	the **r** on the last day."
Acts	2:31	David spoke of the **r** of the
Rom	1: 4	holiness by **r** from the dead,
1 Cor	15:13	If there is no **r** of the dead,
Phil	3:11	I may attain the **r** from the
2 Tim	2:18	the **r** has already taken place.
Heb	6: 2	on of hands, **r** of the dead,
1 Pet	1: 3	through the **r** of Jesus Christ
Rev	20: 5	This is the first **r**.

RETURN
Gen	18:10	I will surely **r** to you in due
Num	10:36	he would say, "**R**, O LORD
Deut	30: 2	and **r** to the LORD your God
2 Sam	12:23	but he will not **r** to me."
2 Chr	30: 9	For as you **r** to the LORD,
Neh	1: 9	but if you **r** to me
Job	16:22	from which I shall not **r**.
Ps	104:29	they die and **r** to their dust.
Isa	10:21	A remnant will **r**,
Jer	4: 1	If you **r**, O Israel,
Lam	3:40	our ways, and **r** to the LORD.
Hos	6: 1	Come, let us **r** to the LORD;
Joel	2:12	says the LORD, **r** to me
Am	4: 6	yet you did not **r** to me,
Zech	10: 9	shall rear their children and **r**.
Mal	3: 7	**R** to me, and I will
Rom	9: 9	I will **r** and Sarah

REVEAL
Esth	2:10	Esther did not **r** her people
Sir	1:30	The Lord will **r** your secrets
Dan	2:11	and no one can **r** it to the king
Mt	11:27	whom the Son chooses to **r**

REVELATION (S)
2 Sam	7:27	have made this **r** to your
2 Cor	12: 1	to visions and **r** of the Lord.

REVERE

Josh	24:14	Now therefore **r** the LORD,
Tob	4:5	"**R** the Lord all your days
Ps	119:48	I **r** your commandments,
Mal	4: 2	But for you who **r** my name

REWARD

Gen	15: 1	your **r** shall be very great."
1 Sam	24:19	So may the LORD **r** you with
Ps	19:11	keeping them there is great **r**.
Prov	25:22	and the LORD will **r** you.
Sir	11:22	of the Lord is the **r** of the
Isa	49: 4	and my **r** with my God."
Mt	5:12	for your **r** is great in heaven,
Lk	6:35	Your **r** will be great,
1 Cor	3:14	the builder will receive a **r**.
Col	3:24	the inheritance as your **r**;
Heb	11:26	looking ahead to the **r**.
2 Jn	1: 8	but may receive a full **r**.
Rev	22:12	my **r** is with me,

RICH

Gen	26:13	the man became **r**;
2 Sam	12: 1	the one **r** and the other poor.
Job	34:19	regards the **r** more than the
Ps	49:16	afraid when some become **r**,
Prov	13: 7	Some pretend to be **r**, yet have
Eccl	5:12	the **r** will not let them sleep
Isa	53: 9	and his tomb with the **r**,
Ezek	34:14	they shall feed on **r** pasture
Mt	19:23	will be hard for a **r** person
Lk	6:24	woe to you who are **r**,
2 Cor	8: 9	that though he was **r**,
Eph	2: 4	But God, who is **r** in mercy,
1 Tim	6: 9	those who want to be **r** fall
Jas	2: 5	to be **r** in faith
Rev	3:17	I am **r**, I have prospered,

RIGHT

Gen	13: 9	I will go to the **r**;
Ex	15: 6	Your **r** hand, O LORD,
Deut	6:18	Do what is **r** and good
Josh	1: 7	turn from it to the **r** hand
1 Sam	12:23	in the good and the **r** way.
1 Kings	15: 5	David did what was **r**
Neh	9:13	and gave them **r** ordinances
Job	42: 7	spoken of me what is **r**,
Ps	4: 5	Offer **r** sacrifices,
Prov	4:27	Do not swerve to the **r**
Isa	30:10	prophesy to us what is **r**;
Ezek	18: 5	does what is lawful and **r**
Hos	14: 9	the ways of the Lord are **r**,
Am	3:10	how to do **r**, says the Lord,
Jon	4:11	who do not know their **r** hand
Zech	3: 1	Satan standing at his **r** hand
Mt	5:29	If your **r** eye causes you to sin
Mk	14:62	at the **r** hand of the Power,'
Jn	7:24	but judge with **r** judgment."
Acts	7:55	Jesus standing at the **r** hand of
Rom	9:21	Has the potter no **r** over the
1 Cor	9: 4	Do we not have the **r** to our
2 Cor	8:21	is **r** not only in the Lord's sight
Eph	6: 1	the Lord, for this is **r**.
Col	3: 1	seated at the **r** hand of God.
2 Thess	3:13	weary in doing what is **r**.
Heb	1:13	Sit at my **r** hand
1 Pet	3:14	for doing what is **r**,
1 Jn	3: 7	who does what is **r** is righteous,
Rev	1:16	In his **r** hand he held seven

RIGHTEOUS

Gen	6: 9	Noah was a **r** man,
1 Sam	24:17	You are more **r** than I;
Neh	9: 8	for you are **r**.
Tob	3:2	"You are **r**, O Lord,
1 Macc	2:24	He gave vent to **r** anger
Job	4:17	Can mortals be **r** before God?
Ps	5:12	For you bless the **r**, O LORD;
Prov	4:18	But the path of the **r** is like
Eccl	3:17	God will judge the **r** and the
Wis	5:15	**r** live forever, and their reward
Isa	26: 7	The way of the **r** is level;
Jer	33:15	I will cause a **r** Branch
Ezek	18: 5	man is **r** and does what is
Hab	2: 4	but the **r** live by their faith.
Zeph	3: 5	The LORD within it is **r**;
Mal	3:18	between the **r** and the wicked,
Mt	5:45	rain on the **r** and on the
Mk	2:17	to call not the **r** but sinners."
Acts	3:14	rejected the Holy and **R** One
Rom	1:17	The one who is **r** will live by
2 Tim	4: 8	the Lord, the **r** judge,
Heb	10:38	my **r** one will live by faith
Jas	5:16	The prayer of the **r** is powerful
1 Pet	3:18	the **r** for the unr,
2 Pet	2: 7	if he rescued Lot, a **r** man
1 Jn	3: 7	does what is right is **r**,
Rev	19: 8	the fine linen is the **r** deeds

RISE (N)

Num	24:17	a scepter shall **r** out of Israel;
Ps	3: 7	**R** up, O LORD! Deliver me
Isa	26:19	their corpses shall **r**.
Dan	12:13	you shall **r** for your reward
Am	8:14	they shall fall, and never **r**
Mal	4: 2	of righteousness shall **r**,
Mt	27:63	After three days I will **r** again.'
Mk	13: 8	For nation will **r** against
Lk	18:33	the third day he will **r** again."
Jn	20: 9	that he must **r** from the dead.
Acts	17: 3	and to **r** from the dead,
Eph	5:14	Sleeper, awake! **R** from the
1 Thess	4:16	the dead in Christ will **r** first.

RIVER (S)

Gen	2:10	A **r** flows out of Eden
Deut	1: 7	as far as the great **r**,
Ps	46: 4	a **r** whose streams make glad
Isa	48:18	would have been like a **r**,
Ezek	47:12	on both sides of the **r**,
Rev	22: 1	the angel showed me the **r**

ROBE

Gen	37: 3	him a long **r** with sleeves.
Ex	28: 4	a breastpiece, an ephod, a **r**,
1 Sam	15:27	the hem of his **r**, and it tore.
2 Sam	13:18	wearing a long **r** with sleeves;
Isa	6: 1	and the hem of his **r** filled the
Bar	5:2	on the **r** of the righteousness
Lk	15:22	Quickly, bring out a **r**
Jn	19: 5	of thorns and the purple **r**.
Rev	6:11	They were each given a white **r**

ROCK

Gen	49:24	the Shepherd, the **R** of Israel,
Ex	33:22	in a cleft of the **r**,
Num	20: 8	command the **r** before their
Deut	32: 4	The **R**, his work is perfect,
1 Sam	2: 2	there is no **R** like our God.
2 Sam	22: 2	The LORD is my **r**, my fortress,
Ps	18: 2	The LORD is my **r**, my fortress,
Wis	11:4	was given them out of flinty **r**
Sir	51:12	*Give thanks to the r of Isaac,*
Isa	44: 8	There is no other **r**; I know not
Mt	16:18	you are Peter, and on this **r**
Mk	15:46	hewn out of the **r**.
Rom	9:33	**r** that will make them fall
1 Cor	10: 4	they drank from the spiritual **r**
1 Pet	2: 8	and a **r** that makes them fall."

ROD

2 Sam	7:14	will punish him with a **r**
Ps	23: 4	your **r** and your staff
Prov	13:24	Those who spare the **r** hate
Isa	11: 4	the earth with the **r** of his
Heb	9: 4	and Aaron's **r** that budded,
Rev	19:15	will rule them with a **r** of iron;

ROOT (ED)

1 Macc	1:10	them came forth a sinful **r**,
Prov	12:12	but the **r** of the righteous
Sir	47:22	to David a **r** from his own
Isa	53: 2	like a **r** out of dry ground;
Mt	13:21	such a person has no **r**,
Rom	15:12	The **r** of Jesse shall come,
1 Tim	6:10	money is a **r** of all kinds of
Rev	5: 5	the **R** of David,

RULE

Gen	3:16	and he shall **r** over you."
Deut	15: 6	you will **r** over many nations,
Judg	8:22	**R** over us,
Ps	110: 2	**R** in the midst of your foes.
Prov	17: 2	who deals wisely will **r** over a
Isa	3: 4	and babes shall **r** over them.
Zech	6:13	shall sit and **r** on his throne.
Rom	15:12	who rises to **r** the Gentiles;
1 Cor	7:17	my **r** in all the churches.
Eph	1:21	far above all **r** and authority
Col	3:15	let the peace of Christ **r**
Rev	12: 5	who is to **r** all the nations

S

SABBATH

Ex	20: 8	Remember the **s** day,
Num	15:32	gathering sticks on the **s** day.
Deut	5:12	Observe the **s** day and keep it
2 Chr	36:21	lay desolate it kept **s**,
Neh	13:17	profaning the **s** day?
Isa	56: 2	keeps the **s**, not profaning it,
Jer	17:21	bear a burden on the **s** day
Mt	12: 1	the grainfields on the **s**;
Mk	2:28	lord even of the **s**."
Lk	6: 9	to do harm on the **s**,

SACRIFICE

Ex	5:17	Let us go and **s** to the LORD.'
Lev	3: 1	If the offering is a **s** of well-
1 Sam	15:22	to obey is better than **s**,
Ps	50:14	God a **s** of thanksgiving,
Prov	15: 8	The **s** of the wicked
Dan	9:27	he shall make **s** and offering
Hos	6: 6	desire steadfast love and not **s**,
Zeph	1: 7	the LORD has prepared a **s**,
Mt	9:13	I desire mercy, not **s**.'

Rom	3:25	God put forward as a **s** of
1 Cor	10:20	I imply that what pagans **s**,
Eph	5: 2	fragrant offering and **s** to God.
Phil	4:18	a **s** acceptable and pleasing to
Heb	9:26	remove sin by the **s** of himself.
1 Jn	2: 2	he is the atoning **s** for our sins,

SADDUCEES
Mt	16: 1	The Pharisees and **S** came,
Mk	12:18	Some **S**, who say there is no
Acts	23: 7	the Pharisees and the **S**,

SAINTS
Ps	31:23	all you his **s**.
Acts	9:13	done to your **s** in Jerusalem;
Rom	8:27	the Spirit intercedes for the **s**
1 Cor	6: 2	the **s** will judge the world?
Eph	1:18	inheritance among the **s**,
Col	1:12	inheritance of the **s** in the
1 Thess	3:13	Lord Jesus with all his **s**.
Philem	1: 7	the **s** have been refreshed
Jude	1: 3	for all entrusted to the **s**.
Rev	5: 8	are the prayers of the **s**.

SAKE
Gen	12:16	And for her **s** he dealt well
Josh	23: 3	all these nations for your **s**,
1 Sam	12:22	for his great name's **s**,
1 Kings	11:12	the **s** of your father David
Ps	25:11	For your name's **s**, O LORD,
Isa	43:25	transgressions for my own **s**,
Jer	14:21	spurn us, for your name's **s**;
Bar	2:14	and for your own **s** deliver us,
Ezek	20:14	But I acted for the **s** of my
Dan	9:17	and for your own **s**, Lord,
Mt	10:39	who lose their life for my **s**
Mk	13:20	but for the **s** of the elect,
Rom	8:36	For your **s** we are being killed
1 Cor	9:23	do it all for the **s** of the gospel,
2 Cor	4:11	given up to death for Jesus' **s**,
1 Pet	2:13	For the Lord's **s** accept the
3 Jn	1: 7	their journey for the **s** of Christ,

SALVATION
Gen	49:18	I wait for your **s**, O LORD.
Ex	15: 2	he has become my **s**;
Deut	32:15	at the Rock of his **s**.
2 Sam	22: 3	horn of my **s**, my stronghold
1 Chr	16:23	Tell of his **s** from day to day.
2 Chr	6:41	be clothed with **s**,
Job	13:16	This will be my **s**,
Ps	13: 5	heart shall rejoice in your **s**.
Wis	6:24	wise is the **s** of the world
Isa	12: 2	Surely God is my **s**;
Jer	3:23	God is the **s** of Israel.
Lam	3:26	quietly for the **s** of the LORD.
Bar	4:29	everlasting joy with your **s**.
Mic	7: 7	for the God of my **s**;
Hab	3:18	in the God of my **s**.
Lk	2:30	my eyes have seen your **s**,
Jn	4:22	for **s** is from the Jews.
Acts	4:12	There is **s** in no one else,
Rom	11:11	But through their stumbling **s**
2 Cor	6: 2	day of **s** I have helped you."
Eph	6:17	Take the helmet of **s**,
Phil	2:12	work out your own **s** with fear
1 Thess	5: 8	a helmet the hope of **s**.
2 Thess	2:13	the first fruits for **s**
2 Tim	2:10	the **s** that is in Christ Jesus
Titus	2:11	bringing **s** to all,

Heb	2: 3	if we neglect so great a **s**?
1 Pet	1: 9	the **s** of your souls.
2 Pet	3:15	patience of our Lord as **s**.
Jude	1: 3	to you about the **s** we share,
Rev	7:10	**S** belongs to our God

SAMARITAN
Lk	10:33	But a **S** while traveling came
Jn	4: 7	A **S** woman came to draw

SANCTIFY (SANCTIFIED)
Lev	11:44	**s** yourselves therefore, and be
Jn	17:17	**S** them in the truth;
1 Thess	5:23	the God of peace himself **s**
Heb	13:12	in order to **s** the people
1 Pet	3:15	in your hearts **s** Christ as Lord.

SANCTUARY
Ex	15:17	the **s**, O LORD,
Num	3:28	to the duties of the **s**.
1 Kings	6:19	The inner **s** he prepared
1 Chr	22:19	Go and build the **s** of the LORD
1 Macc	4:36	cleanse the **s** and dedicate it."
Ps	60: 6	God has promised in his **s**:
Isa	8:14	He will become a **s**,
Lam	1:10	invade her **s**,
Ezek	5:11	because you have defiled my **s**
Dan	8:11	overthrew the place of his **s**.
Heb	8: 5	They offer worship in a **s**

SATAN
1 Chr	21: 1	**S** stood up against Israel,
Job	1: 6	and **S** also came among them.
Zech	3: 2	the LORD said to **S**,
Mt	4:10	Away with you, **S**!
Mk	4:15	**S** immediately comes and
Lk	22: 3	Then **S** entered into Judas
Jn	13:27	**S** entered into him.
Acts	5: 3	why has **S** filled your heart
Rom	16:20	of peace will shortly crush **S**
1 Cor	7: 5	so that **S** may not tempt you
2 Cor	11:14	Even **S** disguises himself as an
2 Thess	2: 9	**S**, who uses all power,
1 Tim	5:15	turned away to follow **S**.
Rev	2: 9	but are a synagogue of **S**.

SAVE (D)
2 Sam	22: 3	my savior; you **s** me from
1 Chr	16:35	**S** us, O God
Ps	6: 4	O LORD, **s** my life;
Prov	6: 3	my child, and **s** yourself,
Isa	35: 4	He will come and **s** you."
Jer	15:20	I am with you to **s** you
Lam	4:17	a nation that could not **s**.
Ezek	7:19	Their silver and gold cannot **s**
Hos	1: 7	of Judah, and I will **s** them by
Zeph	1:18	nor their old will be able to **s**
Zech	8: 7	I will **s** my people from the
Mt	16:25	For those who want to **s** their
Lk	19:10	to seek out and to **s** the lost."
Jn	12:47	but to **s** the world.
Acts	2:40	**S** yourselves from this corrupt
Rom	11:14	and thus **s** some of them.
1 Cor	9:22	I might by all means **s** some.
1 Tim	1:15	Jesus came into the world to **s**
Heb	7:25	to **s** those who approach God
Jas	2:14	Can faith **s** you?
Jude	1:23	**s** others by snatching them

SAVIOR
2 Sam	22: 3	my **s**; you save me from
2 Kings	13: 5	the LORD gave Israel a **s**,
Jdt	9:11	**s** of those without hope.
1 Macc	4:30	"Blessed are you, O **S** of
Ps	106:21	They forgot God, their **S**,
Wis	16:7	but by you, the **S** of all.
Isa	43: 3	Holy One of Israel, your **S**.
Jer	14: 8	its **s** in time of trouble,
Hos	13: 4	there is no **s**.
Lk	1:47	rejoices in God my **S**.
Jn	4:42	this is truly the **S** of the
Acts	13:23	to Israel a **S**, Jesus,
Eph	5:23	he is the **S**.
Phil	3:20	we are expecting a **S**,
1 Tim	2: 3	the sight of God our **S**,
2 Tim	1:10	our **S** Christ Jesus,
Titus	1: 4	Christ Jesus our **S**.
2 Pet	1: 1	God and **S** Jesus Christ:
1 Jn	4:14	sent his Son as the **S** of the
Jude	1:25	to the only God our **S**,

SCRIPTURE
Mk	12:10	Have you not read this **s**:
Lk	4:21	Today this **s** has been fulfilled
Jn	7:42	the **s** said that the Messiah
Acts	1:16	Friends, the **s** had to be
1 Tim	4:13	the public reading of **s**,
2 Tim	3:16	All **s** is inspired by God
2 Pet	1:20	no prophecy of **s**

SEA
Gen	32:12	as the sand of the **s**,
Ex	14:16	out your hand over the **s**
Num	34: 6	you shall have the Great **S**
Deut	30:13	Neither is it beyond the **s**,
1 Kings	7:23	Then he made the molten **s**;
2 Kings	25:13	and the bronze **s**
Neh	9:11	you divided the **s** before them,
Job	11: 9	and broader than the **s**.
Ps	74:13	You divided the **s** by your
Eccl	1: 7	All streams run to the **s**,
Isa	48:18	like the waves of the **s**;
Bar	3:30	Who has gone over the **s**,
Dan	7: 3	beasts came up out of the **s**,
Jon	1: 4	a great wind upon the **s**,
Mic	7:19	into the depths of the **s**.
Hab	2:14	as the waters cover the **s**.
Zech	9:10	dominion shall be from **s** to **s**,
Mt	18: 6	in the depth of the **s**.
Mk	11:23	up and thrown into the **s**,'
1 Cor	10: 1	all passed through the **s**,
Heb	11:29	passed through the Red **S**
Jas	1: 6	like a wave of the **s**,
Jude	1:13	wild waves of the **s**,
Rev	4: 6	like a **s** of glass,

SEAL
Esth	8: 8	and **s** it with the king's ring;
Song	8: 6	Set me as a **s** upon your heart,
Isa	8:16	**s** the teaching among my
Dan	8:26	As for you, **s** up the vision,
Jn	6:27	the Father has set his **s**."
1 Cor	9: 2	are the **s** of my apostleship
2 Cor	1:22	by putting his **s** on us
Eph	4:30	you were marked with a **s**
Rev	6: 3	When he opened the second **s**,

SEARCH
Deut	4:29	if you **s** after him with all your

Ezra	5:17	have a **s** made in the royal
Ps	139:23	**S** me, O God,
Prov	2: 4	and **s** for it
Jer	17:10	LORD test the mind and **s** the
Ezek	34:11	I myself will **s** for my sheep,
Mt	2: 8	Go and **s** diligently for the
Lk	15: 8	and **s** carefully until she

SEAT (S)

Ex	25:17	make a mercy **s** of pure gold;
Lev	16: 2	the mercy **s** that is upon the
2 Kings	25:28	gave him a **s** above the other **s**
Ps	1: 1	or sit in the **s** of scoffers;
Prov	31:23	taking his **s** among the elders
Mt	23: 2	Pharisees sit on Moses' **s**;
Rom	14:10	before the judgment **s** of God.
2 Cor	5:10	the judgment **s** of Christ,
Heb	9: 5	overshadowing the mercy **s**.

SEE

Gen	8: 8	to **s** if the waters had subsided
Ex	12:13	when I **s** the blood, I will pass
Num	14:23	shall **s** the land
Deut	34: 4	I have let you **s** it with your
Tob	11:8	regain his sight and **s** the
Job	19:26	in my flesh I shall **s** God,
Ps	34: 8	O taste and **s** that the LORD is
Isa	40: 5	and all people shall **s** it
Ezek	8:12	The LORD does not **s** us,
Dan	3:25	But I **s** four men unbound,
Joel	2:28	young men shall **s** visions.
Mic	7: 9	I shall **s** his vindication.
Mt	7: 5	will **s** clearly to take the speck
Mk	14:62	you will **s** the Son of Man
Lk	3: 6	flesh shall **s** the salvation of
Jn	9:25	I was blind, now I **s**."
Acts	2:17	your young men shall **s**
1 Cor	13:12	For now we **s** in a mirror,
2 Cor	13: 5	Examine yourselves to **s**
Heb	12:14	no one will **s** the Lord.
1 Jn	3: 2	for we will **s** him as he is.
Rev	1: 7	every eye will **s** him,

SEED (S)

Gen	1:11	yielding **s**, and fruit trees
Eccl	11: 6	In the morning sow your **s**,
Isa	6:13	The holy **s** is its stump.
Mt	13:31	heaven is like a mustard **s**
Mk	4:31	It is like a mustard **s**,
Lk	8:11	The **s** is the word of God
2 Cor	9:10	He who supplies **s** to the
1 Pet	1:23	but of imperishable **s**,
1 Jn	3: 9	because God's **s** abides in

SEEK

Deut	4:29	you will **s** the LORD your God,
1 Chr	28: 9	If you **s** him, he will be found
2 Chr	7:14	pray, **s** my face,
Ezra	9:12	and never **s** their peace
Ps	4: 2	and **s** after lies?
Prov	17:11	Evil people **s** only rebellion,
Sir	24:34	but for all who **s** wisdom.
Isa	55: 6	**S** the Lord while he may be
Jer	29:13	if you **s** me with all your heart
Hos	10:12	it is time to **s** the LORD,
Am	5: 6	**S** the LORD and live,
Zeph	2: 3	**S** the LORD, all you humble
Lk	19:10	Son of Man came to **s** out and
Jn	5:30	because I **s** to do not my own
Acts	15:17	other peoples may **s** the Lord

Rom	10:20	those who did not **s** me;
1 Cor	7:18	Let him not **s** to remove
Heb	11: 6	he rewards those who **s** him.
1 Pet	3:11	let them **s** peace and pursue it.

SELF-CONTROL (LED)

Prov	25:28	is one who lacks **s**.
Acts	24:25	he discussed justice, **s**,
1 Cor	7: 5	because of your lack of **s**.
Titus	1: 8	upright, devout, and **s**.
2 Pet	1: 6	and knowledge with **s**, and **s**

SELFISH (NESS)

Ps	119:36	and not to **s** gain.
2 Cor	12:20	anger, **s**, slander,
Phil	1:17	Christ out of **s** ambition,
Jas	3:16	there is envy and **s** ambition,

SEND

Gen	7: 4	in seven days I will **s** rain on
Ex	33: 2	I will **s** an angel before you,
Deut	28:20	The Lord will **s** upon you
1 Sam	5:11	**S** away the ark of the God of
Ps	57: 3	He will **s** from heaven and
Eccl	11: 1	**S** out your bread upon the
Isa	6: 8	Whom shall I **s**, and who will
Mal	4: 5	Lo, I will **s** you the prophet
Mt	24:31	And he will **s** out his angels
Lk	20:13	I will **s** my beloved son;
Jn	3:17	God did not **s** the Son into the
Acts	3:20	that he may **s** the Messiah
1 Cor	1:17	For Christ did not **s** me

SERPENT

Gen	3: 1	Now the **s** was more crafty
Num	21: 9	So Moses made a **s** of bronze,
2 Kings	18: 4	broke in pieces the bronze **s**
Isa	27: 1	Leviathan the fleeing **s**,
2 Cor	11: 3	the **s** deceived Eve by its
Rev	12: 9	that ancient **s**, who is called

SERVANT

Ex	14:31	the LORD and in his **s** Moses.
Num	12: 7	Not so with my **s** Moses;
1 Sam	3:10	Speak, for your **s** is listening."
1 Kings	8:56	he spoke through his **s** Moses.
Job	1: 8	you considered my **s** Job?
Ps	19:13	Keep back your **s** also
Prov	11:29	the fool will be **s** to the wise.
Isa	42: 1	Here is my **s**,
Jer	30:10	have no fear, my **s** Jacob,
Ezek	34:24	my **s** David shall be prince
Zech	3: 8	going to bring my **s** the Branch.
Mt	8:13	And the **s** was healed in that
Lk	1:54	He has helped his **s** Israel,
Jn	12:26	where I am, there will my **s** be
Acts	3:13	has glorified his **s** Jesus,
Rom	1: 1	Paul, a **s** of Jesus Christ,
Gal	2:17	is Christ then a **s** of sin?
Col	1:23	I, Paul, became a **s** of this
1 Tim	4: 6	you will be a good **s** of Christ
2 Tim	2:24	the Lord's **s** must not be
Heb	3: 5	in all God's house as a **s**,
Rev	19:10	I am a fellow **s** with you

SERVE (D)

Gen	25:23	the elder shall **s** the younger."
Ex	28: 1	to **s** me as priests
Deut	10:12	to **s** the LORD your God
Josh	24:14	and **s** him in sincerity

1 Sam	12:20	but **s** the LORD with all your
2 Kings	17:35	bow yourselves to them or **s**
Neh	9:35	they did not **s** you
Job	36:11	If they listen, and **s** him,
Ps	2:11	**S** the LORD with fear,
Isa	60:12	that will not **s** you shall perish;
Jer	25: 6	other gods to **s** and worship
Dan	3:17	If our God whom we **s** is able
Mt	6:24	No one can **s** two masters;
Mk	10:45	to be **s** but to **s**,
Lk	16:13	No slave can **s** two masters;
Rom	1: 9	be ardent in spirit, **s** the Lord.
1 Thess	1: 9	to **s** a living and true God
1 Tim	6: 2	they must **s** them all the more,
1 Pet	4:10	**s** one another with whatever

SEVEN (SEVENTH)

Gen	7: 2	Take with you **s** pairs of all
Ex	12:15	**S** days you shall eat
Num	23: 1	Build me **s** altars here,
Deut	7: 1	**s** nations mightier and more
Josh	6: 4	**s** priests bearing **s** trumpets
Judg	16:13	If you weave the **s** locks of my
1 Sam	2: 5	The barren has borne **s**,
1 Kings	19:18	Yet I will leave **s** thousand in
2 Kings	5:10	Go, wash in the Jordan **s**
Tob	3:8	she had been married to **s**
1 Macc	6:53	because it was the **s** year;
Ps	119:164	**S** times a day I praise you
Prov	9: 1	she has hewn her **s** pillars.
Sir	40:8	but to sinners **s** times more,
Isa	4: 1	**S** women shall take hold
Dan	3:19	the furnace heated up **s** times
Zech	4: 2	are **s** lamps on it, with **s** lips
Mt	18:22	Not **s** times,
Mk	12:20	There were **s** brothers;
Lk	11:26	brings **s** other spirits more evil
Rom	11: 4	I have kept for myself **s**
Rev	1:12	I saw **s** golden lampstands,

SEVENTY

Gen	46:27	who came into Egypt were **s**.
Ex	24: 1	and **s** of the elders of Israel
Num	11:25	and put it on the **s** elders;
2 Chr	36:21	to fulfill **s** years.
Ps	90:10	the days of our life are **s** years,
Jer	25:12	after **s** years are completed,
Dan	9:24	**S** weeks are decreed for your

SHAME

Ps	4: 2	shall my honor suffer **s**?
Prov	18:13	it is folly and **s**.
Isa	30: 5	everyone comes to **s**
Jer	8: 9	The wise shall be put to **s**,
Ezek	39:26	They shall forget their **s**,
Dan	12: 2	to **s** and everlasting contempt.
Hos	4: 7	changed their glory into **s**.
Joel	2:26	never again be put to **s**.
Rom	9:33	will not be put to **s**."
1 Cor	1:27	foolish in the world to **s** the
Phil	3:19	their glory is in their **s**;
Heb	12: 2	disregarding its **s**,
1 Pet	2: 6	will not be put to **s**."
1 Jn	2:28	and not be put to **s** before him

SHARE

Num	18:20	nor shall you have any **s**
2 Sam	20: 1	no **s** in the son of Jesse
2 Chr	10:16	What **s** do we have in David
Neh	2:20	but you have no **s** or claim

Prov	31:31	Give her a **s** in the fruit
Lk	3:11	Whoever has two coats must **s**
Acts	8:21	You have no part or **s** in this,
Rom	1:11	that I may **s** with you
2 Cor	1: 7	as you **s** in our sufferings,
Eph	4:28	something to **s** with the needy.
Col	1:12	to **s** in the inheritance
1 Tim	6:18	and ready to **s**,
2 Tim	2: 6	ought to have the first **s** of the
Heb	12:10	that we may **s** his holiness.
Jude	1: 3	about the salvation we **s**,
Rev	22:19	will take away that person's **s**

SHEEP

Gen	4: 2	Abel was a keeper of **s**,
Num	27:17	be like **s** without a shepherd."
Deut	17: 1	an ox or a **s** that has a defect,
1 Sam	15:14	is this bleating of **s** in my ears,
1 Kings	22:17	like **s** that have no shepherd;
Ps	44:22	as **s** for the slaughter.
Isa	53: 6	All we like **s** have gone astray;
Jer	50: 6	My people have been lost **s**;
Ezek	34:15	the shepherd of my **s**,
Zech	13: 7	that the **s** may be scattered;
Mt	9:36	like **s** without a shepherd.
Lk	15: 4	having a hundred **s** and losing
Jn	10: 3	and the **s** hear his voice.
Acts	8:32	Like a **s** he was led
Rom	8:36	accounted as **s** to be
Heb	13:20	the great shepherd of the **s**,
1 Pet	2:25	you were going astray like **s**,

SHEPHERD

Gen	48:15	God who has been my **s** all
Num	27:17	like sheep without a **s**."
2 Sam	7: 7	I commanded to **s** my people
1 Kings	22:17	like sheep that have no **s**;
1 Chr	11: 2	shall be **s** of my people Israel,
Ps	23: 1	The LORD is my **s**,
Eccl	12:11	that are given by one **s**.
Isa	40:11	feed his flock like a **s**;
Jer	31:10	will keep him as a **s** a flock."
Ezek	34: 5	because there was no **s**; and
Zech	11: 9	I will not be your **s**.
Mt	25:32	as a **s** separates the sheep
Mk	6:34	like sheep without a **s**;
Jn	10:11	I am the good **s**.
Heb	13:20	Jesus, the great **s** of the sheep,
1 Pet	5: 4	And when the chief **s** appears,
Rev	7:17	the throne will be their **s**,

SHINE (S)

Num	6:25	LORD make his face to **s** upon
Ps	37: 6	your vindication like the
Isa	60: 1	Arise, for your light has
Dan	12: 3	Those who are wise shall **s**
Mt	5:16	let your light **s** before others,
2 Cor	4: 6	Let light **s** out of darkness,"
Eph	5:14	and Christ will **s** on you."
Phil	2:15	you **s** like stars in the world
Rev	21:23	sun or moon to **s** on it,

SHOW

Gen	12: 1	the land that I will **s** you.
Ex	9:16	to **s** you my power,
Deut	4: 6	for this will **s** your wisdom
1 Sam	20:14	**s** me the faithful love
2 Sam	9: 1	to whom I may **s** kindness
Ps	18:26	with the pure you **s** yourself
Prov	12:16	Fools **s** their anger at once,

Isa	30:18	he will rise up to **s** mercy to
Jer	32:18	You **s** steadfast love
Joel	2:30	I will **s** portents
Mic	7:20	You will **s** faithfulness to Jacob
Zech	7: 9	true judgments, **s** kindness
Mt	22:19	**S** me the coin
Jn	14: 8	Lord, **s** us the Father,
Acts	2:19	I will **s** portents in the heaven
1 Cor	12:31	And I will **s** you a still more
2 Cor	11:30	the things that **s** my weakness.
Eph	2: 7	he might **s** the immeasurable
Titus	3: 2	and to **s** every courtesy to
Jas	2:18	**S** me your faith apart from
Rev	4: 1	and I will **s** you what must

SICK

Prov	13:12	deferred makes the heart **s**,
Ezek	34: 4	you have not healed the **s**,
Mt	8:16	and cured all who were **s**.
Acts	19:12	were brought to the **s**,
Jas	5:14	Are any among you **s**?

SIGHT

Gen	6:11	earth was corrupt in God's **s**,
Ex	3: 3	look at this great **s**,
Ps	51: 4	what is evil in your **s**,
Prov	3: 4	in the **s** of God and of people
Jer	18:10	it does evil in my **s**,
Mt	11: 5	the blind receive their **s**,
Acts	4:19	Whether it is right in God's **s**
2 Cor	5: 7	walk by faith, not by **s**.
1 Pet	3: 4	is very precious in God's **s**.

SIGN

Gen	9:12	This is the **s** of the covenant
Ex	12:13	The blood shall be a **s** for you
Num	16:38	shall be a **s** to the Israelites.
Judg	6:17	show me a **s** that it is you
1 Kings	13: 3	He gave a **s** the same day,
Isa	55:13	for an everlasting **s**
Ezek	24:24	Ezekiel shall be a **s** to you;
Mt	12:38	we wish to see a **s** from you."
Mk	8:12	this generation ask for a **s**?
Lk	2:12	This will be a **s** for you:
Jn	2:18	What **s** can you show us
Rom	4:11	received the **s** of circumcision
1 Cor	14:22	a **s** not for believers
2 Cor	12:12	The **s** of a true apostle

SILENT

Ps	39: 2	I was **s** and still;
Prov	17:28	keep **s** are considered wise;
Isa	53: 7	before its shearers is **s**,
Jer	4:19	I cannot keep **s**;
Zeph	1: 7	Be **s** before the Lord GOD!
Mk	14:61	was **s** and did not answer.
Acts	8:32	lamb **s** before its shearer,
1 Cor	14:34	should be **s** in the churches.
1 Tim	2:12	she is to keep **s**.

SILVER

Gen	37:28	for twenty pieces of **s**.
Ex	20:23	shall not make gods of **s**
Deut	17:17	**s** and gold he must not
Josh	7:21	two hundred shekels of **s**,
2 Chr	1:15	The king made **s** and gold as
1 Macc	1:23	He took the **s** and the gold,
Ps	66:10	you have tried us as **s** is tried.
Prov	3:14	her income is better than **s**,
Isa	48:10	but not like **s**;

Ezek	22:18	all of them, **s**, bronze,
Dan	5: 4	gods of gold and **s**, bronze,
Hag	2: 8	The **s** is mine, and the gold
Zech	11:12	my wages thirty shekels of **s**.
Mal	3: 3	a refiner and purifier of **s**,
Mt	26:15	paid him thirty pieces of **s**.
Acts	3: 6	I have no **s** or gold,
1 Cor	3:12	the foundation with gold, **s**,
2 Tim	2:20	not only of gold and **s**
1 Pet	1:18	perishable things like **s** or

SIN (S) (SINNED)

Gen	4: 7	**s** is lurking at the door
Ex	32:32	you will only forgive their **s**
Num	32:23	sure your **s** will find you out.
1 Sam	15:23	rebellion is no less a **s**
1 Kings	8:46	If they **s** against you
2 Chr	7:14	and will forgive their **s**
Neh	13:26	King Solomon of Israel **s**
Tob	12:10	but those who commit **s**
Job	1:22	In all this Job did not **s**
Ps	32: 5	I acknowledged my **s** to you,
Prov	5:22	in the toils of their **s**.
Eccl	5: 6	your mouth lead you into **s**,
Wis	10:13	but delivered him from **s**.
Sir	7:8	Do not commit a twice;
Isa	3: 9	proclaim their **s** like Sodom,
Jer	16:18	their iniquity and their **s**,
Dan	9:20	praying and confessing my **s**
Mic	6: 7	for the **s** of my soul?"
Mt	5:29	your right eye causes you to **s**,
Mk	3:29	is guilty of an eternal **s**"
Jn	8: 7	without **s** be the first to throw
Acts	7:60	Lord, do not hold this **s**
Rom	5:12	just as **s** came into the world
1 Cor	15:56	The sting of death is **s**,
2 Cor	5:21	him to be **s** who knew no **s**,
Eph	4:26	Be angry but do not **s**;
1 Tim	5:20	for those who persist in **s**,
Heb	4:15	as we are, yet without **s**.
Jas	1:15	it gives birth to **s**,
1 Pet	2:22	He committed no **s**,
1 Jn	1: 8	If we say that we have no **s**,

SINAI

Ex	19:20	descended upon Mount **S**,
Num	1:19	in the wilderness of **S**.
Ps	68:17	the Lord came from **S**
Gal	4:25	Hagar is Mount **S** in Arabia

SLANDER

Ps	15: 3	do not **s** with their tongue,
Prov	10:18	whoever utters **s** is a fool.
Sir	28:15	**S** has driven virtuous women
Mt	15:19	theft, false witness, **s**.
2 Cor	12:20	selfishness, **s**, gossip,
Eph	4:31	**s**, together with all malice,
Col	3: 8	malice, **s**, and abusive
1 Pet	2: 1	insincerity, envy, and all **s**.
2 Pet	2:10	they are not afraid to **s**
Jude	1: 8	and **s** the glorious ones.

SLAUGHTER

Ex	29:11	and you shall **s** the bull
Deut	12:15	you may **s** and eat meat
Prov	7:22	like an ox to the **s**,
Isa	53: 7	that is led to the **s**,
Jer	11:19	like a gentle lamb led to the **s**.
Zech	11: 4	of the flock doomed to **s**.
Acts	8:32	he was led to the **s**,

SLAVE (S) (SLAVERY)

Gen	9:26	and let Canaan be his **s**.
Mk	10:44	first among you must be **s** of
Lk	7: 2	A centurion there had a **s**
Jn	8:34	who commits sin is a **s** to sin.
Rom	7:25	I am a **s** to the law of God
1 Cor	7:21	Were you a **s** when called?
Gal	3:28	there is no longer **s** or free
Phil	2: 7	taking the form of a **s**,
Col	3:11	**s** and free
1 Tim	6: 1	are under the yoke of **s**
Philem	1:16	longer as a **s** but more than a **s**
2 Pet	2:19	for people are **s** to whatever
Rev	13:16	both free and **s**

SLEEP (ING)

Gen	2:21	LORD God caused a deep **s**
Ex	22:27	what else shall that person **s**?
Deut	24:12	shall not **s** in the garment
1 Sam	26:12	a deep **s** from the LORD
Ps	4: 8	both lie down and **s** in peace
Prov	6:10	A little **s**, a little slumber
Eccl	5:12	Sweet is the **s** of laborers
Isa	29:10	a spirit of deep **s**
Dan	12: 2	who **s** in the dust of
Mt	9:24	girl is not dead but **s**.
Acts	20: 9	Overcome by **s**,
1 Thess	5: 7	those who **s s** at night.

SLOW

Ex	4:10	I am **s** of speech and **s** of
Num	14:18	The LORD is **s** to anger
Judg	18: 9	Do not be **s** to go
Ps	86:15	**s** to anger and abounding in
Prov	14:29	Whoever is **s** to anger
Joel	2:13	**s** to anger, and abounding in
Nah	1: 3	The Lord is **s** to anger but
Lk	24:25	how **s** of heart to believe all
Jas	1:19	**s** to speak, **s** to anger
2 Pet	3: 9	The Lord is not **s** about his

SON (S)

Gen	5: 3	became the father of a **s**'"
Ex	4:23	I will kill your firstborn **s**.
Deut	18:10	who makes a **s** or daughter
2 Sam	7:14	and he shall be a **s** to me.
1 Kings	3:23	and your **s** is dead
2 Kings	6:29	So we cooked my **s** and ate
1 Chr	22:10	He shall be a **s** to me
1 Macc	1:48	to leave their **s** uncircumcised.
Ps	127: 3	**S** are indeed a heritage
Prov	3:12	the **s** in whom he delights.
Isa	7:14	and shall bear a **s**
Jer	31:20	Is Ephraim my dear **s**?
Hos	11: 1	Out of Egypt I called my **s**.
Am	7:14	nor a prophet's **s**
Mal	1: 6	A **s** honors his father
Mt	1: 1	the **s** of David, the **s** of
Mk	1:11	"You are my **S**
Lk	1:32	the **S** of the Most High
Jn	1:34	this is the **S** of God."
Acts	7:56	the **S** of Man
Rom	1: 4	declared to be **S** of God
1 Cor	15:28	then the **S** himself
Col	1:13	the kingdom of his beloved **S**,
1 Thess	1:10	wait for his **S** from heaven,
Heb	1: 2	spoken to us by a **S**,
Jas	2:21	he offered his **s** Isaac
2 Pet	1:17	"This is my **S**,
1 Jn	1: 3	with his **S** Jesus

Rev	1:13	like the **S** of Man

SONG (SING)

Ex	15: 1	sang this **s** to the LORD.
Deut	31:21	this **s** will confront them
Jdt	16:13	I will **s** to my God a new **s**:
Ps	33: 3	**S** to him a new **s**;
Isa	54: 1	burst into **s**
Rev	5: 9	**s** a new **s**:

SOUL (S)

Deut	6: 5	with all your **s**,
2 Kings	23:25	with all his **s**,
Ps	16: 9	and my **s** rejoices;
Prov	13:19	sweet to the **s**,
Lam	3:20	My **s** continually thinks
Mic	6: 7	for the sin of my **s**?"
Mt	10:28	cannot kill the **s**;
Lk	1:46	"My **s** magnifies the Lord,
1 Thess	5:23	spirit and **s** and body
Heb	4:12	divides **s** from spirit,
Jas	5:20	save the sinner's **s**
1 Pet	2:11	war against the **s**.
3 Jn	1: 2	it is well with your **s**.
Rev	6: 9	**s** of those who had been

SOUND

Gen	3: 8	heard the **s** of the Lord
Ex	32:18	it is the **s** of revelers
Deut	4:12	the **s** of words
Ps	66: 8	let the **s** of his praise
Ezek	1:24	like the **s** of mighty waters,
Joel	2: 1	**s** the alarm
Jn	3: 8	hear the **s** of it,
Acts	2: 2	came a **s** like the rush
1 Cor	14: 8	gives an indistinct **s**,
1 Tim	1:10	contrary to the **s**
2 Tim	1:13	standard of **s** teaching
Titus	1: 9	preach with **s** doctrine
Rev	1:15	like the **s** of many waters.

SOW

Ex	23:10	shall **s** your land
Job	4: 8	and **s** trouble
Ps	126: 5	those who **s** in tears
Eccl	11: 6	In the morning **s** your seed,
Hos	8: 7	they **s** the wind,
Mt	6:26	they neither **s** nor reap
1 Cor	15:36	What you **s** does not come
2 Pet	2:22	"The **s** is washed only to

SPEAK

Gen	18:27	upon myself to **s** to the Lord
Ex	4:12	teach you what you are to **s**."
Num	12: 8	I **s** face to face
Deut	18:20	presumes to **s** in my name
1 Sam	3: 9	'S, LORD, for your servant
2 Kings	18:26	"Please **s** to your servants
Job	13: 3	I would **s** to the Almighty
Ps	49: 3	mouth shall **s** wisdom;
Prov	23: 9	Do not **s** in the hearing
Eccl	3: 7	and a time to **s**;
Sir	4:5	Never **s** against the truth,
Isa	28:11	he will **s** to this people,
Jer	10: 5	they cannot **s**;
Ezek	3:18	**s** to warn the wicked
Dan	7:25	shall **s** words against
Mt	13:13	I **s** to them in parables
Mk	7:37	the mute to **s**."
Jn	12:49	what to say and what to **s**.

Acts	2: 4	began to **s** in other languages
1 Cor	12:30	Do all **s** in tongues?
Eph	4:25	let all of us **s** the truth
Jas	1:19	quick to listen, slow to **s**,

SPIRIT

Gen	6: 3	"My **s** shall not abide
Ex	31: 3	filled him with divine **s**,
Num	11:25	the **s** rested upon them,
Deut	34: 9	full of the **s** of wisdom,
Judg	6:34	the **s** of the LORD took
1 Sam	10: 6	the **s** of the LORD will possess
2 Sam	23: 2	The **s** of the LORD speaks
2 Kings	2: 9	a double share of your **s**."
2 Chr	18:21	be a lying **s**
Neh	9:20	gave your good **s**
Job	33: 4	The **s** of God has made me
Ps	31: 5	I commit my **s**;
Wis	1:6	For wisdom is a kindly **s**,
Isa	11: 2	The **s** of the LORD shall rest
Ezek	3:12	the **s** lifted me up,
Dan	4: 8	endowed with a **s**
Joel	2:28	I will pour out my **s**
Mt	1:18	child from the Holy **S**.
Mk	1: 8	baptize you with the Holy **S**."
Lk	1:15	filled with the Holy **S**.
Jn	1:33	you see the **S** descend
Acts	1: 5	baptized with the Holy **S**
Rom	7: 6	new life of the **S**.
1 Cor	2:10	the **S**; for the **S** searches
2 Cor	1:22	giving us his **S**
Gal	3: 2	receive the **S**
Eph	1:13	seal of the promised Holy **S**;
Col	2: 5	I am with you in **s**,
1 Thess	5:19	Do not quench the **S**.
2 Thess	2:13	sanctification by the **S**
1 Tim	4:1	vindicated in **s**,
2 Tim	1: 7	**s** of cowardice,
Heb	2: 4	by gifts of the Holy **S**,
1 Pet	1: 2	sanctified by the **S**
2 Pet	1:21	moved by the Holy **S**
1 Jn	3:24	by the **S** that he has given
Jude	1:20	pray in the Holy **S**;
Rev	1:10	in the **s** on the Lord's day

STAFF

Gen	38:25	cord and the **s**."
Ex	4: 4	became a **s** in his hand—
Num	17: 6	the **s** of Aaron was among
Ps	23: 4	your rod and your **s**—
Mic	7:14	your people with your **s**,
Zech	11:10	I took my **s** Favor

STAND (ING)

Gen	18:22	Abraham remained **s**
Ex	3: 5	on which you are **s** is holy
Num	22:23	saw the angel of the LORD **s**
Josh	4:10	remained **s** in the middle
2 Chr	18:18	host of heaven **s**
Sir	5:10	**S** firm for what you know,
Am	7: 7	Lord was **s** beside a wall
Zech	1: 8	He was **s** among the myrtle
Acts	7:55	Jesus **s** at the right hand
1 Cor	10:12	you think you are **s**,
1 Tim	3:13	deacons gain a good **s**
Jas	5: 9	Judge is **s** at the doors!
Rev	3:20	I am **s** at the door,

STAR (S)

Gen	1:16	rule the night—and the **s**.

50

Num 24:17 a **s** shall come out of Jacob.
Deut 1:10 numerous as the **s** of heaven.
Job 38: 7 morning **s** sang together
Ps 148: 3 praise him, all you shining **s**!
Eccl 12: 2 and the moon and the **s** are
Isa 14:13 above the **s** of God;
Dan 12: 3 like the **s** forever
Joel 2:10 **s** withdraw their shining.
Mt 2: 2 observed his **s** at its rising,
Mk 13:25 the **s** will be falling
Phil 2:15 you shine like **s** in the world.
Rev 1:16 right hand he held seven **s**,

STEADFAST
Ex 15:13 "In your **s** love you led
Num 14:18 and abounding in **s** love,
2 Sam 7:15 will not take my **s** love from
Neh 9:32 keeping covenant and **s** love
Ps 13: 5 trusted in your **s** love;
Isa 26: 3 Those of **s** mind
Joel 2:13 abounding in **s** love,
Heb 6:19 sure and **s** anchor of the soul,
1 Pet 5: 9 **s** in your faith,

STONE (D) (S)
Gen 28:18 took the **s** that he had put
Ex 28: 9 take two onyx **s**,
Deut 4:13 he wrote them on two **s**
Josh 7:25 Israel **s** him to death;
1 Sam 7:12 Samuel took a **s**
Ps 91:12 dash your foot against a **s**.
Isa 8:14 a **s** one strikes against;
Jer 3: 9 committing adultery with **s**
Ezek 11:19 heart of **s** from their flesh
Zech 3: 9 a single **s** with seven facets,
Mt 4: 6 dash your foot against a **s**.'"
Mk 12:10 'The **s** that the builders
Lk 4: 3 this **s** to become a loaf of
Jn 8: 7 first to throw a **s** at her."
Acts 4:11 'the **s** that was rejected
Rom 9:32 stumbled over the stumbling **s**,
2 Cor 3: 3 not on tablets of **s**
1 Pet 2: 4 a living **s**, though rejected
Rev 2:17 I will give a white **s**,

STRAIGHT
Ps 107: 7 led them by a **s** way,
Prov 3: 6 he will make **s** your paths.
Isa 40: 3 make **s** in the desert
Mt 3: 3 Lord, make his paths **s**.'"
Jn 1:23 'Make **s** the way of the Lord
Acts 9:11 street called **S**,
2 Pet 2:15 left the **s** road

STRANGER (S)
Gen 23: 4 "I am a **s** and an alien
Deut 10:19 love the **s**, for you were **s**
1 Macc 1:38 she became a dwelling of **s**;
Mt 25:35 I was a **s** and you welcomed
Jn 10: 5 They will not follow a **s**,
3 Jn 1: 5 even though they are **s** to you;

STRENGTH (EN) (ENS) (STRONG)
Ex 15: 2 LORD is my **s**
Deut 33:25 as your days, so is your **s**.
Judg 16:15 what makes your **s** so great."
1 Sam 2: 1 my **s** is exalted in my God
2 Sam 22:33 girded me with **s**
1 Chr 16:11 Seek the Lord and his **s**,
Neh 8:10 LORD is your **s**."

1 Macc 3:19 but **s** comes from Heaven.
Job 12:13 "With God are wisdom and **s**;
Ps 18: 1 LORD, my **s**.
Prov 24: 5 those who have **s**;
Isa 12: 2 God is my **s**
Mic 5: 4 feed his flock in the **s**
Hab 3:19 Lord, is my **s**;
Mk 12:30 with all your **s**.'
Lk 1:15 never drink wine or **s** drink;
Acts 15:32 encourage and **s** the believers.
1 Cor 1:25 stronger than human **s**.
Phil 4:13 things through him who **s** me.
2 Tim 4:17 gave me **s**,
Heb 11:34 won **s** out of weakness,
1 Pet 4:11 with the **s** that God supplies,

STRIKE
Gen 3:15 he will **s** your head,
Ex 3:20 **s** Egypt with all my wonders
Isa 11: 4 he shall **s** the earth
Zech 13: 7 **S** the shepherd,
Mal 4: 6 **s** the land with a curse
Mk 14:27 'I will **s** the shepherd,
Rev 11: 6 to **s** the earth

STUMBLE (STUMBLING)
Ps 37:24 though we **s**, we shall not fall
Prov 3:23 foot will not **s**.
Jer 13:16 before your feet **s**
Ezek 14: 3 iniquity as a **s** block
Hos 14: 9 transgressors **s** in them
Mal 2: 8 caused many to **s**
Mt 18: 9 eye causes you to **s**,
Jn 11: 9 during the day do not **s**,
Rom 9:33 stone that will make people **s**,
1 Pet 2: 8 "A stone that makes them **s**,

SUFFER (ING) (INGS)
Job 2:13 his **s** was very great.
Zech 10: 2 they **s** for lack of a shepherd
Lk 22:15 with you before I **s**;
24:26 Messiah should **s** these things
24:46 Messiah is to **s**
Acts 3:18 Messiah would **s**.
Rom 5: 3 our **s**, knowing that **s**
1 Cor 3:15 builder will **s** loss;
Heb 9:26 had to **s** again
1 Pet 3:17 better to **s** for doing good,
Rev 2:10 you are about to **s**.

SUN
Josh 10:13 the **s** stood still,
Judg 5:31 like the **s** as it rises
Ps 72: 5 while the **s** endures,
Eccl 1: 9 nothing new under the **s**.
Song 6:10 bright as the **s**,
Isa 60:19 **s** shall no longer be your light
Joel 2:31 **s** shall be turned to darkness
Mic 3: 6 **s** shall go down
Mal 4: 2 the **s** of righteousness shall
Mt 5:45 makes his **s** rise
Mk 13:24 **s** will be darkened,
Acts 2:20 **s** shall be turned to darkness
Eph 4:26 do not let the **s** go down
Rev 1:16 face was like the **s**

SWEAR (SWORE) (SWORN)
Gen 22:16 "By myself I have **s**,
Ex 6: 8 land that I **s** to give
Deut 10:20 by his name you shall **s**.

Josh 2:12 **s** to me by the Lord
Ps 24: 4 do not **s** deceitfully.
Isa 45:23 every tongue shall **s**."
Mt 5:34 Do not **s** at all,
Heb 6:13 one greater by whom to **s**,
Jas 5:12 do not **s**, either by heaven

SWEET (ER)
Ex 15:25 water became **s**.
Judg 14:18 "What is **s** than honey?
Job 20:12 wickedness is **s** in their
Ps 119:103 How **s** are your words
Prov 9:17 "Stolen water is **s**,
Eccl 5:12 **S** is the sleep of laborers
Isa 5:20 who put bitter for **s** and **s**
Ezek 3: 3 as **s** as honey.
Joel 3:18 shall drip **s** wine,
Rev 10:10 it was **s** as honey

SWORD (S)
Gen 3:24 a **s** flaming and turning
Ex 18: 4 delivered me from the **s**
Num 14: 3 fall by the **s**?
Deut 32:41 when I whet my flashing **s**,
Josh 5:13 before him with a drawn **s**
1 Sam 17:45 come to me with **s**
2 Sam 12:10 the **s** shall never depart
1 Chr 21:30 he was afraid of the **s**
Neh 4:18 builders had his **s**
Ps 22:20 Deliver my soul from the **s**,
Prov 5: 4 sharp as a two-edged **s**.
Sir 21:3 lawlessness is like a two-edged **s**
Isa 2: 4 shall not lift up **s**
Jer 15: 2 destined for the **s**, to the **s**;
Lam 1:20 the **s** bereaves;
Ezek 5: 2 strike with the **s**
Hos 2:18 abolish the bow, the **s**,
Mic 4: 3 beat their **s** into plowshares,
Mt 10:34 bring peace, but a **s**.
Lk 2:35 a **s** will pierce your own soul
Acts 12: 2 killed with the **s**.
Rom 13: 4 does not bear the **s**
Eph 6:17 and the **s** of the Spirit, which
Heb 4:12 sharper than any two-edged **s**,
Rev 1:16 sharp, two-edged **s**,

SYNAGOGUE (S)
Mt 4:23 teaching in their **s**
Lk 4:16 he went to the **s**
Jn 18:20 taught in **s**
Acts 13:14 they went into the **s**
Rev 2: 9 but are a **s** of Satan.

T

TABERNACLE
Ex 25: 9 of the **t** and of all its furniture
Lev 8:10 anointed the **t**
Num 1:50 appoint the Levites over the **t**
1 Chr 6:48 of the **t** of the house of God.

TABLET (S)
Ex 31:18 two **t** of the covenant,
Prov 3: 3 write them on the **t**
Isa 30: 8 before them on a **t**,
Lk 1:63 asked for a writing **t**

2 Cor	3: 3	not on **t** of stone

TAKE (N)

Gen	2:23	for out of Man this one was **t**."
Ex	6: 7	I will **t** you as my people.
Num	1: 2	**T** a census
Deut	1: 8	**t** possession of the land.
1 Sam	8:11	he will **t** your sons
1 Kings	11:34	I will not **t** the whole kingdom
1 Chr	17:13	**t** my steadfast love
Job	23:10	he knows the way that I **t**;
Ps	2:12	Happy are all who **t**
Sir	44:16	pleased the Lord and was **t**
Hos	1: 2	**t** for yourself a wife
Mt	1:20	afraid to **t** Mary
Mk	2: 9	'Stand up and **t** your mat
Lk	21: 7	this is about to **t** place?"
Acts	1:20	'Let another **t** his position
Eph	6:13	Therefore **t** up the whole
1 Tim	3: 5	how can he **t** care of God's
Heb	11: 5	Enoch was **t**
Rev	1: 1	what must soon **t** place;

TASTE (D)

Ex	16:31	the **t** of it was like wafers
Ps	34: 8	O **t** and see that the Lord is
Prov	24:13	sweet to your **t**.
Song	2: 3	sweet to my **t**.
Mt	16:28	will not **t** death
Col	2:21	Do not **t**, Do not touch"?
Heb	6: 4	have **t** the heavenly gift

TEACH

Ex	4:12d	**t** you what you are
Deut	6: 1	God charged me to **t**
1 Kings	8:36	when you **t** them the good
Job	6:24	**T** me, and I will be
Ps	25: 4	**t** me your paths.
Prov	9: 9	**t** the righteous
Jer	31:34	they **t** one another,
Mic	4: 2	that he may **t** us his ways
Mal	4: 4	the **t** of my servant Moses, the
Mt	10:24	disciple is not above the **t**,
Lk	11: 1	"Lord, **t** us to pray,
Jn	14:26	will **t** you everything,
Ac	5:28	orders not to **t** in this name,
Rom	2:21	that **t** others, will you not **t**
1 Cor	11:14	nature itself **t** you
Col	3:16	**t** and admonish one another
1 Tim	1: 3	instruct certain people not to **t**
2 Tim	2: 2	able to **t** others as well.
Titus	2: 1	**t** what is consistent
Heb	5:12	**t** you again the basic
Jas	3: 1	who **t** will be judged
2 Pet	2: 1	false **t** among you,
1 Jn	2:27	do not need anyone to **t** you.
Rev	2:20	is **t** and beguiling my servants

TEMPLE

Judg	4:21	drove the peg into his **t**,
1 Sam	3: 3	lying down in the **t**
1 Kings	6: 7	was heard in the **t**
2 Chr	2:12	build a **t** for the LORD,
Ezra	3:10	foundation of the **t**
Tob	14:5	they will rebuild the **t** of God,
1 Macc	4:48	and the interior of the **t**,
Ps	11: 4	LORD is in his holy **t**;
Isa	6: 1	his robe filled the **t**.
Jer	7: 4	"This is the **t** of the LORD,
Ezek	8:16	entrance of the **t**

Dan	5: 2	taken out of the **t**
Mic	1: 2	Lord from his holy **t**.
Hab	2:20	LORD is in his holy **t**;
Mt	4: 5	pinnacle of the **t**,
Mk	15:38	curtain of the **t** was torn
Lk	21: 5	speaking about the **t**,
Jn	2:14	**t** he found people selling
Acts	2:46	time together in the **t**,
1 Cor	3:16	you are God's **t**
2 Cor	6:16	we are the **t**
Eph	2:21	grows into a holy **t**
2 Thess	2: 4	seat in the **t**
Rev	3:12	pillar in the **t**

TEMPT (ED) (TEMPTER)

Mt	4: 1	to be **t** by the devil.
Mk	1:13	**t** by Satan;
Lk	4: 2	forty days he was **t**
1 Cor	7: 5	Satan may not **t** you
Gal	6: 1	you yourselves are not **t**.
1 Thess	3: 5	somehow the **t** had **t** you
Jas	1:13	God cannot be **t** by evil

TEST (ED)

Gen	22: 1	God **t** Abraham.
Deut	6:16	LORD your God to the **t**,
1 Kings	10: 1	she came to **t** him
1 Macc	2:52	found faithful when **t**,
Ps	26: 2	**t** my heart and mind.
Sir	44:20	he was **t** he proved faithful.
Jer	9: 7	refine and **t** them,
Mal	3:10	put me to the **t**,
Lk	4:12	God to the **t**.'"
Acts	5: 9	the Spirit of the Lord to the **t**?
1 Cor	3:13	fire will **t** what sort of work
2 Cor	13: 5	**T** yourselves.
Gal	6: 4	All must **t** their own work.
1 Thess	5:21	**t** everything; hold fast
Heb	3: 9	ancestors put me to the **t**,
Jas	1:12	stood the **t**
1 Jn	4: 1	**t** the spirits
Rev	3:10	**t** the inhabitants of the earth

TESTIFY (TESTIFIED) (TESTIFIES) (TESTIMONY)

Isa	59:12	sins **t** against us.
Jer	14: 7	our iniquities **t**
Lk	22:71	What further **t** do we need?
Jn	1: 7	witness to **t**
Acts	10:43	prophets **t** about him
1 Jn	5: 6	Spirit is the one that **t**,
Rev	1: 9	the **t** of Jesus.

THANK (S)

Lev	7:12	offer with the **t** offering
1 Chr	16: 8	give **t** to the LORD,
2 Chr	29:31	brought sacrifices and **t**
Ps	52: 9	I will **t** you forever,
Isa	38:18	Sheol cannot **t** you,
Lk	18:11	'God, I **t** you
Jn	11:41	"Father, I **t** you for having
Phil	1: 3	I **t** my God every time
1 Thess	3: 9	can we **t** God enough

THIEF (THIEVES)

Ex	22: 1	**t** shall pay
Mt	6:19	where **t** break in
Lk	12:39	hour the **t** was coming,
Jn	10:10	**t** comes only to steal
1 Thess	5: 2	come like a **t** in the night.

1 Pet	4:15	a murderer, a **t**, a criminal,
Rev	16:15	I am coming like a **t**!

THIRST (Y)

Ex	17: 3	livestock with **t**?"
Deut	28:48	hunger and **t**,
Ps	107: 9	he satisfies the **t**,
Mt	5: 6	those who hunger and **t**
Rom	12:20	if they are **t**,
Rev	7:16	**t** no more;

THOUSAND (S)

Deut	7: 9	to a **t** generations,
Josh	23:10	puts to flight a **t**,
1 Sam	18: 7	"Saul has killed his **t**,
Ps	50:10	cattle on a **t** hills.
Song	5:10	distinguished among ten **t**.
Mt	14:21	were about five **t** men,
2 Pet	3: 8	one day is like a **t** years,
Jude	1:14	Lord is coming with ten **t**
Rev	20: 4	reigned with Christ a **t** years.

THREE (THIRD)

Gen	6:10	Noah had **t** sons,
Ex	23:14	**T** times in the year
Deut	19:15	two or **t** witnesses
1 Sam	31: 8	Saul and his **t** sons
2 Sam	23: 9	among the **t** warriors
Job	2:11	when Job's **t** friends
Prov	30:15	**T** things are never satisfied;
Ezek	5:12	One **t** of you shall die
Dan	3:24	"Was it not **t** men
Am	1: 3	For **t** transgressions
Jon	1:17	of the fish **t** days and **t** nights
Zech	11: 8	disposed of the **t** shepherds,
Mt	12:40	Jonah was **t** days and **t** nights
Mk	8:31	after **t** days rise again.
Jn	2:19	in **t** days I will raise it
1 Cor	13:13	these **t**; and the greatest
2 Cor	12: 8	**T** times I appealed
1 Jn	5: 7	There are **t** that testify:
Rev	4: 7	**t** living creature

THRONE (S)

2 Sam	7:13	**t** of his kingdom
1 Chr	17:12	I will establish his **t**
Ps	11: 4	LORD's **t** is in heaven.
Prov	20:28	**t** is upheld by righteousness.
Isa	6: 1	Lord sitting on a **t**,
Jer	33:21	reign on his **t**,
Ezek	1:26	something like a **t**,
Dan	7: 9	Ancient One took his **t**,
Mt	5:34	it is the **t** of God,
Lk	1:32	give to him the **t**
Acts	7:49	'Heaven is my **t**,
Col	1:16	whether **t** or dominions
Heb	1: 8	"Your **t**, O God, is forever
Rev	2:13	where Satan's **t**

TIME (S)

Gen	4:26	At that **t** people
Ex	23:14	Three **t** in the year
Deut	32:35	the **t** when their foot shall slip
Esth	4:14	at such a **t** as this,
Ps	119:126	It is **t** for the LORD
Eccl	3: 1	a **t** for every matter
Sir	20:12	but pay for it seven **t** over.
Dan	7:25	for a **t**, two **t**,
Hos	10:12	it is **t** to seek the LORD,
Lk	21: 8	'The **t** is near!'

Rom 5: 6 right **t** Christ died
1 Cor 4: 5 judgment before the **t**,
2 Cor 6: 2 now is the acceptable **t**;
Gal 4: 4 fullness of **t** had come,
Eph 5:16 making the most of the **t**,
1 Tim 4: 1 in later **t** some will
Heb 9:28 appear a second **t**,
1 Pet 4:17 **t** has come for judgment
Rev 1: 3 for the **t** is near.

TONGUE (S)

Ex 4:10 and slow of **t**."
Job 33: 2 **t** in my mouth
Ps 34:13 Keep your **t** from evil,
Prov 6:17 a lying **t**,
Song 4:11 milk are under your **t**;
Isa 45:23 every **t** shall swear."
Jer 23:31 who use their own **t**
Mk 7:33 spat and touched his **t**.
Lk 16:24 cool my **t**;
Rom 14:11 every **t** shall give praise
1 Cor 14: 2 those who speak in a **t**
Phil 2:11 every **t** should confess
Jas 3: 5 **t** is a small member,

TOUCH (ED)

Gen 3: 3 nor shall you **t** it,
Ex 19:12 to **t** the edge of it.
Num 4:15 must not **t** the holy things,
1 Sam 10:26 whose hearts God had **t**.
Ps 105:15 "Do not **t** my anointed ones;
Wis 3: 1 no torment will ever **t** them.
Isa 52:11 **T** no unclean thing;
Ezek 9: 6 **t** no one who has
Dan 10:16 one in human form **t** my lips,
Mt 9:21 "If I only **t** his cloak,
Lk 18:15 that he might **t** them;
2 Cor 6:17 **t** nothing unclean;
Col 2:21 Do not taste, Do not **t**"?
Heb 11:28 would not **t** the firstborn

TRANSFIGURED

Mt 17: 2 he was **t** before them,

TRANSGRESSION (S)

Ex 23:21 pardon your **t**;
Ps 19:13 innocent of great **t**.
Isa 53: 8 stricken for the **t**
Dan 9:24 finish the **t**, to put an end to
Mic 1: 5 **t** of Jacob
Gal 6: 1 anyone is detected in a **t**,
2 Pet 2:16 rebuked for his own **t**;

TREASURE (S) (D)

Ex 19: 5 you shall be my **t** possession
Deut 33:19 hidden of the sand,
Ps 119:11 I **t** your word
Sir 41:14 wisdom and unseen **t**—
Isa 33: 6 fear of the Lord is Zion's **t**.
Mt 6:21 where your **t** is,
Lk 12:33 unfailing **t** in heaven,
2 Cor 4: 7 we have this **t** in clay jars,
1 Tim 6:19 the **t** of a good foundation
2 Tim 1:14 Guard the good **t** entrusted to

TREE (S)

Gen 1:29 every **t** with seed
Deut 21:23 night upon the **t**;

---

1 Kings 14:23 every green **t**;
Ps 52: 8 like a green olive **t**
Prov 3:18 She is a **t** of life
Isa 65:22 like the days of a **t**
Jer 17: 8 like a **t** planted by water,
46:22 like those who fell **t**.
Ezek 17:24 bring low the high **t**,
Dan 4:10 a **t** at the center of the earth.
Hos 9:10 fruit on the fig **t**,
Hab 3:17 Though the fig **t** does not
Zech 3:10 under your vine and fig **t**."
Mt 3:10 root of the **t**;
Mk 11:13 fig **t** in leaf,
Lk 19: 4 climbed a sycamore **t**
Acts 5:30 hanging him on a **t**
Rom 11:24 into their own wild olive **t**
Jas 3:12 Can a fig **t**,
Jude 1:12 autumn **t** without fruit,
Rev 2: 7 eat from the **t** of life

TRIBE (S)

Gen 49:28 these are the twelve **t**
Num 1: 4 man from each **t**
Josh 13:14 **t** of Levi
Judg 21: 6 **t** is cut off
1 Kings 11:13 give one **t** to your son,
Ps 122: 4 To it the **t** go up, the **t**
Heb 7:13 belonged to another **t**,
Rev 5: 5 Lion of the **t** of Judah,

TROUBLE (D)

Josh 7:25 "Why did you bring **t** on us?
Job 5: 7 are born to **t**
Ps 9: 9 stronghold in times of **t**.
Eccl 12: 1 days of **t** come,
Sir 51:10 forsake me in the days of **t**,
Isa 33: 2 salvation in the time of **t**.
Nah 1: 7 stronghold in a day of **t**;
Mt 6:34 Today's **t** is enough
Jn 14: 1 not let your hearts be **t**.

TRUE (TRUTH)

Gen 42:16 whether there is **t** in you;
Num 11:23 word will come **t**
Deut 18:22 does not take place or prove **t**,
1 Sam 9: 6 he says always comes **t**.
1 Kings 10: 6 "The report was **t**
2 Chr 15: 3 without the **t** God,
Ps 119:151 commandments are **t**.
Prov 22:21 what is right and **t**,
Jer 10:10 Lord is the **t** God;
Lk 16:11 entrust to you the **t**
Jn 1: 9 The **t** light,
Rom 3: 4 let God be proved **t**,
Eph 4:24 likeness of God in **t**
Phil 4: 8 whatever is **t**,
1 Thess 1: 9 living and **t** God,
1 Jn 2: 8 commandment that is **t**
2 Jn 1: 1 I love in the **t**,
3 Jn 1:12 testimony is **t**.
Rev 3: 7 of the holy one, the **t** one,

TRUMPET

Ex 19:16 blast of a **t**
Isa 27:13 on that day a great **t**
Ezek 33: 5 sound of the **t**
Joel 2:15 Blow the **t** in Zion;
Zech 9:14 God will sound the **t**
Mt 24:31 angels with a loud **t**
1 Cor 15:52 at the last **t**. For the **t**

---

1 Thess 4:16 sound of God's **t**,
Rev 1:10 voice like a **t**

TRUST (TRUSTWORTHY)

Ex 19: 9 so **t** you ever after."
Num 20:12 you did not **t** in me,
Deut 1:32 you have no **t**
Judg 11:20 Sihon did not **t**
1 Sam 3:20 Samuel was a **t** prophet
1 Chr 9:22 them in their office of **t**.
Job 4:18 servants he puts no **t**,
Ps 4: 5 put your **t** in the Lord.
Prov 3: 5 **T** in the Lord
Sir 2:6 **T** in him, and he will help
Isa 26: 4 **T** in the Lord forever,
Jer 2:37 those in whom you **t**,
Mic 7: 5 no **t** in a friend,
Titus 1: 9 word that is **t** in
Heb 2:13 "I will put my **t** in him."

TURN (ED)

Ex 23:27 enemies **t** their backs
Num 32:15 you **t** away from following
Deut 5:32 you shall not **t**
Josh 1: 7 do not **t** from it
2 Chr 7:14 **T** from their wicked ways,
Ps 6: 4 **T**, O Lord, save my life
Isa 6:10 **t** and be healed."
Jer 18:11 **T** now, all of you
Ezek 33: 9 warn the wicked to **t**
Joel 2:14 he will not **t** and relent,
Jon 3: 9 may **t** from his fierce anger,
Mal 4: 6 will **t** the hearts of parents
Mt 5:39 **t** the other also;
Lk 1:17 to **t** the hearts
Jn 12:40 with their heart and **t**—
Acts 3:19 **t** to God
Rom 3:12 All have **t** aside,
Gal 4: 9 how can you **t** back
2 Tim 4: 4 will **t** away from listening
1 Pet 3:11 let them **t** away

TWELVE

Gen 35:22 sons of Jacob were **t**.
Ex 24: 4 set up **t** pillars,
Josh 4: 3 'Take **t** stones
1 Kings 11:30 tore it into **t** pieces.
Mt 10: 1 summoned his **t** disciples
Lk 9:17 **t** baskets of broken pieces.
Jas 1: 1 To the **t** tribes
Rev 12: 1 crown of **t** stars.

TWO (TWO-EDGED)

Gen 1:16 God made the **t** great lights
Ex 31:18 gave him the **t** tablets
Deut 4:13 wrote them on **t** stone
1 Kings 3:16 **t** women who were prostitutes
Prov 30: 7 **T** things I ask of you
Eccl 4: 9 **T** are better than one,
Isa 6: 2 with **t** they covered their faces,
Ezek 1:11 each creature had **t** wings,
Dan 8: 3 It had **t** horns.
Zech 4:11 **t** olive trees
Mt 6:24 "No one can serve **t** masters;
Mk 6: 7 send them out **t** by **t**,
Lk 9:30 they saw **t** men,
1 Cor 6:16 "The **t** shall be one flesh."
Gal 4:24 women are **t** covenants.
Eph 5:31 will become one flesh."
Heb 4:12 sharper than any **t** sword,

Rev	11: 3	my **t** witnesses authority

U

UNBELIEF (UNBELIEVER) (UNBELIEVERS)

Mk	6: 6	he was amazed at their **u**.
Rom	11:20	broken off because of their **u**,
1 Cor	7:12	wife who is an **u**,
2 Cor	4: 4	blinded the minds of the **u**,
1 Tim	1:13	acted ignorantly in **u**,
Heb	3:19	enter because of **u**.

UNCLEAN

Lev	5: 2	any of you touch any **u** thing
1 Macc	1:47	sacrifice swine and other **u**
Ps	106:39	became **u** by their acts,
Eccl	9: 2	to the clean and the **u**,
Isa	6: 5	man of **u** lips,
Mk	3:11	Whenever the **u** spirits
Acts	10:14	anything that is profane or **u**."
Rom	14:14	nothing is **u** in itself;
2 Cor	6:17	touch nothing **u**;
Rev	21:27	nothing **u** will enter it,

UNDERSTAND (ING)

Gen	11: 7	not **u** one another's speech,"
Ex	36: 1	skill and **u** to know how
Tob	4:19	For none of the nations has **u**,
Job	42: 3	have uttered what I did not **u**,
Ps	73:16	I thought how to **u** this,
Prov	2: 5	then you will **u** the fear
Isa	1: 3	people do not **u**.
Jer	17: 9	who can **u** it?
Dan	9:25	Know therefore and **u**:
Hos	14: 9	Those who are wise **u**
Mt	13:15	**u** with their heart
Mk	4:13	"Do you not **u** this parable?
Lk	24:45	minds to **u** the scriptures,
Jn	13: 7	later you will **u**."
Acts	8:30	you **u** what you are reading?"
Rom	7:15	I do not **u** my own actions.
1 Cor	2:12	so that we may **u**
Eph	5:17	**u** what the will
Heb	11: 3	By faith we **u**
Jas	3:13	Who is wise and **u**
2 Pet	1:20	you must **u** this,
1 Jn	5:20	and has given us **u**

UNRIGHTEOUS (NESS)

Ps	92:15	there is no **u** in him.
Mt	5:45	righteous and on the **u**.
1 Pet	3:18	righteous for the **u**,
2 Pet	2: 9	keep the **u** under punishment
1 Jn	1: 9	cleanse us from all **u**.

UPRIGHT

Gen	37: 7	sheaf rose and stood **u**;
Deut	32: 4	just and **u** is he;
Job	1: 1	man was blameless and **u**,
Ps	7:10	saves the **u** in heart.
Prov	2: 7	wisdom for the **u**;
Titus	1: 8	prudent, **u**, devout,

USE (FUL)

Ex	20: 7	make wrongful **u**

Deut	5:11	wrongful **u** of the name
Rom	9:21	**u** and another for ordinary **u**
Gal	5:13	do not **u** your freedom
Eph	4:29	only what is **u** for building up,
2 Tim	2:20	some for special **u**,

V

VAIN (VANITY)

Lev	26:16	sow your seed in **v**,
Ps	2: 1	peoples plot in **v**?
Eccl	1: 2	**V** of vanities,
Isa	65:23	shall not labor in **v**,
Ezek	6:10	not threaten in **v**
Mt	15: 9	in **v** do they worship me,
Acts	4:25	peoples imagine **v** things?
1 Cor	15: 2	have come to believe in **v**.
2 Cor	6: 1	grace of God in **v**.
Gal	2: 2	had not run, in **v**.
Phil	2:16	did not run in **v** or labor in **v**.

VENGEANCE

Gen	4:15	suffer a sevenfold **v**."
Num	31: 3	execute the LORD's **v**
Ps	94: 1	God of **v**, you God of **v**,
Sir	28:1	vengeful will face the Lord's **v**,
Isa	34: 8	day of **v**,
Jer	50:15	this is the **v** of the LORD:
Nah	1: 2	LORD takes **v**

VICTORY

1 Sam	2: 1	rejoice in my **v**.
2 Sam	8: 6	Lord gave **v** to David
Ps	33:17	vain hope for **v**.
Prov	21:31	**v** belongs to the LORD.
Zeph	3:17	warrior who gives **v**;
1 Cor	15:54	swallowed up in **v**."
1 Jn	5: 4	**v** that conquers the world,

VINE (YARD)

Gen	9:20	first to plant a **v**.
Deut	32:32	Their **v** comes
1 Kings	21: 1	had a **v** in Jezreel,
Ps	80: 8	brought a **v** out of Egypt;
Isa	36:16	eat from your own **v**
Jer	2:21	planted you as a choice **v**,
Ezek	17: 6	became a **v** spreading
Hos	10: 1	Israel is a luxuriant **v**
Mk	14:25	fruit of the **v**
Jn	15: 1	"I am the true **v**,
1 Cor	9: 7	Who plants a **v**
Rev	14:18	clusters of the **v**

VIOLENT (VIOLENCE)

Gen	6:11	earth was filled with **v**.
Prov	3:31	Do not envy the **v**
Ezek	18:10	son who is **v**,
Mt	11:12	**v** take it by force.
1 Tim	3: 3	not **v** but gentle,
Titus	1: 7	**v** or greedy for gain;

VIRGIN

1 Kings	1: 2	"Let a young **v**
Jer	31:21	Return, O **v** Israel,
Lam	2:13	O **v** daughter Zion?
Mt	1:23	**v** shall conceive

Lk	1:34	since I am a **v**?"
1 Cor	7:28	if a **v** marries,
2 Cor	11: 2	chaste **v** to Christ.

VISION (S)

Gen	15: 1	Abram in a **v**,
Num	24: 4	sees the **v** of the Almighty,
1 Sam	3:15	tell the **v** to Eli.
Ps	89:19	spoke in a **v**
Isa	22: 1	valley of **v**.
Jer	23:16	speak **v** of their own minds,
Dan	7: 2	saw in my **v**
Lk	1:22	he had seen a **v**
Acts	9:10	said to him in a **v**,
Rev	9:17	saw the horses in my **v**:

VOICE

Gen	3:17	listened to the **v**
Deut	4:33	heard the **v** of a god
1 Sam	15:22	obeying the **v**
Job	40: 9	thunder with a **v**
Ps	19: 4	their **v** goes out
Prov	1:20	she raises her **v**.
Isa	40: 3	A **v** cries out:
Jer	31:15	A **v** is heard
Dan	9:14	disobeyed his **v**.
Mt	2:18	"A **v** was heard
Mk	1: 3	**v** of one crying out
Jn	10:18	"I am the **v**
Rom	10:18	"Their **v** has gone out
Heb	3: 7	if you hear his **v**,
2 Pet	1:17	that **v** was conveyed
	1:18	this **v** come from heaven,
	2:16	with a human **v** and restrained
Rev	3:20	you hear my **v**

VOW (S)

Gen	28:20	Jacob made a **v**,
Num	6: 2	women make a special **v**,
Deut	23:21	If you make a **v**
Judg	11:30	Jephthah made a **v**
1 Sam	1:11	She made this **v**:
Ps	22:25	my **v** I will pay
Eccl	5: 4	make a **v** to God,
Sir	18:23	Before making a **v**, prepare
Jon	1:16	LORD and made **v**.
Acts	18:18	he was under a **v**.

W

WAIT (S)

Ps	27:14	**W** for the LORD;
Prov	1:18	they lie in **w**—
Sir	6:19	and **w** for her good harvest.
Isa	30:18	Therefore the Lord **w**
Lam	3:26	should **w** quietly
Hab	2: 3	**w** for it;
Acts	1: 4	**w** there for the promise
Rom	8:23	while we **w** for adoption,
Gal	5: 5	we eagerly **w** for the hope
1 Thess	1:10	**w** for his Son from heaven
Titus	2:13	we **w** for the blessed hope

WALK (ED) (ING)

Gen	5:24	Enoch **w** with God;
Deut	10:12	**w** in all his ways,

Josh	22: 5	**w** in all his ways,
Ps	15: 2	**w** blamelessly,
Prov	4:12	When you **w**,
Isa	2: 3	we may **w** in his paths."
Jer	6:16	**w** in it, and find rest
Dan	4:37	**w** in pride.
Am	3: 3	Do two **w** together
Mic	4: 5	**w** in the name of the LORD
Zech	10:12	**w** in his name,
Mt	14:26	disciples saw him **w**
Mk	2: 9	take your mat and **w**?
Jn	8:12	**w** in darkness
Acts	3: 8	stood and began to **w**,
2 Cor	5: 7	we **w** by faith,
1 Jn	1: 7	we **w** in the light
2 Jn	1: 6	we **w** according to his
3 Jn	1: 3	you **w** in the truth.
Rev	9:20	cannot see or hear or **w**.

WANT (ING)

Ps	23: 1	I shall not **w**.
Dan	5:27	on the scales and found **w**;
Lk	18:41	"What do you **w** me
Rom	7:15	do not do what I **w**,
2 Cor	12:14	I do not **w** what is yours
Phil	3:10	I **w** to know Christ

WAR (WARRIOR)

Ex	17:16	LORD will have **w**
Josh	11:23	rest from **w**.
1 Chr	28: 3	are a **w** and have shed blood.'
1 Macc	2:66	has been a mighty **w**
Ps	68:30	delight in **w**.
Eccl	3: 8	time for **w**,
Isa	2: 4	they learn **w** any more.
Dan	7:21	horn made **w**
Rom	7:23	another law at **w**
2 Cor	10: 3	we do not wage **w**
1 Pet	2:11	wage **w** against the soul.
Rev	12: 7	**w** broke out

WASH (ED)

2 Kings	5:14	**w** in the Jordan
Ps	51: 7	**w** me, and I shall be whiter
Jer	4:14	**w** your heart clean
Lk	11:38	he did not first **w**
Jn	9: 7	**w** in the pool
1 Cor	6:11	you were **w**, you were
Rev	22:14	those who **w** their robes,

WATER (S)

Gen	1: 2	over the face of the **w**.
Ex	7:20	struck the **w**
Num	5:19	be immune to this **w**
2 Kings	2: 8	struck the **w**; the **w** was parted
Ps	1: 3	planted by streams of **w**,
Prov	5:15	Drink **w**
Eccl	11: 1	bread upon the **w**,
Sir	15:3	him the **w** of wisdom to drink.
Isa	12: 3	With joy you will draw **w**
Jer	2:13	fountain of living **w**,
Ezek	36:25	sprinkle clean **w**
Mt	14:29	walking on the **w**,
Lk	5: 4	"Put out into the deep **w**
Jn	4:10	steward tasted the **w**
Eph	5:26	washing of **w** by the word
Heb	10:22	washed with pure **w**.
Jas	3:11	brackish **w**?
1 Jn	5: 6	who came by **w**
Rev	7:17	springs of the **w**

WAY (S)

Gen	3:24	guard the **w**
Ex	13:21	lead them along the **w**,
Deut	1:33	before you on the **w**
1 Sam	12:23	right **w**.
2 Sam	22:31	his **w** is perfect;
1 Kings	8:36	good **w** in which they should
2 Chr	6:27	teach them the good **w**
Job	23:10	he knows the **w**
Ps	1: 6	over the **w** of the righteous
Prov	3: 6	In all your **w** acknowledge
Sir	2:15	who love him keep his **w**.
Isa	30:21	"This is the **w**;
Jer	21: 8	before you the **w** of life
Mal	3: 1	prepare the **w** before me,
Mt	3: 3	'Prepare the **w**
Lk	7:27	prepare your **w**
Jn	14: 6	"I am the **w**,
Acts	1:11	come in the same **w**
1 Cor	9:24	Run in such a **w**
Eph	4:20	That is not the **w**
Col	3: 7	These are the **w**
Heb	9: 8	indicates that the **w**
2 Pet	2:21	never to have known the **w**
Rev	15: 3	Just and true are your **w**,

WEAK

Judg	16: 7	I shall become **w**,
Ps	72:13	He has pity on the **w**
Ezek	34: 4	strengthened the **w**,
Mt	26:41	flesh is **w**."
Acts	20:35	we must support the **w**,
Rom	14: 1	**w** in faith,
1 Cor	1:27	God chose what is **w**
2 Cor	12:10	whenever I am **w**,
Gal	4: 9	turn back again to the **w**
1 Thess	5:14	help the **w**,
Heb	7:18	because it was **w**

WEALTH

Deut	8:17	hand have gotten me this **w**."
2 Chr	1:11	**w**, honor,
Ps	49: 6	trust in their **w**
Prov	13: 7	yet have great **w**.
Eccl	5:10	nor the lover of **w**,
Song	8: 7	all the **w** of his house,
Sir	11:14	and **w**, come from the Lord.
Mt	13:22	lure of **w**
Lk	16:11	dishonest **w**,
Rev	5:12	receive power and **w**

WEEP (ING)

Ps	6: 8	heard the sound of my **w**.
Eccl	3: 4	a time to **w**,
Jer	3:21	plaintive **w** of Israel's children,
Lam	1:16	For these things I **w**;
Lk	6:21	"Blessed are you who **w**
Rom	12:15	**w** with those who **w**.

WHEAT

Ex	34:22	fruits of **w** harvest,
Mt	3:12	gather his **w**
Lk	22:31	sift all of you like **w**,
Jn	12:24	unless a grain of **w**

WHITE (R)

Ps	51: 7	I shall be **w** than snow.
Dan	7: 9	clothing was **w** as snow,
Zech	1: 8	**w** horses.
Mt	5:36	make one hair **w**

Acts	1:10	men in **w** robes
Rev	1:14	hair were **w** as **w** wool,

WICKED (NESS)

Gen	13:13	people of Sodom were **w**,
Ex	23: 1	hands with the **w**
Num	14:35	all this **w** congregation
2 Kings	17:11	They did **w** things,
2 Chr	7:14	turn from their **w** ways,
Job	15:20	**w** writhe in pain
Ps	1: 1	advice of the **w**,
Prov	4:14	enter the path of the **w**,
Eccl	7:15	there are **w** people
Wis	2:21	for their **w** blinded them,
Sir	15:20	commanded anyone to be **w**,
Isa	11: 4	he shall kill the **w**.
Ezek	3:18	If I say to the **w**,
Dan	12:10	**w** shall continue to act **w**
Lk	6:35	ungrateful and the **w**.
Acts	1:18	with the reward of his **w**;
1 Cor	5:13	"Drive out the **w**
2 Tim	2:19	turn away from **w**."
Heb	1: 9	righteousness and hated **w**;

WIDOW (S)

Ex	22:22	shall not abuse any **w**
Deut	10:18	orphan and the **w**,
Ruth	4: 5	**w** of the dead man,
Jdt	8:4	Judith remained as a **w** for
Ps	68: 5	protector of the **w**
Isa	1:17	plead for the **w**.
Lam	1: 1	How like a **w**
Ezek	22: 7	and the **w** are wronged in you.
Mk	12:19	marry the **w**
Lk	2:37	**w** to the age of eighty-four.
1 Tim	5: 4	**w** has children
Rev	18: 7	no **w**, and I will never see grief

WIFE (WIVES)

Gen	2:24	clings to his **w**,
Ex	20:17	covet your neighbor's **w**,
Num	5:12	man's **w** goes astray
Ruth	4:13	she became his **w**.
2 Sam	12:10	taken the **w** of Uriah
Ezra	10:11	from the foreign **w**."
Tob	8:6	his **w** Eve as a helper and
Ps	128: 3	**w** will be like a fruitful
Prov	5:18	rejoice in the **w** of your youth,
Eccl	9: 9	Enjoy life with the **w**
Sir	26:1	is the husband of a good **w**;
Hos	1: 2	take for yourself a **w**
Mal	2:14	between you and the **w**
Mt	1:20	take Mary as your **w**,
Mk	6:18	have your brother's **w**."
Lk	17:32	Remember Lot's **w**.
1 Cor	7: 2	man should have his own **w**
Eph	5:23	head of the **w**
Rev	21: 9	**w** of the Lamb."

WILL (ING)

Num	30: 5	LORD **w** forgive her,
1 Sam	2:25	it was the **w** of the LORD
2 Kings	24: 4	LORD was not **w** to pardon.
1 Chr	13: 2	it is the **w** of the LORD
Ezra	7:18	according to the **w**
Tob	12:18	not acting on my own **w**,
2 Macc	12:16	the town by the **w** of God.
Ps	40: 8	delight to do your **w**,
Wis	14:5	your **w** that works of your
Isa	30:19	He **w** surely be gracious

Jer 3:17 follow their own evil **w**.
Ezek 16:27 up to the **w** of your enemies,
Dan 11:28 shall work his **w**,
Mt 6:10 Your **w** be done,
Mk 3:35 Whoever does the **w**
Lk 22:42 not my **w** but yours be done."
Jn 1:51 you **w** see heaven
Acts 21:14 "The Lord's **w** be done."
Rom 2:18 know his **w**
1 Cor 1: 1 by the **w** of God,
2 Cor 1:10 he **w** rescue us again,
Gal 1: 4 according to the **w**
Eph 1: 5 good pleasure of his **w**,
Phil 2:13 enabling you both to **w**
Col 1: 9 knowledge of God's **w**
1 Thess 4: 3 this is the **w** of God,
2 Tim 3: 1 distressing times **w** come.
Heb 2: 4 distributed according to his **w**.
Jas 3: 4 wherever the **w** of the pilot
1 Pet 2:15 it is God's **w**
2 Pet 1:21 ever came by human **w**,
1 Jn 2:17 those who do the **w** of God
Rev 4:11 by your **w** they existed

WIND (WHIRLWIND)

Gen 1: 2 **w** from God swept
1 Kings 19:11 there was a great **w**,
2 Kings 2:11 Elijah ascended in a **w**
Ps 1: 4 chaff that the **w** drives away,
Prov 11:29 households will inherit **w**,
Eccl 1:14 vanity and chasing after **w**.
Ezek 5: 2 shall scatter to the **w**,
Hos 8: 7 they sow the **w**,
Jon 1: 4 LORD hurled a great **w**
Nah 1: 3 His way is in **w** and storm,
Mk 6:51 the **w** ceased.
Jn 3: 8 **w** blows where it chooses,
Acts 2: 2 rush of a violent **w**,
Eph 4:14 every **w** of doctrine,
Jas 1: 6 tossed by the **w**;

WINE

Gen 9:21 drank some of the **w**
Num 6: 3 separate themselves from **w**
Deut 33:28 land of grain and **w**,
Judg 13: 4 be careful not to drink **w**
1 Sam 1:15 have drunk neither **w**
Neh 13:15 people treading **w** presses
Ps 4: 7 grain and **w** abound.
Prov 3:10 vats will be bursting with **w**,
Eccl 2: 3 cheer my body with **w**
Song 1: 2 love is better than **w**,
Sir 31:29 **W** drunk to excess leads to
Isa 1:22 **w** is mixed with water.
Dan 1: 8 rations of food and **w**;
Joel 2:24 overflow with **w** and oil.
Am 5:11 shall not drink their **w**.
Mic 2:11 preach to you of **w**
6:15 tread grapes, but not drink **w**.
Zeph 1:13 they shall not drink **w** from
Mt 9:17 new **w** put into old **w**skins;
Lk 1:15 must never drink **w**
Jn 2: 3 "They have no **w**."
Acts 2:13 "They are filled with new **w**."
Rom 14:21 eat meat or drink **w**
Eph 5:18 Do not get drunk with **w**,
1 Tim 3: 8 not indulging in much **w**,
Rev 14: 8 nations drink of the **w**

WINGS

Ex 19: 4 on eagles' **w**
Ruth 2:12 under whose **w**
1 Kings 8: 7 spread out their **w**
Ps 17: 8 in the shadow of your **w**,
Isa 6: 2 each had six **w**:
Ezek 1: 6 each of them had four **w**.
Zech 5: 9 was in their **w**; they had **w**
Mal 4: 2 with healing in its **w**.
Lk 13:34 brood under her **w**,
Rev 4: 8 each of them with six **w**,

WISDOM

Deut 4: 6 show your **w** and discernment
1 Kings 4:29 gave Solomon very great **w**,
2 Chr 1:10 Give me now **w**
Job 11: 6 of **w**! For **w** is many-sided
Ps 37:30 righteous utter **w**,
Prov 1: 7 fools despise **w**
Eccl 1:13 search out by **w**
Isa 11: 2 spirit of **w**
Jer 9:23 boast in their **w**,
Bar 3:12 forsaken the foundatin of **w**
Ezek 28:12 full of **w**
Dan 5:14 excellent **w** are found
Mic 6: 9 is sound **w** to fear your name
Mt 11:19 Yet **w** is vindicated
Lk 2:52 Jesus increased in **w**
Acts 6:10 could not withstand the **w**
Rom 11:33 riches and **w**
1 Cor 1:19 destroy the **w**
Eph 1:17 spirit of **w**
Col 1: 9 all spiritual **w**
Jas 1: 5 lacking in **w**,
Rev 7:12 Blessing and glory and **w**

WISE

Gen 41:39 discerning and **w** as you.
Ex 7:11 Pharaoh summoned the **w**
Deut 4: 6 nation is a **w**
1 Kings 2: 9 you are a **w** man;
Job 9: 4 He is **w** in heart,
Ps 94: 8 when will you be **w**?
Prov 3:35 **w** will inherit honor,
Eccl 2:14 **w** have eyes in their head
Sir 7:19 Do not dismiss a **w** and good
Isa 29:14 wisdom of their **w** shall
Jer 8: 9 **w** shall be put to shame
Dan 2:21 gives wisdom to the **w**
Mt 25: 4 **w** took flasks of oil
Rom 1:22 Claiming to be **w**,
1 Cor 1:19 destroy the wisdom of the **w**,
Eph 5:15 unwise people but as **w**,
Jas 3:13 Who is **w** and understanding

WITNESS (ES)

Gen 31:44 **w** between you
Num 35:30 testimony of a single **w**.
Deut 19:15 evidence of two or three **w**
Josh 22:27 **w** between us and you,
Judg 11:10 LORD will be **w** between us;
1 Sam 12: 5 LORD is **w** against you,
Job 16:19 my **w** is in heaven,
Prov 12:17 false **w** speaks deceitfully.
Rom 2:15 conscience also bears **w**;
Heb 10:28 testimony of two or three **w**."
1 Pet 5: 1 **w** of the sufferings of Christ
Rev 1: 5 Christ, the faithful **w**,

WOMAN (WOMEN)

Gen 2:22 he made into a **w**
Ex 3:22 each **w** shall ask her neighbor
Num 30: 3 When a **w** makes a vow
Deut 20: 7 become engaged to a **w**
Judg 4: 9 into the hand of a **w**."
Ruth 3:11 you are a worthy **w**.
1 Sam 1:15 I am a **w** deeply troubled,
2 Sam 11: 2 from the roof a **w** bathing;
1 Kings 17:24 the **w** said to Elijah,
2 Kings 4: 8 where a wealthy **w** lived,
Jdt 8:31 a God-fearing **w**, pray for us
Job 2:10 speak as any foolish **w**
Ps 113: 9 gives the barren **w** a home,
Prov 11:16 gracious **w** gets honor,
Sir 9:3 Do not go near a loose **w**,
Isa 54: 1 children of the desolate **w**
Mt 5:28 looks at a **w** with lust
Mk 7:25 **w** whose little daughter
Lk 1:42 "Blessed are you among **w**,
Jn 4: 7 Samaritan **w** came to draw
Acts 16:14 certain **w** named Lydia,
Rom 7: 2 married **w** is bound
1 Cor 14:34 **w** should be silent
Gal 4: 4 Son, born of a **w**,
1 Tim 2:11 Let a **w** learn in silence
2 Tim 3: 6 captivate silly **w**,
Titus 2: 3 tell the older **w** to be reverent
Rev 12: 1 **w** clothed with the sun,

WONDERFUL

Gen 18:14 anything too **w** for the LORD?
Judg 13:18 It is too **w**."
2 Sam 1:26 your love to me was **w**,
1 Chr 16: 9 tell of all his **w** works.
Job 42: 3 things too **w** for me,
Ps 105: 2 tell of all his **w** works.
Sir 11:4 works of the Lord are **w**,
Isa 9: 6 he is named **W** Counselor,
Lk 13:17 rejoicing at all the **w** things

WONDERS

Ex 3:20 strike Egypt with all my **w**
Ps 77:14 God who works **w**;
Sir 18:6 to fathom the **w** of the Lord
Dan 4: 3 how mighty his **w**!
Jn 4:48 "Unless you see signs and **w**
2 Cor 12:12 and **w** and mighty works.
2 Thess 2: 9 all power, signs, lying **w**,
Heb 2: 4 testimony by signs and **w**

WORD (S)

Gen 15: 1 After these things the **w**
Ex 20: 1 Then God spoke all these **w**:
Num 30: 2 he shall not break his **w**;
Deut 8: 3 every **w** that comes from the
1 Sam 3: 1 **w** of the LORD was rare
1 Kings 8:56 not one **w** has failed
1 Chr 17: 3 **w** of the LORD came
2 Chr 36:22 fulfillment of the **w** of the
Tob 14:4 None of all their **w** will fail
Ps 33: 4 **w** of the LORD is upright
Prov 12:25 a good **w** cheers it up.
Eccl 5: 2 therefore let your **w** be few.
Sir 32:8 Be brief; say much in few **w**;
Isa 1:10 Hear the **w** of the LORD,
Jer 5:13 the **w** is not in them.
Dan 9: 2 according to the **w** of the LORD
Mk 4:14 sower sows the **w**.
Lk 1: 2 servants of the **w**,

Jn	1: 1	was the **W**, and the **W**
Acts	4: 4	heard the **w** believed;
Rom	9: 6	not as though the **w** of God
2 Cor	2:17	peddlers of God's **w**
Gal	6: 6	taught the **w**
Eph	6:17	which is the **w** of God.
Phil	2:16	holding fast to the **w**
Col	3:16	Let the **w** of Christ dwell
2 Thess	2:15	either by **w** of mouth
Heb	1: 3	all things by his powerful **w**.
Jas	1:21	meekness the implanted **w**
1 Pet	1:23	enduring **w** of God.
2 Pet	3: 5	by the **w** of God
1 Jn	1: 1	concerning the **w** of life—
Rev	3: 8	you have kept my **w**

WORK (S)

Gen	2: 2	God finished the **w**
Ex	20:10	you shall not do any **w**—
Deut	14:29	bless you in all the **w**
1 Chr	22:16	Now begin the **w**,
2 Chr	2: 7	artisan skilled to **w** in gold,
Ezra	4:24	the **w** on the house of God
Job	1:10	You have blessed the **w**
Ps	8: 6	dominion over the **w**
Eccl	11: 5	you do not know the **w**
Isa	2: 8	they bow down to the **w**
Jer	48:10	slack in doing the **w**
Lk	13:14	six days on which **w**
Jn	6:27	Do not **w** for the food
Acts	13:25	John was finishing his **w**,
Rom	4: 6	righteousness apart from **w**:
1 Cor	3:13	**w** of each builder
Gal	6: 4	All must test their own **w**;
Eph	3:20	power at **w** within us
Phil	1: 6	one who began a good **w**
1 Thess	4:11	to **w** with your hands,
2 Thess	2: 7	lawlessness is already at **w**,
1 Tim	6:18	to be rich in good **w**,
2 Tim	2:21	ready for every good **w**
Heb	6:10	overlook your **w**

WORLD

1 Chr	16:30	**w** is firmly established;
Ps	9: 8	the **w** with righteousness;
Isa	13:11	punish the **w** for its evil,
Mt	5:14	are the light of the **w**.
Jn	1:10	He was in the **w**, and the **w**
Acts	17:31	the **w** judged in righteousness
Rom	3:19	whole **w** may be held
1 Cor	1:27	foolish in the **w**
2 Cor	5:19	reconciling the **w** to himself,
Gal	6:14	by which the **w** has been
1 Tim	1:15	Jesus came into the **w**
Heb	1: 6	firstborn into the **w**,
Jas	1:27	unstained by the **w**.
1 Pet	1:20	foundation of the **w**.
1 Jn	2: 2	sins of the whole **w**.
Rev	11:15	"The kingdom of the **w**

WORSHIP

Ex	4:23	that he may **w** me."
Deut	12: 4	You shall not **w** the LORD
2 Kings	17:37	You shall not **w** other gods;
1 Chr	16:29	**W** the LORD in holy splendor
Ps	95: 6	come, let us **w**
Sir	35:10	Be generous when you **w** the
Dan	3:28	serve and **w** any god
Jon	1: 9	"I **w** the LORD,
Zech	14:17	go up to Jerusalem to **w**

Mt	4: 9	fall down and **w** me."
Lk	4: 8	'W the Lord your God,
Jn	4:24	who **w** him must **w** in spirit
Rom	12: 1	God, which is your spiritual **w**.
1 Cor	10:14	friends, flee from the **w** of idols.
Rev	4:10	**w** the one who lives forever

WORTHY

2 Sam	22: 4	who is **w** to be praised,
Mt	10:37	is not **w** of me;
Lk	15:19	I am no longer **w** to be called
Jn	1:27	I am not **w** to untie the thong
Eph	4: 1	lead a life **w** of the calling
Phil	1:27	manner **w** of the gospel of
Col	1:10	may lead lives **w** of the Lord,
Heb	3: 3	Yet Jesus is **w** of more glory
3 Jn	1: 6	on in a manner **w** of God;
Rev	5:12	"W is the Lamb that was

WRATH

Num	16:46	For **w** has gone out
1 Chr	27:24	yet **w** came upon Israel for
2 Chr	36:16	until the **w** of the LORD
1 Macc	1:64	Very great **w** came upon Israel
Ps	2: 5	speak to them in his **w**,
Prov	15: 1	A soft answer turns away **w**,
Isa	13:13	the **w** of the LORD of hosts
Jer	6:11	I am full of the **w** of the LORD;
Lam	4:11	gave full vent to his **w**;
Ezek	20: 8	I would pour out my **w** upon
Zeph	1:15	will be a day of **w**,
Mt	3: 7	flee from the **w** to come?
Jn	3:36	must endure God's **w**.
Rom	2: 5	storing up **w** for yourself
Eph	2: 3	were by nature children of **w**,
1 Thess	5: 9	has destined us not for **w**
Rev	6:17	great day of their **w** has come,

WRITE (WRITING) (WRITTEN) (WROTE)

Ex	24: 4	Moses **w** down all the words
	34:27	LORD said to Moses: **W** these
Num	17: 2	**W** each man's name on his
Deut	10: 2	I will **w** on the tablets
1 Kings	2:3	as it is **w** in the law of Moses,
Prov	3: 3	**w** them on the tablet of
Jer	31:33	I will **w** it on their hearts;
Dan	5:7	"Whoever can read this **w**
Lk	1: 3	to **w** an orderly account for
Heb	8:10	and **w** them on their hearts,
1 Jn	2: 7	**w** you no new commandment,
Rev	21:27	are **w** in the Lamb's book of life

Y

YEAR (S)

Gen	1:14	seasons and for days and **y**,
Ex	12:40	was four hundred thirty **y**.
Num	1: 1	in the second **y** after they had
Deut	2: 7	These forty **y** the LORD your
2 Sam	21: 1	for three **y**, **y** after **y**;
2 Chr	36:21	sabbath, to fulfill seventy **y**.
Ezra	5:11	house that was built many **y**
Neh	9:21	Forty **y** you sustained them

Job	36:26	of his **y** is unsearchable.
Ps	90: 4	For a thousand **y** in your sight
Prov	9:11	and **y** will be added
Eccl	6: 6	live a thousand **y** twice over,
Jer	25:12	Then after seventy **y** are
Dan	9: 2	in the first **y** of his reign,
Joel	2:25	will repay you for the **y**
Mt	2:16	who were two **y** old or under,
Lk	3:23	Jesus was about thirty **y** old
Jn	2:20	construction for forty-six **y**,
Gal	4:10	months, and seasons, and **y**.
Heb	3:17	whom was he angry forty **y**?
2 Pet	3: 8	thousand **y**, and a thousand **y**
Rev	20: 2	bound him for a thousand **y**,

YEAST

Mt	16: 6	of the **y** of the Pharisees and
1 Cor	5: 6	little **y** leavens the whole

YOKE

Deut	28:48	He will put an iron **y** on your
1 Kings	12: 4	"Your father made our **y**
Mt	11:30	For my **y** is easy,
Gal	5: 1	submit again to a **y** of slavery.

YOUNG

Deut	22: 6	take the mother with the **y**.
Ruth	2: 5	"To whom does this **y** woman
1 Sam	2:17	sin of the **y** men was very great
2 Chr	10:14	with the advice of the **y** men,
Ps	37:25	I have been **y**, and now am
Prov	7: 7	a **y** man without sense,
Eccl	11: 9	**y** man, while you are **y**
Lam	1:18	my **y** women and **y** men
Dan	1: 4	**y** men without physical defect
Joel	2:28	your **y** men shall see visions.
Mk	14:51	A certain **y** man was following
Lk	2:24	turtledoves or two **y** pigeons."
1 Jn	2:13	I am writing to you, **y** people,

YOUTH

Gen	8:21	human heart is evil from **y**;
1 Sam	17:33	been a warrior from his **y**."
Ps	71: 5	my trust, O Lord, from my **y**.
Prov	2:17	forsakes the partner of her **y**
Eccl	4:13	is a poor but wise **y**
Isa	65:20	years will be considered a **y**,
Ezek	16:60	in the days of your **y**,
Mal	2:14	and the wife of your **y**,

Z

ZEAL (OUS) (ZEALOT)

Num	25:11	manifesting such **z** among
	25:13	because he was **z** for his God,
2 Kings	10:16	see my **z** for the LORD."
1 Macc	2:27	"Let every one who is **z** for the
Ps	69: 9	It is **z** for your house
Isa	37:32	The **z** of the LORD of hosts
Lk	6:15	Simon, who was called the **Z**,
Jn	2:17	"Z for your house will
Rom	10: 2	testify that they have a **z** for
2 Cor	7:11	alarm, what longing, what **z**,
Phil	3: 6	**z**, a persecutor of the church

ZION

2 Sam	5: 7	took the stronghold of **Z**,

Zion

2 Kings	19:31	Mount **Z** a band of survivors.	Lam	2:13	O virgin daughter **Z**?	Rom	9:33	"See, I am laying in **Z**
Ps	2: 6	set my king on **Z**, my holy	Joel	3:21	for the LORD dwells in **Z**.	Heb	12:22	you have come to Mount **Z**
Song	3:11	O daughters of **Z**, at King	Am	1: 2	The LORD roars from **Z**,	1 Pet	2: 6	"See, I am laying in **Z** a
Sir	24:10	and so I was established in **Z**.	Mic	3:12	**Z** shall be plowed	Rev	14: 1	Lamb, standing on Mount **Z**!
Isa	2: 3	of **Z** shall go forth instruction,	Zech	1:17	the LORD will again comfort **Z**			
Jer	50: 5	shall ask the way to **Z**,	Mt	21: 5	"Tell the daughter of **Z**,			

Notes

Notes